ABOUT THE AUTHORS

Penelope Quest is a qualified teacher with fifteen years' experience as a lecturer and senior manager in further and higher education, where she taught marketing, management, communication and personal development. Her academic qualifications include a Masters degree in Health and Healing Science, and a BA in Psychology and Education.

She first became interested in Reiki in 1990, and worked part-time as a Reiki practitioner for three years before becoming a Reiki Master Teacher of both the Usui and Usui/Tibetan traditions in 1994, and a Karuna Reiki® Master in 1996. Since then she has taught Reiki to thousands of students, and in 2000 and 2003 she gained further experience and qualifications in the original Reiki techniques from the Japanese traditions and lineage. In addition she has extended her knowledge by studying a wide range of other subjects, including meditation, Neuro-linguistic Programming (NLP); Emotional Freedom Technique (EFT); sound healing; shamanism; dowsing; kinesiology and other topics which promote understanding, personal growth and a holistic view of the person.

Her books – *The Basics of Reiki, Reiki for Life, Self-healing with Reiki* and *Living the Reiki Way* – have become bestsellers in the UK and internationally. She is a former Vice-Chairman and Education Co-ordinator for the UK Reiki Federation, and was involved with the Reiki Regulatory Working Group (RRWG) during the initial process of formulating the new guidelines for professional Reiki practice. She has also been a consultant on Reiki for both the Open University and the NHS, and now teaches Reiki and leads occasional shamanic retreats and workshops on personal and spiritual development, energy psychology, earth energies and abundance theory.

Kathy Roberts is a graduate with over fifteen years of teaching and training experience, including teaching in primary and secondary schools; working as a freelance training consultant; and writing, organising and delivering a variety of courses within both the private and public sectors. In addition to working in her chosen career she has always maintained an interest in the holistic approach to health, and has been qualified to Reiki level 2 since 1994.

THE
Reiki
MANUAL

A Training Guide for Reiki Students, Practitioners and Masters

PENELOPE QUEST

with Kathy Roberts

piatkus

PIATKUS

First published in Great Britain in 2010 by Piatkus

5 7 9 10 8 6

A CIP catalogue record for this book
is available from the British Library.

ISBN 978-0-7499-4251-9

Designed and typeset in Adobe Garamond by Paul Saunders
Illustrations by Rodney Paull
Printed and bound by CPI Group (UK) Ltd, Croydon, CR0 4YY

Papers used by Piatkus are from well-managed forests
and other responsible sources.

MIX
Paper from
responsible sources
FSC® C104740

Piatkus
An imprint of
Little, Brown Book Group
Carmelite House
50 Victoria Embankment
London EC4Y 0DZ

An Hachette UK Company
www.hachette.co.uk

www.piatkus.co.uk

Thank you to all of our past students, who over the years have helped us experience the joy of teaching, and have helped us to learn as much as we hope we have helped them. Without you, this manual would not have been possible.

DISCLAIMER

This book gives non-specific, general advice and should not be relied on as a substitute for proper medical consultation. Reiki does not replace normal allopathic medical treatment. Reiki helps to enhance the process of harmony of the mind, body, emotions and spirit, and is a means of supporting and complementing medical treatment or other complementary therapies. If you have any acute or chronic disease you should consult a qualified medical practitioner.

Whilst all suggested treatments are offered in good faith, the authors and publisher accept no liability for damage of any nature resulting directly or indirectly from the application or use of information in this book, or from the failure to seek medical advice from a doctor. Furthermore, it is the readers' responsibility to ensure that they comply with any and all laws relating to their practise of Reiki in whichever country they work, and to make sure that they keep up to date with changes in legislation by regularly checking for any new or revised information.

CONTENTS

Part Four · SETTING UP AS A PROFESSIONAL PRACTITIONER

Part Five · BECOMING A REIKI MASTER (LEVEL 3)

Part Six · APPENDICES

ACKNOWLEDGEMENTS

We would like to express our heartfelt gratitude to the many people who have helped, directly or indirectly, with this manual, especially to our family and past academic teachers who helped so much to prepare us to be writers. Thanks also go to the Reiki teachers with whom we've worked, including Kristin Bonney, William Lee Rand, Andy Bowling, Richard Rivard, Robert Jefford and Frans Stiene, and to the many Reiki students who have brought love, learning and laughter to Reiki courses and other Reiki events over the years.

We would also like to thank the many Reiki friends who have inspired and helped us, including Helen Galpin, Jackie Gleeson and, especially, Doreen Sawyer from the UK Reiki Federation (UKRF) and the members of the Reiki Regulatory Working Group (RRWG) and the Reiki Council. In addition, thanks go to Gill Bailey, Claudia Dyer and Rebecca Woods from Piatkus, our copyeditor Charlotte Ridings, and to our wonderful illustrator, Rodney Paull.

INTRODUCTION

Reiki as a holistic healing therapy has been taught in the West since 1938 and in Japan since the early 1920s, and now there are millions of people all over the world who have trained in Reiki, at least at the first level, and even more who have experienced a Reiki treatment.

In recent years there have been attempts in a number of countries to formalise the requirements for the professional practice of Reiki, to ensure common standards so that clients receive the best possible treatment from fully trained, professional practitioners. The route into professional practice at the moment in most countries is for a student to attend one or more courses taught by a Reiki Master (Teacher). However, because all Reiki Masters currently operate independently, they have to produce their own teaching materials, and obviously the standard of documentation – and teaching – varies enormously.

In Britain the various Reiki organisations got together in 2003 to discuss the idea that there was a need for a more structured approach to Reiki training for those wishing to practise professionally, so they began the process of working towards voluntary self-regulation. Their initial task was to produce National Occupational Standards (NOS) for Reiki, with the ultimate aim of setting up a single Register of Professional Reiki Practitioners. As Vice-President and Education Co-ordinator of the UK Reiki Federation in 2005/06, I was a member of the Education and Accreditation Committee of the Reiki Regulatory Working Group responsible for producing an acceptable Core Curriculum for Reiki practitioner training.

Because training in Reiki can be so variable, and is sometimes achieved in just a few days, it is unlikely that the current courses offered by most Reiki Masters will be sufficient to meet the NOS, so students will have to gain further knowledge and experience so that they can fulfil the new requirements. This is what motivated my co-author, Kathy Roberts, and myself to write *The Reiki Manual*, because we wanted to provide a source of information about good practice, not only for those wishing to practise Reiki informally on family or friends, but particularly for anyone wanting to practise Reiki professionally. Moreover, because the principles of good practice are the same wherever you are working, it will provide any practitioner in any country with a really comprehensive guide to the professional practice of Reiki.

As many of you will know, I have been involved in Reiki since 1990, and have been teaching it since 1994, and lots of you will have already come across my other books – *Reiki for Life, Self-Healing with Reiki, The Basics of Reiki* and *Living the Reiki Way*. However, this time I have collaborated with my daughter Kathy Roberts, because writing books and writing manuals can be quite different skills, and she has many years' experience not only in Reiki, but also in writing course manuals as part of her job as a trainer, so her input has been invaluable. Our combined knowledge and experience has put us in a unique position to produce this complete manual for Reiki practice, which we hope you will find not only very useful and interesting, but also enjoyable!

Part One

THE REIKI TRAINING PROGRAMME

Definitions of Terms

·

The Reiki Training Levels

·

Different Types of Training

·

Choosing Your Reiki Master

·

Continuing Your Training

Chapter One

HOW TO USE THIS MANUAL

In the 1920s a Japanese Buddhist priest, Mikao Usui, rediscovered an ancient way of channelling healing energy, creating the Usui Spiritual Energy Healing System, or Usui Reiki Ryoho, which has become better known in the West simply as 'Reiki'. Reiki is a safe, gentle, non-intrusive healing technique for use on oneself, other people, or on animals, but it is much more than a physical therapy. It is a holistic system for balancing, healing and harmonising body, mind, emotions and spirit, promoting relaxation, a sense of wholeness and well-being, and encouraging self-awareness, personal growth and spiritual development. *The Reiki Manual* is a training guide that takes you through all the theory and practice needed for the three levels of training which enable you to use Reiki, but if you don't already know much about what Reiki is, you might find it helpful to go straight to Chapter 3 – 'What is Reiki' – before reading the rest of this chapter, or Chapter 2, 'Reiki Training'.

WHO CAN USE THIS MANUAL?

The Reiki Manual can be used by anyone who has an interest in the subject of Reiki, but particularly Reiki students, Reiki practitioners and Reiki Masters. Their use of the manual may differ slightly, but the essence remains the same; it will become a valuable resource text to consult when learning, practising or teaching Reiki.

DEFINITIONS

At this early stage perhaps it would be useful to define some of the terms we'll be using in this, and later, chapters.

Reiki student – Someone who is learning how to use Reiki on themselves, on other people, on animals and so on. People are usually referred to as Reiki students at any of the levels of training, whether they are just beginning (Reiki level 1), learning additional techniques (Reiki 2) or learning how to teach Reiki to others (Reiki 3 or Master).

Reiki practitioner – Someone who is practising Reiki professionally, either carrying out Reiki treatments on clients and receiving payment, or working voluntarily in hospices or other similar settings.

Recipient or client – Someone receiving Reiki from a person who has already undertaken at least the first level of Reiki training. The term 'client' is used primarily when someone is paying a professional Reiki practitioner for their treatment – it is not usual to refer to such a person as a 'patient', as Reiki is not a medical treatment. The term 'recipient' covers *anyone* receiving Reiki from a person who has done at least the first level of training, so this could be a relative, a friend or acquaintance, or a colleague at work, for example.

Reiki Master – Someone who is qualified to teach Reiki to others, often referred to as 'Reiki Master Teacher', because sometimes the term 'Reiki Master Practitioner' is used to denote a person who has learned some extra skills to offer their clients, but who has not yet undertaken the additional training required to be able to teach Reiki.

Reiki Students

From the Reiki student's perspective, this manual provides a basic summary of the essentials of Reiki, so it can be used as pre-course reading, post-course revision or for refresher knowledge if anything has been forgotten. As the teaching of Reiki can differ quite significantly from teacher to teacher, it can also bridge the gap between what was taught to you on your Reiki course and what you need to know to have a good all-round knowledge to be able to start practising, whether on friends and family, or on paying clients.

Information that is particularly useful to Reiki students can be found in Parts One, Two, Three and Six of *The Reiki Manual*.

Reiki Practitioners

Reiki practitioners will find that this manual is a good place to start identifying ideal practice standards, responsibilities and legal implications when practising Reiki professionally, as it contains substantial information about what is required to comply with the new National Occupational Standards (NOS) recently introduced in the UK (see Chapter 14), and which may well be replicated by other countries in due course.

In Britain the various Reiki organisations got together in 2003 to set up the Reiki Regulatory Working Group (now called the Reiki Council). Its aim was to produce NOS for Reiki, and to work towards the creation of a single UK Register of Professional Reiki Practitioners. Now that the Register of Practitioners has come into operation, there is a need for a more structured approach to Reiki training for those wishing to practise professionally, and it is unlikely that the current courses offered by most Reiki Masters will be sufficient so students will have to gain further knowledge and experience in order to fulfil the requirements of the NOS – although if you only want to practise Reiki on friends and family, you won't need to register, and therefore the NOS won't apply to you.

Reiki practitioners need to be familiar with all the theory and practice of Reiki, so information that is useful to them can be found in Parts Two, Three and Six of *The Reiki Manual*, and most particularly in Part Four, which is specifically about setting up and working as a professional practitioner, as well as giving more detailed information about the National Occupational Standards.

Reiki Masters

For those of you who have committed to becoming a Reiki Master, there are many challenging aspects to your role: passing on your knowledge in a responsible manner as a teacher; continuing to gain experience by being a practitioner; and remaining a life-long student of Reiki. In any of these scenarios *The Reiki Manual* can help to provide you with the information you need.

Within your teaching role, perhaps the most time-consuming aspect of it is to prepare course documentation to provide for students when they attend your courses. *The Reiki Manual,* however, has all of the essential subjects covered on Reiki courses presented in a succinct (but comprehensive) style. It can therefore be used as your course text, and being widely available in bookshops and on relevant websites it means that either your students can purchase their own copy before attending your course, or you can buy copies for them and incorporate the cost of the manual into your course charges.

If you choose to use *The Reiki Manual* as your course text there are many ways in which you could do this. Between sessions you could ask your students to read a particular chapter, which could then lead to a discussion on the subject; you can use the Revision Questions in each chapter to check their understanding of the subject; or you could use the Revision Activities to vary the learning methods on your course and check your students' understanding in a way other than just a question and answer session, to give but a few examples.

In Part Five of the manual there are valuable Teaching Notes for you, to help you prepare the structure of your sessions, as well as tips on the delivery of the course, and further activities to introduce during your teaching to ensure all learning styles are covered. This should help to increase your students' knowledge retention and satisfaction with their course.

As a course teacher, much as we would like to be able to remember every little detail between courses, we are all just human! So it's not just the students who can use *The Reiki Manual* as a learning tool: you can use it to refresh your memory if there has been a significant gap since the last time you taught.

Parts Two and Three cover all the theory and practice you need to teach your Reiki level 1 and level 2 students, with some additional information in the Appendices in Part Six, and Part Four will be especially useful if you want to help your students prepare to be professional Reiki practitioners. Part Five is designed to help you to prepare for and structure your courses.

WHAT *THE REIKI MANUAL* DOES NOT DO

However comprehensive a manual on Reiki you read, it does not enable you to teach yourself Reiki and then to be able to practise, as this can only be done by going through the spiritual attunement process with a qualified Reiki Master (see Chapter 3). Having said that, please don't be put off acquiring knowledge of Reiki before attending a course, as the better prepared you are, the more benefit you are likely to get from attending an official session.

In addition, it is worth noting for Reiki Masters that although tips on teaching are mentioned in this manual, it does not replace structured teacher training, so you may wish to investigate additional courses on this subject.

Chapter Two

REIKI TRAINING

Reiki is probably the simplest and easiest holistic healing method available to us, so anyone can learn to use Reiki, whatever their age, gender, religion or origin – although in the case of young children, it is best if they understand what it is, and of course they need permission from a parent or guardian before taking a Reiki course. No specific knowledge or experience is required before beginning your Reiki training; just an interest in it and some time to attend a short course or workshop. For beginners this is at the first level of Reiki, usually called Reiki 1 or Reiki First Degree.

REIKI TRAINING LEVELS

Reiki is now used and taught in almost every country around the world, and many other similar forms of healing have been developed in recent years, derived from the original method devised by Dr Mikao Usui – more about him in Chapter 4. The way Reiki is taught today in the West is usually in three levels – Reiki 1, Reiki 2 and Reiki 3 (or Reiki Master) – but as you will see below, sometimes other levels are added. The method of acquiring the ability to let Reiki flow through you is called an 'attunement', and this is explained in more detail in Chapter 3.

1. **Reiki 1, or Reiki First Degree,** is often a two-day course, although some-times it is taught in one day, or over four separate days, or as an evening

class spread over a term at a college. It is traditional to receive four separate attunements during this time to open up your inner healing channel and allow the Reiki healing energy to flow through you, although some Reiki Masters prefer to use one single integrated attunement instead of separating them out, a tradition which comes from the Usui/Tibetan form of Reiki developed by an American Reiki Master, William Lee Rand. The emphasis at this level is on self-healing, so you should be shown the basic hand positions, and how to do a self-treatment, but you will also be taught how to carry out a treatment on family members and friends, either seated in a chair or lying on a therapy couch, so there is often a chance to practise Reiki treatments on your fellow students. You will also be told about the history and origins of Reiki, and how to use Reiki on animals and plants.

2. **Reiki 2, or Reiki Second Degree,** is sometimes regarded as practitioner level, although as you will have noted from Chapter 1, the UK is leading the way in regulating practitioner training for the benefit of both practitioners and clients, and there is more information about these changes in Part Four. You should be aware that many people decide to progress to this level because of the additional scope it gives them for personal healing and spiritual development, rather than because they want to practise Reiki professionally. It is usually a two-day course, but as with Reiki 1 it is sometimes taught in one day, or during a term of evening classes, and it includes at least one more attunement (and sometimes two or three), which enables you to access even more Reiki. You will learn three sacred symbols (calligraphic shapes) – the Power, Mental/Emotional and Distant symbols (sometimes called the Focus, Harmony and Connection symbols) – and their mantras (sacred names) and some special ways of using them, including for self-treatments and treatments on other people and animals. You will also be taught a form of distant healing which enables you to 'send' a Reiki treatment to anyone, anywhere, at any time, with the same effectiveness as if that person was with you having a 'hands-on' treatment.

3. **Reiki 3, or Reiki Third Degree,** is the level of a Reiki Master (Teacher) (see also Reiki 4, below). The training used to be like an apprenticeship, with a student working alongside a qualified Reiki Master for about a year, but it is more usual now to take a course. This may be taught as a whole or divided into several parts, from a one-, two- or three-day workshop, to a residential course lasting a week or more. So the training varies considerably from one Master to another. This training level will include the

Master (Empowerment) symbol, and one or two attunements, some advanced healing techniques, plus training in how to carry out the special attunement processes for each level of Reiki. However, this level should be regarded as much more than gaining an extra qualification or some additional skills, because it really means making a life-long commitment to the mastery of Reiki. The term Reiki 'Master' is a rough translation of the Japanese 'sensei', meaning 'respected teacher'. In reality, no one can 'master' Reiki, because it is a powerful spiritual energy, so in essence being a 'Reiki Master' means being on a voyage of self-discovery and self-mastery, which can be physically, mentally, emotionally and spiritually demanding, even though it can also be very rewarding, so training at this level shouldn't be undertaken lightly, or without adequate preparation.

4. **Reiki 4, or Reiki Fourth Degree.** There are now many different types of Reiki being taught around the world, and some of these include more than three levels. It is quite common for Reiki to be divided into four levels, with the first and second levels being as described above, but the third level being divided into two separate courses. The first of these leads to Master Practitioner level, sometimes called Reiki 3A, or Advanced Reiki Training (ART), where the student is taught the Usui Master (or Empowerment) symbol and some advanced healing techniques. The fourth level is then Master Teacher, where the student is taught the attunement processes for each of the levels, and is sometimes taught two or more additional symbols which do not come from the original Usui Reiki but may be from channelled sources, i.e. someone has 'received' the shapes and meanings of the symbols during meditation or trance.

OTHER REIKI SYSTEMS

There are now more than fifty different types of Reiki in existence around the world, although all of them are based in some way on Dr Usui's original healing system. The most popular is probably **Usui/Tibetan Reiki**, devised by the American Reiki Master William Lee Rand, which includes two additional symbols at Master level which apparently come from Tibet. Kathleen Milner's **Tera Mai** (or **Tera Mai Seichem**) **Reiki** is another popular system that originally included twelve to fifteen symbols, but which can now include more than thirty. **Karuna Reiki**® is another system devised by William Lee Rand which is only taught to those who have already qualified as Usui Reiki Masters; it includes four levels and twelve symbols. The **Radiance Technique®**, now called **Authentic Reiki®** or **Real Reiki®**, was developed by Dr Barbara Ray and it has seven levels. Some of these systems have been taught since the 1990s or earlier, whereas others have come into existence more recently. *The Reiki Manual* focuses mainly on the traditional Western-style of Usui Reiki (see Chapters 3 and 4), although the Japanese traditions are also referred to. If you would like to know more about other Reiki styles and systems there is more information in Appendix 1.

TYPES OF TRAINING

There are various ways in which people can train in Reiki, particularly at Reiki 1 and 2 levels. Some attend a one- or two-day course or a practical workshop where the theory of Reiki is explained and demonstrated by the Reiki Master, and they get a chance to practise Reiki treatments and other techniques on their fellow students. Others receive just an attunement to Reiki with perhaps an hour or two of brief explanation from the Reiki Master and a few pages of notes to take home, whilst still others receive a 'distant' attunement, which may or may not be supported by written notes or a CD or DVD; they don't have any 'in person' contact with the Reiki Master.

In the UK there is a move towards setting down a minimum number of training hours to be required by someone who wishes to become a professional practitioner, and 'distant' attunements will not be considered sufficient. Even if you're not sure that practising professionally is something you might wish to do in the future, it would be wise to check the new NOS requirements (see the Core Curriculum in Chapter 14) to see if the course you're choosing will fulfil the criteria.

TIME BETWEEN LEVELS

Some Reiki Masters insist on specific time gaps between the various levels of Reiki training, the most usual being three months between Reiki 1 and Reiki 2, and three years between Reiki 2 and Reiki Master. However, since the 1990s there has been an increasing number of Masters who have either shortened the gaps between levels, or even dispensed with them altogether. It is now not uncommon to have Reiki 1 taught one day followed immediately by Reiki 2 the next day, and sometimes Reiki Master level on the following weekend, or perhaps just a month or two later. There are also some Masters who teach all three levels over a single weekend, but this is relatively unusual.

CHOOSING YOUR REIKI MASTER

When you decide you would like to learn Reiki, you will need to decide what type of training you would prefer, and which Reiki Master to go to. Every Master is unique, and each one of them brings something of themselves to their teaching, so it is important that you should feel that he or she is someone you can like, trust and respect. At this stage you probably won't know whether you would like to practise Reiki professionally in the future, but if you think that might be possible you would need to attend a Reiki course or workshop in person, because (as we have seen) the new regulations for professional practitioners in the UK preclude distant attunements, and other countries may follow.

Perhaps the most sensible way to make your decision is to ask for recommendations from people you know who have already attended a course, or to ask for leaflets from a number of Masters, and/or access their website if they have one, and then contact the Masters you feel most drawn to and ask some questions, such as:

- How long have you been teaching Reiki?

- What is included in your course?

- How long do your courses last (e.g. hours/days) and what time intervals do you recommend between the levels?

- Is there time on the course for supervised practise of treatments?

- Do you provide a certificate at the end of the training?

- Do you offer post-course support for your students?

You might also find it useful to have a Reiki treatment from them before the course, so you can get to know them – and that could be the ideal time to ask your questions! If you like practical, no-nonsense people, then you'll probably be attracted to train with someone similar; if you are a real go-getter who can't bear to wait for things, then you're more likely to prefer a Master who is willing to let you progress quickly through the levels. If you love history and tradition, then you'll probably choose a very traditional Reiki Master who recommends you to take your time; and if you are interested in spirituality, you'll probably be more interested in finding a Master who teaches mainly from that perspective.

There are Reiki organisations and associations now in most countries, and many of these keep lists of Reiki Masters, although these shouldn't be regarded as recommendations or guarantees of particular standards – it is still up to you to decide if a particular Master is the right one for you. In the Resources section at the back of this manual there are website addresses and contact details for some of these organisations in the UK, as well as in many other countries, so you should be able to find a suitable Master near to you. Some Masters teach in only one location, whilst others travel around to different areas or even to different countries.

PREPARING FOR A REIKI COURSE

When you've found the right Reiki Master, you're ready to book on to a course or workshop at a convenient time and place. Some Masters suggest that it can be an advantage to prepare yourself for about a week beforehand by eating very healthily, drinking plenty of water, limiting your consumption of alcohol and perhaps by doing some meditation or spending some time with nature. These suggestions are intended to encourage a state of harmony and balance, but they are optional, and there are no serious disadvantages to not preparing yourself in this way, so please don't be concerned if you don't have the time – or inclination – to follow these ideas.

AFTER A REIKI COURSE

At each level of attunement to Reiki the frequency or rate of vibration of your energies is raised (see Appendix 2 for details about your energy bodies and their relationship with Reiki), and in order for this to happen there has to be a clearing of old physical, mental, emotional and spiritual patterns and thoughts which can inhibit your personal growth and spiritual development. One of the major effects of a course, therefore, is what is sometimes called the 'Twenty-one-day Clearing Cycle', where your physical and energy bodies are cleansed and cleared by the Reiki.

This can be described as a sort of energetic 'spring cleaning', where the Reiki gently flows through you and breaks down the blockages in your whole energy system. The effects of this release can vary from feeling more emotional or irritable than usual, or having the urge to laugh or cry, to a sense of detachment and the need to spend more time alone. Physically you may need to visit the toilet more frequently than usual, as Reiki helps to flush out toxins, and occasionally there may be a temporary 'healing crisis', such as a cold; this is simply the toxins being released from the body and is perfectly natural (if a little uncomfortable!). The whole process can be made easier if you drink plenty of fluids (especially water) during the three weeks, to help your body to get rid of any toxins, and also if you carry out a self-treatment on yourself each day (see Chapter 7).

> **Note:** If you have any health problems related to water retention, please seek medical advice before drinking extra water.

REIKI TRAINING IN JAPAN

What we have been describing so far is the Western way of Reiki training, sometimes referred to as Usui Shiki Ryoho, meaning the 'Usui Natural Healing Method', which is the most prevalent system in the Western world. However, Reiki originated in Japan, and some aspects of the Japanese way of training in Reiki, usually referred to as Usui Reiki Ryoho, or the 'Usui Spiritual Energy Healing Method', are now also taught in the West, so you may come across Reiki Masters who prefer to teach in this way. Most of these Masters choose to teach in three levels, which is very similar to the more familiar Western way.

1. **Shoden** ('the entrance') is equivalent to Reiki 1 or our First Degree

2. **Okuden** ('the deep inside') is like Reiki 2 or Second Degree

3. **Shinpiden** ('the mystery/secret teachings') is similar to our Reiki 3/Reiki Master

You may be taught the Western way of carrying out treatments, which is via a series of twelve or more hand positions, or you may be shown the Japanese way, which is to use your intuition to allow yourself to be guided to the places on a person's body which need Reiki. Sometimes you will be taught additional special techniques which come from the Japanese tradition, including a combined meditation and self-treatment technique called Hatsurei-ho (see

Appendix 3), and at Shinpiden level you will be taught an alternative attunement/spiritual empowerment called Reiju. You will find more information about Japanese Reiki training in Chapter 4.

CONTINUING YOUR TRAINING

It is possible to become a Reiki practitioner (treating members of the public and charging money) at any level – Reiki 1, 2 or Master. However, as you will see later in this manual, the steps to becoming a professional practitioner are changing, so if this is something you would like to do, whether now or in the future, you will find Part Four especially useful.

In order to teach others about Reiki, you obviously will need to have plenty of knowledge about, and experience in, Reiki, which can take a number of years to acquire. You might find it useful to read books and attend courses with several different Reiki Masters in order to broaden your experience, so the information in all parts of this manual will be useful if you are training to become a Reiki Master. However, Part Five is specifically about becoming a Reiki Master, and how to structure your own Reiki classes when you start teaching.

In the meantime Part Two explains what you need to know when you are starting out on your Reiki journey.

Part Two

REIKI THEORY
AND PRACTICE FOR
LEVEL 1/FIRST DEGREE

What is Reiki?

·

The Origins and History of Reiki

·

The Reiki Principles

·

The Hand Positions Used in Reiki Treatments

·

How to Use Reiki for Self-healing

·

Using Reiki to Treat Family and Friends

·

Using Reiki to Treat Animals and Plants

·

Using Reiki to Help Heal Personal and Global Situations

Chapter Three

WHAT IS REIKI?

Reiki can be explained in three ways: as a word, as an energy, and as a holistic healing system.

REIKI AS A WORD

Reiki (pronounced 'RAY KEE') is a Japanese word which is most often translated as 'universal life-force energy', although this could just refer to the second part of the word, Ki, so perhaps a more precise translation is 'spiritual energy'. You will often see the word Reiki written in one of the following ways:

These are representations in the calligraphy of the Japanese kanji, or alphabet; the top shape is the word 'Rei' and the bottom shape is the word 'Ki'. On the left is the older version, in the middle is the more modern version, and on the right is the version which often appears in print. Japanese is quite a complex language, so words often have many different meanings. For instance, Rei can be translated as 'soul', 'spirit', 'wisdom', 'divine', 'essence' and 'sacred' or 'mysterious power', whilst Ki usually refers to 'life-force energy', although it is sometimes translated as 'cosmic' or 'universal energy'.

REIKI AS AN ENERGY

Reiki is 'spiritual energy', as referred to above, but what does this mean? The second part of the word, Ki, refers to life-force energy, and you may have heard of other versions of this word from other languages, such as 'Chi' or 'Qi' in Chinese (as in Tai Chi or Qi Gong), or 'Prana' from India, where it is a central concept in Yoga and Ayurveda. These words all signify a vital, life-sustaining energy which is believed to flow throughout the human body (and through all living things) through a network of fine subtle channels called meridians, as well as flowing outside the physical body as an energy field called an aura. This 'Ki' is an energy which operates at high vibrations and fast frequencies which makes it difficult to see, but it can be detected by various forms of electro-magnetic equipment, and identifying and removing blockages in its flow has for centuries been central to acupuncture. Most complementary and alternative therapies work at an energetic level – indeed the physical body is energy, but vibrating at a slower frequency which is denser, and therefore visible. See Appendices 2 and 3 for more information about energy theory and the human energy field.

Reiki, as a spiritual energy, operates at an even higher and faster vibration than the Ki that is present in the physical body and the aura, so it can move through all parts of the human energy field to break through energetic blockages and promote healing. The source of this high spiritual energy can be described in various ways, depending upon what you are happy to accept – God, the Source, the All-That-Is, the Universe – or you can think of it as part of your Soul or Spirit or Higher Self that you can access to help you.

REIKI AS A HOLISTIC HEALING SYSTEM

What we call Reiki in the West refers to a holistic healing system originally devised by a Japanese priest, Dr Mikao Usui, in the early part of the twentieth century (Chapter 4 has more information about Dr Usui). Reiki is a healing process that anyone can benefit from in the normal course of their life and which may also bring help and comfort to people suffering from a range of conditions. However, it should not be regarded as a cure for such conditions, and neither is it a religion nor a belief system. As a natural form of healing Reiki can support and enhance other forms of treatment, including conventional medical treatments as well as alternative or complementary therapies – more about this in Chapters 7 and 8.

> The whole Reiki healing system consists of:
>
> Training in three or more levels
>
> The origins and history of Reiki
>
> Spiritual principles for living
>
> The method of acquiring the ability to use Reiki (the 'attunements')
>
> Instruction in how to apply Reiki with the hands for treatments on yourself, other people and animals
>
> A number of symbols (shapes) and mantras (sacred words) that can be used to enhance Reiki's effectiveness
>
> In some traditions, meditation and cleansing techniques, and specific hand positions for treating particular conditions
>
> All of these aspects of Reiki are dealt with in this part of the manual, with additional information included in Parts Three and Six.

The most common way of experiencing Reiki for most people is by receiving a Reiki treatment from a Reiki practitioner, where the recipient remains fully clothed and lies on a therapy couch or sits on a chair and relaxes. The practitioner gently places their hands non-intrusively on or near the body, in a sequence of positions (see Chapter 6). There is no pressure, massage or manipulation and the whole person is treated rather than specific symptoms. Reiki is 'holistic' because it affects the whole person – body, mind and spirit – encouraging deep relaxation and a sense of well-being, and assisting the physical body's own healing ability to operate more effectively and efficiently. It is possible to give yourself a Reiki treatment if you have attended at least one Reiki course – see Chapter 7 – and to receive Reiki at a distance – see Chapters 8 and 13; and Reiki can also be used in a similar way to treat animals, birds and other creatures.

THE EFFECTS OF REIKI

When receiving Reiki during a treatment people often experience warmth or tingling wherever the practitioner's hands are placed, although some get no particular sensations but simply feel pleasantly calm and relaxed. Some people report 'seeing' beautiful colours, dreams or visions, or find that long-forgotten memories arise during or soon after having Reiki, and most experience a wonderful feeling of peace and radiance afterwards. Some people do get quite emotional during or just after a Reiki treatment, so tears or laughter are not uncommon, and some also find that their body shakes or their arms or legs suddenly jerk. These reactions are quite normal, and just indicate that the Reiki is breaking through energy blockages, and the body needs to throw off the negative energy which has been encountered.

The benefits of Reiki can be enjoyed without necessarily feeling any of these sensations. Most people achieve a very deep state of relaxation during a treatment, which allows physical, mental or emotional stress to leave the body, re-establishing equilibrium and a feeling of well-being. Basically, Reiki balances and works on four levels – physical, emotional, mental and spiritual – and as it flows through the person it adjusts to the recipient so that each person receives exactly what they need at that time.

The Physical Level: The physical body and any pain or illness

Reiki supports and accelerates your body's own natural ability to heal itself, usually alleviating pain and relieving other symptoms whilst helping the body to rid itself of poisons and toxins. It balances and harmonises the whole energy field (see Appendix 2), promoting a sense of wholeness, a state of positive wellness and an overall feeling of well-being. It also helps you develop greater awareness of your body's real needs, such as good nutrition, and regular exercise.

The Emotional Level: What you are feeling and experiencing

Reiki inspires you to examine your emotional responses, encouraging you to let go of negative emotions such as anger or resentment, and promoting the qualities of loving, caring, sharing, trusting and good will. It can also help you to channel emotional energy into creativity.

The Mental Level: Your thoughts and attitudes

Reiki leads to a state of deep relaxation, with the consequent release of stress and tension. It allows you to let go of negative thoughts, concepts and attitudes, replacing them with positive thoughts, peace and serenity. It can also enhance your intuitive abilities and encourages you to pursue your personal potential through greater insight and self-awareness.

The Spiritual Level: Your capacity to love yourself and others unconditionally

Reiki helps you to accept and love your whole self, and fosters a non-judgemental approach to humankind, allowing you to accept every person as a beautiful and pure soul energy as well as a human being. It promotes the qualities of love, compassion, understanding and acceptance, and encourages you on your individual path towards personal growth and spiritual development.

BECOMING 'ATTUNED' TO REIKI

The strand of healing energy we call Reiki isn't automatically accessible to us simply by thinking we can use it, although everyone has an innate ability to use their own life-force energy for healing. For example, if a child falls over and hurts itself we often place our hands quite naturally on the cut or bruise, and of course we cuddle them to make them feel better, and this often seems to have a healing effect.

The way in which we access Reiki is to undergo a process called an 'attunement'. This is sometimes referred to as an initiation, as it 'initiates' the student into a new life with Reiki (initiate means 'to begin'), and 'attunes' the student to the unique energetic vibrations of the Reiki spiritual healing energy (attune means 'to bring into harmony with'). We also sometimes refer to the process as a 'spiritual empowerment' – a sacred ceremony that empowers a part of our spirit – Reiki – which we did not consciously know how to access before, so that we become aware of it for the first time, and can begin to use it. Once a person has been 'attuned' to Reiki in this way, they will always be able to access it easily and simply by just intending to use it for self-healing, or with others. There are no complicated rituals to follow. Energy follows thought, so simply thinking that you want to use Reiki is what 'switches it on'.

In Usui Reiki there are a number of these attunements spread out between the various levels of training, so that the student has time to 'acclimatise' to the levels of energy involved. There are usually four attunements at the level of Reiki 1, one attunement at Reiki 2, and one attunement at Reiki Master level. (There's more about the levels of training in Chapter 2.)

The first attunements activate an energetic channel in the student, through which the Reiki energy can flow from the Source (or God, All-That-Is, or the Universe, as you prefer), through their Soul energy and into the top of the student's head, where an energy centre called the crown chakra is located (see Appendix 2 and the illustration below). It then flows through the energy pathways called meridians to the heart chakra, and from there it flows down the arms and out through the hands.

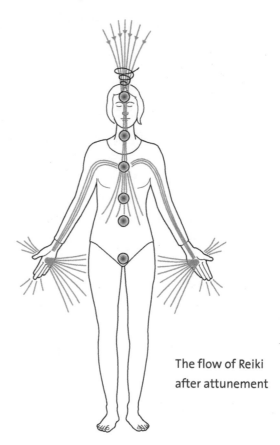

The flow of Reiki
after attunement

Any additional attunements, or attunements at the different levels, further expand this energetic channel, increasing the amount of Reiki which can flow through it. It is the attunement process, or spiritual empowerment, which is what makes Reiki unique and is the reason why the ability to heal can be developed so quickly and yet so permanently. Once you have been attuned to Reiki you are able to use it for the rest of your life; the ability to channel Reiki never wears off or wears out, and there is always a limitless supply.

Experiencing an Attunement

Reiki Masters differ in the way they arrange things for the attunements. Some prefer to work one-on-one, whilst others like to work with groups (although the attunement will be given to each individual in turn). It is usually carried out in silence, with perhaps some soft, relaxing music playing in the background, with each student sitting on a chair with their eyes closed and their hands held in the 'gassho' or prayer position, palms together in front of their chest.

Gassho hand position

At various stages during the process there may be some gentle touching on the student's head and hands, and they may be asked to raise their hands above their head for a few moments, but everything is done in a very gentle, supportive and restful manner. The attunement is a very special, meditative experience, and the silent contemplation with eyes closed is for two reasons.

The first is because, as a sacred and spiritual ceremony, the procedures are intended to be kept secret until such time as any individual student trains to be a Reiki Master. The second, less obvious reason is that when someone has their eyes closed, this reduces any external distractions around them, so that they are more easily able to stay in an appropriate meditative state.

Everyone's experience of a Reiki attunement is slightly different, even though the process carried out by the Reiki Master will be identical for everyone. After an attunement is over, students sometimes describe the beautiful spiritual or mystical experiences they have had, such as 'seeing' wonderful colours or visions, receiving personal messages or profound healing, or simply having a feeling of complete peace. Some people go through a real shift in their awareness immediately afterwards, describing the sensation as almost like being reborn, so that they experience everything around them more intensely. Colours are brighter, their senses of smell and taste are enhanced, and sounds are sharper. Others feel a buzzing or heightened sensitivity on the top of their head for a short while, or describe a sense of floating or light-headedness. All of these reactions are absolutely normal, but so is experiencing very little, which, whilst perhaps a little disappointing for some students, does not mean the attunement hasn't worked! An attunement always works, provided a qualified Reiki Master carries out the attunement process with you, so you will be able to channel Reiki afterwards.

REVISION QUESTIONS

1. What does the word 'Reiki' translate as?

2. What is kanji?

3. Why is Reiki 'holistic'?

4. What are a few of the sensations people may experience when receiving Reiki?

5. What are the four levels that Reiki can work on?

6. How long are you able to give Reiki for, following your attunements?

(Answers in Appendix 8)

REVISION ACTIVITIES

1. Identify how Reiki has helped you on all four levels.

2. Draw one of the Reiki kanji symbols at the beginning of this chapter – choose whichever one you're attracted to.

Chapter Four

THE ORIGINS
AND HISTORY OF REIKI

Reiki originated in Japan in the 1920s when Dr Mikao Usui rediscovered a way of channelling healing energy. However, there are two slightly different versions of the Reiki history. The first one was primarily told as an oral history in the West from the late 1930s until the early 1990s, and which some Reiki Masters still prefer to use now, whilst the second came to light in the 1990s as a result of some Reiki Masters (particularly Frank Arjava Petter) doing research in Japan. There are similarities between the two stories, and each has its merits and will appeal to some people more than others. So your Reiki Master may tell you one version or the other, or perhaps a bit of both!

THE TRADITIONAL WESTERN VERSION OF THE REIKI HISTORY

This story told that Dr Mikao Usui (1865–1926) was a learned scholar who taught in a Christian seminary in Japan where he was one day challenged by one of his students, who asked him if he believed in the stories in the Bible of Jesus healing, and if so, when were they going to be taught how to heal? It was said that, as an honourable Japanese gentleman, upon realising that he could not teach his students any healing techniques, Dr Usui dedicated the rest of his life to finding out how Jesus and the Buddha had been able to heal. He was said to have travelled widely and learned other languages in order to research both Christian scriptures and Buddhist teachings, before finally ending up in a Zen Buddhist monastery where the abbot advised him to meditate to find the answers he was seeking.

Mikao Usui

At the end of a twenty-one-day fasting retreat on Mount Kurama Dr Usui was apparently struck by a great light, and saw the sacred symbols (calligraphic shapes) he had discovered earlier during his research, and came to a deep understanding of those symbols, received a spiritual empowerment and achieved enlightenment. When it was over, despite his weakness after twenty-one days of fasting, he was able to rush down the mountain. In his haste he injured his foot, and when he quite naturally bent down to hold his toe, he found that the bleeding stopped, the pain went away and he was healed.

At the bottom of the mountain he encountered a food seller and he asked for some food, which the food seller's daughter brought to him. He saw that the girl's face was swollen and that she had been crying, and she told him she had bad toothache which her father couldn't afford to get treated. Remembering what had happened to his toe, Dr Usui asked if he could place his hands on her face, and when he did so, the swelling went down and her pain went away. Later, when he returned to the monastery to tell his friend the abbot what had happened to him, he was told that the abbot's arthritis was very bad and he had taken to his bed. Once again, Dr Usui placed his hands on the abbot and his pain went away. In this way he came to a realisation that he had finally discovered the healing power for which he had been searching.

The story then told that he spent many years healing people in Japan before passing his teachings on to Dr Chujiro Hayashi (1878–1940), a former captain in the Japanese Navy, and a naval doctor. After Dr Usui's death, Dr Hayashi was said to have opened a Reiki clinic where clients were treated, usually by two or more practitioners.

Dr Chujiro Hayashi

In 1935 a young woman from Hawaii called Hawayo Takata (1900–80), who was visiting relatives in Japan, became ill and was taken to hospital. She was about to have an operation but she had an intuition that there was another way to find healing. She left the hospital and went to Dr Hayashi's clinic, where she was treated by several Reiki healers. Apparently she was surprised by the heat in their hands and demanded to know what it was, so they told her about Reiki. She became fully well within a few weeks of daily treatment, and was so impressed with such success that she begged to be able to learn Reiki, and Dr Hayashi eventually agreed to teach her. Mrs Takata then lived with his family and worked without pay in his clinic in exchange for the privilege of being able to learn the first and second levels of this healing system.

Mrs Hawayo Takata

Eventually she went back to Hawaii and in 1937 she opened the first Reiki clinic in the West. A year later Dr Hayashi and his family visited her, and he passed on the final level of the Reiki teachings before he returned to Japan, so that she would be able to teach this healing art to others. The story Mrs

Takata told was that during the Second World War Dr Hayashi and all of his Reiki students in Japan were killed, and that therefore she was the only Reiki teacher left alive.

Mrs Takata continued to teach Reiki and run her clinic in Hawaii, but she also travelled extensively throughout the USA and Canada, treating people with Reiki and training them how to use Reiki for themselves. She held classes in two levels of Reiki training, which she called First Degree and Second Degree, but it wasn't until the 1970s that she began to teach the final level of teachings, the Third Degree, which she called Reiki Master (a rough translation of 'Sensei', 'respected teacher' in Japanese), so that others would be able to pass on the teachings when she had gone. By the time of her death in December 1980, after forty-two years of teaching Reiki, she had trained twenty-two Masters, and it is through those twenty-two Masters that Reiki has spread so widely throughout the Western world.

THE ALTERNATIVE JAPANESE TRADITION

In the 1990s information began to reach the West from Japan which indicated that Dr Usui had been a Buddhist priest, not a Christian priest, and that he had passed his Master level teachings on to seventeen people, not only to Chujiro Hayashi. Nor had all the Reiki Masters in Japan been killed during the Second World War, so Reiki had continued to be taught there since Mikao Usui's death. Indeed, an organisation existed which was dedicated to preserving his original teachings – the Usui Reiki Ryoho Gakkai. This new information came from two men in particular – Frank Arjava Petter, a European Reiki Master, at that time living and working in Japan with his Japanese wife, Chetna Kobayashi, and Hiroshi Doi, a Japanese Reiki Master who has trained in both Japanese and Western Reiki traditions. Others who have contributed to our current knowledge of Reiki in Japan include Dave King, Chris Marsh, Melissa Riggall and Robert Jefford, and more recently Rick Rivard and Andy Bowling, all of whom have spent time researching in Japan.

We now know that Dr Usui was born in Japan on 15 August 1865, and that he began his study of Buddhism at the age of four, when he was sent to a monastery school run by the Tendai Buddhist sect. He studied martial arts from the age of twelve, being awarded the Menkyo Kaiden, a certificate of full proficiency, by his mid-twenties; he also reached high levels of proficiency in other ancient Japanese energy systems as he got older, including Ki-Ko, the Japanese form of the Chinese energy-balancing system known as Qi

Gong. He also learned meditation and healing, and during his life he worked in many different jobs, including as a government officer, a businessman, a journalist and as secretary to the Mayor of Tokyo. As he lived a relatively normal life, and had a wife and children, it is unlikely that he was a cloistered monk, but he is believed to have studied various forms of Buddhism, including Shingon and Zen Buddhism.

Usui grew up during the reign of Emperor Mutsuhito, the Meiji Emperor, during whose reign (1868–1912) a new wave of openness began, as Japan's previously closed borders were opened for the first time in many centuries. The country became more industrialised, which engendered an eagerness to explore the benefits of Western influences, with a consequent freedom for Japanese nationals to travel outside their own country. Many Japanese scholars were sent abroad to study Western languages and sciences, and it states on Dr Usui's memorial, situated in the graveyard of the Saihoji temple in Tokyo, that he visited China, the USA and Europe, and that he was fond of reading, acquiring knowledge of medicine, history, psychology and world religions.

His memorial confirms that he had a mystical enlightenment experience on Mount Kurama, near Kyoto, apparently after advice from a Zen Master to undergo 'shyu gyo', a strict spiritual discipline involving meditation and fasting for twenty-one days, until he either died, or became enlightened. On the last morning of his fast he experienced 'a great Reiki over his head' – a quote from his memorial – which gave him the ability to access healing energy (Reiki) and to pass that ability on to others.

It is a facet of Japanese culture that knowledge or important information is normally kept secret (or sacred – the words are synonymous in the Japanese language) within family groups, so initially it is believed that Dr Usui used Reiki only on himself and his family; it is reported that Reiki cured his wife of a serious illness at that time. However, he eventually realised his discovery was of great importance, so he began to teach people how to access this healing energy, and he made 'Shoden' ('the entrance', the first level of Reiki training, equivalent to our Reiki 1) 'freely available to all of the people', as it says in one of his teaching manuals, the *Usui Reiki Hikkei*. It is believed that about two thousand people learned this level of Reiki from Dr Usui. Between thirty and fifty people may have learned the second level, 'Okuden' ('the deep inside'), and seventeen acquired the third level, 'Shinpiden' ('the mystery or secret teachings'), which is what we call Reiki Master. These included five Buddhist nuns, four naval officers and eight other men, but little else is known about them.

Dr Usui then spent the few years before his death at the age of sixty practising and teaching his healing system, which he called 'Teate', or 'palm healing', but which we now refer to as Usui Reiki Ryoho, or the Usui Spiritual-Energy Healing Method. His memorial states:

> If Reiki can be spread throughout the world it will touch the human heart and the morals of society. It will be helpful for many people, not only healing disease, but the Earth as a whole.

As you can see, the essence of the two stories – the traditional Western one and the alternative Japanese version – is the same. Mikao Usui lived in Japan, researched and discovered a way of channelling spiritual energy which could be used for healing, and taught that system to a number of people, including Dr Chujiro Hayashi, one of the Japanese naval officers, who in turn taught Mrs Takata, which is how Reiki came to the West.

THE DEVELOPMENT OF REIKI IN THE WEST

Mrs Takata established a system of teaching Reiki that survives to this day, although since the early 1990s there have been a number of changes made by various Masters which will be outlined in later chapters. She adapted the teaching to suit Western students; for example she taught First Degree or Second Degree as workshops held over just a few days, to fit in with most Western working lives, rather than expecting students to work in her clinic for months in order to learn, as she had done when she trained with Dr Hayashi. She used the four Reiki symbols she had been taught by Dr Hayashi, three of which she taught at Second Degree, and one at Master level, and she instigated a series of twelve basic hand positions for both self-treatment and the treatment of others, encouraging students to work on themselves with Reiki every day. She advised that each hand position should be held for five minutes, and recommended that students carry out four treatments on each client for maximum benefit (see Chapters 7 and 8 for details about Reiki treatments).

After Hawayo Takata's death, a group of the Masters she had trained met in Hawaii in 1982 to discuss how Reiki should progress, and who should become the next leader or 'Grand Master', which may be how Mrs Takata described herself, since she was the only Reiki Master in the West for so many years. Phyllis Lei Furumoto, Mrs Takata's granddaughter, agreed to follow in her grandmother's footsteps and was therefore elected Grand Master. At that historic first meeting in 1982 the Masters standardised the system. They agreed on the exact form of each of the four Reiki symbols, what should be taught at each of the three levels, the length of time students should allow between learning each level, and other aspects of teaching, including that it should remain an oral tradition which should incorporate Mrs Takata's story of the discovery of Reiki. They also decided to follow her system of hand positions, and the method of spiritual empowerment or attunement she used to transmit the healing ability to students. They also agreed on the wording of the five spiritual Principles of Reiki, as taught by Mrs Takata, although other slight variations were taught by the few Masters who chose not to attend that meeting. The Reiki Principles are discussed in detail in Chapter 5.

At a further meeting in British Columbia in 1983 the Reiki Alliance was formed, an organisation of Reiki Masters who recognised Phyllis Lei Furumoto as the Grand Master, and whose purpose was to support each other as teachers of the Usui System of Reiki. This organisation still exists, with a fairly small membership of Reiki Masters all over the world. Until 1988, only Phyllis Lei Furumoto, as Grand Master, was entitled to train other Masters, which clearly limited the numbers, but at a gathering in Friedricksburg that year she announced that any suitably experienced Master could teach other Masters. This development opened up Reiki in the West to the inevitable changes that result from expansion. By the early 1990s the numbers of Masters and practitioners had grown extensively, and a growing number of Masters moved away from the system agreed by the Reiki Alliance to work independently, introducing changes to the way they taught Reiki.

REIKI'S DEVELOPMENT IN JAPAN

To most people in the West involved in Reiki, whether as students, practitioners or Masters, Reiki is a healing system with a spiritual aspect. In contrast, Dr Usui's emphasis was on a spiritual practice with healing as a by-product. His teaching was more about a spiritual awakening, rather than just physical healing. Mikao Usui referred to his teachings as the 'Method to Achieve Personal Perfection'. He taught that it is by mastering the mysteries of the self that we learn to affect the mysteries of life.

The first teachings (Shoden) were about 'cleansing' (healing and affirmations) and 'opening' (receiving Reiju empowerments, see below), for the healing of the Self. The Inner (Okuden) and the Higher (Shinpiden) teachings were to take the student further on his or her spiritual path, including at a very much later stage of their Shinpiden training learning how to perform the Reiju empowerment, the Japanese form of attunement to the Reiki energy. The importance of self-healing was imparted, as well as the benefits of living a 'proper' life, using the Reiki Principles as a foundation (see Chapter 5). In addition, Dr Usui used 125 inspirational poems (Gyosei) written by Emperor Mutsuhito, and he asked his students to recite the Principles and some of the poems each day as part of their spiritual practice. The Reiki Principles are covered in depth in Chapter 5.

Dr Usui incorporated other aspects of his Buddhist training into his Reiki teaching, including meditation, self-cleansing and the simple method of spiritual empowerment, Reiju, as well as some energy practices from Shinto, a form of religion common in Japan, and Ki-Ko, a Japanese martial art. It seems that he worked intuitively on people, placing his hands wherever seemed in need of healing. However, once he began to teach others to do Reiki Dr Usui found that instructions were needed, and he wrote the *Usui Reiki Hikkei*, a manual to be given to his students (some researchers state that this manual was really written by Dr Hayashi).

Mikao Usui is also credited with founding the Usui Reiki Ryoho Gakkai (the Usui Reiki Healing Method Learning Society), an organisation dedicated to keeping the Reiki teachings alive, although it is possible that his followers started it after his death, naming Usui as the founder as a mark of respect. The Gakkai members follow Dr Usui's teachings very closely, using two manuals said to be produced by Dr Usui. One of these is an explanation of his energy healing method, the Usui Reiki Ryoho, and the other gives details of the various healing techniques, including specific hand positions for different diseases and physical problems.

Even today, when a Japanese Reiki student has received his or her attunement into the first level, Shoden, they are expected to practise Reiki daily, and to live with the five Principles in their daily lives to encourage mental and emotional growth and development. They are also expected to practise Hatsurei-ho daily, a technique for self-cleansing and spiritual enhancement (see Appendix 3), and to continue their spiritual development, partly by attending regular training seminars where they receive more Reiju attunements. This helps them to develop their intuitive skills so that they become better able to detect and treat physical illnesses, a process which is called 'byosen', which means being able to feel energy from a source of illness, and being able to judge a symptom and how many days of healing will be required. Another skill is called 'reiji', where the hands go intuitively to affected areas automatically and start sending Reiki. If (rather than when) they reach a certain level, as determined by their Reiki Master Teacher, they will then be given Okuden, the second level, but there is no time limit for this. Very few people in Japan ever reach the advanced level of Shinpiden, the equivalent of a Western Reiki Master, even after many years of practice.

REIKI DEVELOPMENT IN THE FUTURE

Although the traditional ways of teaching, learning and using Reiki have developed in slightly different ways in Japan and in the West, we now have the opportunity to meld these two systems together, to use what is best in both. Western and Eastern Reiki practices have distinctly different styles. The linear, logical structure of the Western system of hand positions can be balanced with the more intuitive, flexible Japanese system, which develops the practitioner's sensitivity and awareness. Using the two together could give us the best of both worlds, enabling us to develop an even deeper understanding of this amazing healing energy, and leading to even greater health and well-being for ourselves and others.

Reiki is in many ways still true to its ancient spiritual traditions, although clearly there have been some changes along the way. From Dr Usui's experience of enlightenment, and his research into healing techniques from the Buddhist traditions, has come one of the world's most precious gifts – a holistic healing system that is easy to use and easy to learn, and which connects us with a spiritual energy to replenish our physical and energy bodies, and that also helps us to develop personally and spiritually.

THE LINEAGE SYSTEM IN REIKI

In the above sections, we have referred to Dr Hayashi and Mrs Takata 'teaching' Dr Usui's system of healing, but Reiki cannot be 'learned' in any of the ways with which we in the West are familiar. It doesn't actually require any *learning*, in the traditional sense, because it is not knowledge-based. It is *experience*-based. Being able to use Reiki requires that you draw, or channel, the healing energy into yourself, and you cannot acquire the ability to channel Reiki by reading this manual, or any other book, or by attending a lecture, or watching a television programme, video or DVD, although you can learn how to use Reiki in those ways (for example, where to place your hands when carrying out a Reiki treatment).

As explained in Chapter 3, the ability to channel Reiki energy, or draw it into yourself, is passed on from a Reiki Master to a student through an attunement or spiritual empowerment, which can be received either in person or at a distance. This creates a lineage system, which simply means that each Reiki Master can trace their lineage back to the founder, Mikao Usui, rather like a family tree. So for example, in the West most Reiki Masters can trace their lineage thus:

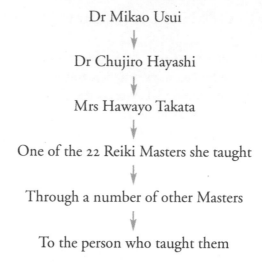

Dr Mikao Usui

↓

Dr Chujiro Hayashi

↓

Mrs Hawayo Takata

↓

One of the 22 Reiki Masters she taught

↓

Through a number of other Masters

↓

To the person who taught them

Each Reiki Master is taught how to carry out the attunement process, and this knowledge is then passed from Master to Master to continue the lineage. Your Reiki Master may give you a copy of his or her lineage at some stage in your Reiki training, and you may need this if you decide to become a professional practitioner – see Chapter 14.

REVISION QUESTIONS

1. In which country did Reiki originate?

2. Who is said to have 'found' Reiki?

3. What are Shoden, Okuden and Shinpiden?

4. Who or what is the Reiki Alliance?

5. How is Reiki passed on from a Reiki Master to a student?

(Answers in Appendix 8)

REVISION ACTIVITY

Ask your Reiki Master about their lineage, and then make a record of your own.

Chapter Five

THE REIKI PRINCIPLES
OR IDEALS

As mentioned in Chapter 4, to help his students Dr Usui taught some principles for living a good life, and normally when you attend a Reiki 1 course you are taught the five Reiki Principles (sometimes referred to as the Reiki Ideals or Reiki Precepts). Versions differ, depending upon how your Reiki Master was taught, but here are two sets of examples:

1. Just for today, do not anger

2. Just for today, do not worry

3. Honour your parents, teachers and elders

4. Earn your living honestly

5. Show gratitude to every living thing

1. Just for today I will let go of anger

2. Just for today I will let go of worry

3. Today I will count my many blessings

4. Today I will do my work honestly

5. Today I will be kind to every living creature

These two versions were taught by two different branches of Reiki, the first by Masters who joined the Reiki Alliance, under the direction of Phyllis

Lei Furumoto, Mrs Takata's granddaughter, and the second by Radiance® Technique Reiki Masters under the direction of Dr Barbara Ray, one of Mrs Takata's twenty-two Reiki Masters.

In the late 1990s, however, the author and Reiki Master Frank Arjava Petter published the original spiritual principles, written in Dr Usui's own hand, as you will see below, which he translated like this (a rough guide to how to pronounce them phonetically is given underneath each):

Kyo dake wa
(Kee oh dah kay wah)

Just today

1. Okoru-na
(Oh koh roo nah)

1. Don't get angry

2. Shinpai suna
(Shin pie soo nah)

2. Don't worry

3. Kansha shi te
(Kan shah shtay)

3. Show appreciation (or be thankful)

4. Goo hage me
(Go oh hah gay may)

4. Work hard (or with diligence)

5. Hito ni shinsetsu ni
(Hee toe nee shin set soo nee)

5. Be kind to others

Below are the Reiki Principles from that original document written in Dr Usui's own handwriting, followed by a more recent translation into English (Japanese text is read from right to left):

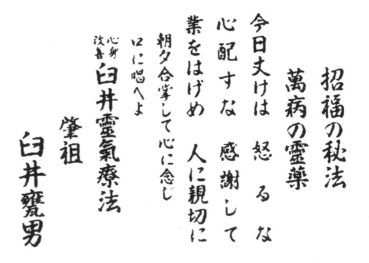

The secret art of inviting happiness
The spiritual medicine of all diseases (of body and mind)
Just for today, do not be angry
Do not be worried and be filled with gratitude
Devote yourself to your work and be kind to people
Every morning and evening sit in the Gassho position,*
Pray these words to your heart
And chant these words with your mouth
Usui Reiki treatment for the improvement of body and mind
— The founder, Mikao Usui

*Gassho position means with your hands clasped in prayer, see page 27.

There is a generally accepted belief that the Reiki Principles taught by Dr Usui were originally written by Emperor Mutsuhito, the Meiji Emperor whose reign coincided with much of Usui's life. However, their real origin is probably much older than that. They are very similar to precepts used for hundreds of years in the Tendai Buddhist sect of Shugendo, with which Usui (and probably Emperor Mutsuhito) would have been familiar:

Do not bear anger,
For anger is illusion.
Do not be worried,
Because fear is distraction.
Be true to your way and your being,
Show compassion to yourself and others,
Because this is the centre of Buddhahood.

Of course the version of the Reiki Principles you learn when you first do Reiki may well be different from the translation above. This might partly be because Japanese is a very complex language, so there are a number of different translations. For example, sometimes 'be kind to people' is translated as 'show compassion to yourself and others', whilst 'devote yourself to your work' is translated as 'work hard' or 'do your work diligently' or 'do your work honestly'.

However, perhaps it isn't surprising that in the West our form of the Principles isn't exactly the same as the more recently revealed version from Japan. Mrs Takata was taught Reiki in the late 1930s, and taught it herself for over forty years as an oral tradition, so the wording probably changed slightly over all that time. Or perhaps some of the Masters she taught didn't remember it accurately. It doesn't really matter why the differences occurred: there are great similarities between all of the versions, so whichever you are taught and choose to follow will help you to live a better life, which is what Dr Usui intended.

JUST TODAY

One of the most important aspects of the Reiki Principles is the phrase 'Just today'. If you were to promise yourself, when repeating the Principles, that you would never again be angry, or never again worry, or always be kind to others – well, that's quite hard to live up to! We are all human, so it's unlikely that any of us will manage to keep permanently to the spirit of the Principles, at least at first. So making a promise to ourselves that we won't get angry *today*, or won't worry *today*, means we only have to try one day at a time. This feels like an achievable goal, whereas 365 days a year feels like a lot of pressure! And if on occasion we don't quite manage to live up to the Principles, well, tomorrow is another day; we can just start again, one day at a time.

The other reason why the words 'Just today' are important is because they highlight the need to live in the moment and be aware of what is going on around you; to live in the present, in the 'Now'. Many people spend much of their time with their minds elsewhere, with thoughts of what happened yesterday, or last week, or last year, such as what they wish they'd said to a colleague yesterday, or regretting that they didn't buy that bargain when they had the chance. Or their thoughts are constantly on what might be in the future – what can I cook for dinner tonight, or where to go on holiday? And of course there are always the 'what if' scenarios to fill the mind: what if I lose this job, or what if my partner fancies someone else?

Whilst these thoughts are spinning through your mind, you are not living life as it really is, in the present, and because of that, you are actually limiting your enjoyment of life. Our happiest times are often when we are really absorbed in something, and paying full attention to it, such as when we're reading a really good book or watching an exciting film, or playing with our children, or taking part in a sport. If you are truly aware of what you are doing now, in this moment, rather than drifting off in other thoughts, your life becomes richer and more fulfilling, and therefore more pleasurable – even if what you're doing is mundane and ordinary.

TODAY, DO NOT ANGER

Anger is a fairly destructive emotion, and it may sometimes feel like the only option, but although it might be uncomfortable to realise it, like many emotions anger is actually a conscious choice, a habitual response you have developed to a given set of circumstances. It is usually triggered when someone or something fails to meet your expectations, or even when you don't come up to your own expectations. Expressing anger towards someone rarely achieves anything other than to make you both feel bad, but you can break the cycle and choose a different response instead. And you *can* find healthier and safer ways of expressing the frustration which often lies behind the anger, by turning the emotion into creativity, or going for a brisk walk, or doing that very old-fashioned thing, counting to ten before you speak! So give yourself the chance to choose, just for today, not to get angry.

TODAY, DO NOT WORRY

Worry is linked with our fear of the future and the unknown, and particularly to our lack of self-belief that we can cope with situations, and it often centres around a 'what if' scenario – a future event which hasn't happened yet, and possibly never will. Worrying can also be a habit we get into, but no matter how much worrying we do, it will never achieve anything or change anything; it just makes us feel dreadful.

Fear is often based on negative beliefs about life or the world, so, for example, if you have a general belief that life is a struggle, or that the world is a dangerous place, it will colour your judgement about what happens to you, and it will become a focus for worrying about things like lack of money, or losing your job, or being alone. Whatever problem or situation you are worried about, if there is some action you can take to improve matters, then take it. Even talking things over with someone else can help, and very few things turn out to be as bad as we've anticipated! So it is possible to choose not to worry – just for today.

SHOW APPRECIATION, OR BE THANKFUL

It is important to value and appreciate many things in our lives and to be grateful for our many blessings – to develop an 'attitude of gratitude', rather than just taking things for granted, or thinking with regret about what we haven't got. Western society today seems to have a culture of wanting bigger, better and more, and it's easy to forget just how much we already have. So take a little time, every day, just to appreciate what you have and what is around you. For example, at the end of every day think of at least five things to be grateful for from that day, and write them in a journal. By the end of one week, you will have a list of thirty-five things to be grateful for and, by the end of a month, give or take a few repetitions, you'll have about a hundred and fifty! And one of the good things about this is that you will naturally begin to feel happier, and less concerned about what you haven't got, because you'll realise that actually your life is pretty good after all! So, just for today, be thankful.

WORK HARD, OR WITH DILIGENCE, OR DO YOUR WORK HONESTLY

In Dr Usui's original Principles, this was probably intended to mean work hard on yourself – in other words, work on your personal and spiritual development with Reiki and meditation. So giving yourself a Reiki treatment every day (see Chapter 7) is a good place to start, and you could also try the Hatsurei-ho Reiki meditation technique in Appendix 3.

Another aspect of this, however, is to do with the wider influence of work in your life, from paid employment to everyday tasks, and how you carry it out. Do you do your work willingly and with a good heart, or are you reluctant, only doing your work because you have to, or because it is the only way you can see to earn a living? It is important to respect any work that you have chosen for yourself and honour yourself by doing your best to create a feeling of satisfaction in it. *All* work is valuable to the extent that you choose to value it, so take satisfaction from even the simplest tasks, and be willing to do everything to the best of your ability.

Doing your work honestly also means being honest with yourself, as well as with others – it means accepting yourself for who you are. We often confuse what we *do* with who we *are*, taking our sense of identity from the kind of job we have, or don't have. What we need to remember is that we are human *beings*, not human *doings*. We are *all* valuable and special; every life, every person has a role to play in the whole and we all impact on each other in many different ways. So just for today, work hard on whatever tasks you have to do, and especially on your personal growth and spiritual development.

BE KIND TO OTHERS, OR SHOW COMPASSION TO YOURSELF AND OTHERS

This is about being kind to every person you meet, so it also incorporates 'honour your parents, teachers and elders'. Of course we all need to honour and respect all of the people we interact with in our lives, not just those who are close to us, because everyone we meet is in some way one of our teachers, whether we love them or loathe them, because every interaction we have helps us to learn and grow personally and spiritually. And as Reiki helps you to grow spiritually, you will realise that there is no place for prejudice, being judgemental, or for cruelty or indifference in a world where everyone and everything has a vital role to play, and should therefore be valued, respected and treated with kindness. It may also seem an obvious statement, but if you are kind to other people, they are usually kind to you, and that's no bad thing! So just for today, be kind to everyone and everything – including yourself of course!

You can explore the Reiki Principles in more detail, including how to live with them in today's busy world, in the book *Living the Reiki Way* by Penelope Quest.

REVISION QUESTIONS

1. What is the Gassho position?

2. What are the five Reiki Principles that your Reiki Master taught you?

(Answers in Appendix 8)

REVISION ACTIVITIES

1. Make a list of how you will implement the five Reiki Principles into the different areas of your life, e.g. every day I will think of five things I am grateful for.

2. Read aloud the Japanese pronunciation of the Reiki Principles.

Chapter Six

THE HAND POSITIONS FOR REIKI TREATMENTS

When you're using Reiki it flows quite naturally out of your hands, and wherever you place them, the Reiki will actually flow around the whole body. However, to be even more effective when treating yourself or someone else, or even when treating animals, you place your hands and hold them still in a number of different positions on the head and body, usually for between three and five minutes in each place. This remains the same whatever level of Reiki you have – 1, 2 or 3.

REIKI TREATMENTS – THE BASICS

Hands On or Hands Off?

Traditionally Reiki is a 'hands-on' treatment, meaning that the hands are placed gently and held still on the head or body, without any pressure, massage or manipulation. However, it is sometimes appropriate to keep the hands slightly away from the body, i.e. 'hands off', especially over areas which are perhaps too sore to touch, or over any intimate areas of the body. (It is never appropriate – nor is it necessary – to place your hands on a woman's breasts or on either male or female genitalia.) There are several advantages to the 'hands-on' approach. For one thing your hands (and arms) are supported by the recipient's body, so it isn't so tiring, and for another, it can be comforting for the recipient to feel a gentle touch.

Treatments are carried out with the recipient fully clothed, either seated in a chair or lying on a therapy couch – see Chapter 8. Often recipients are covered with a soft blanket, so there is no need to touch any bare skin.

Some people, when they first start doing Reiki, are reluctant to place their hands on the recipient's body, feeling that it is in some way intrusive, so they barely allow their hands to touch the body. This results in a hesitant, 'fluttering' feeling which most recipients don't like. If the hands are placed lightly but confidently on the person's head or body, this helps to give the recipient a feeling of security, and as none of the hand positions is 'intimate' there is no invasion of privacy. See illustrations below.

When the hands are intentionally held in the air, usually 5–15 cm (2–6 inches) above the body, the Reiki flows through that person's aura (the energy field surrounding the body, see Appendix 2) into the body, so the recipient receives just as much Reiki as they would if the treatment was 'hands on'. Some practitioners and recipients do prefer this method, and some Reiki Masters do teach this as a way of carrying out a full treatment. However, holding your hands still above the recipient's body without support for several minutes can be more tiring, so you will need to pay special attention to your stance, or how you are seated, to ensure your maximum comfort.

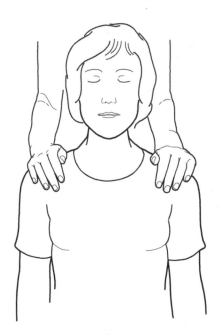

An example of the 'hands-on' approach to treating someone with Reiki

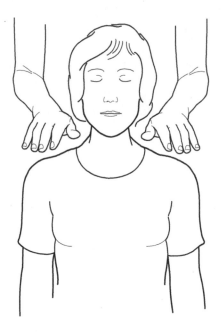

An example of the 'hands-off' approach to treating someone with Reiki

One Hand or Two?

Our Western way of treating with Reiki is to use two hands, usually placed one on each side of the body, which has a naturally balancing effect. However, it is perfectly acceptable to use only one hand; apparently Dr Usui often used only one hand at a time when treating his patients. Reiki flows in response to your *intention* to use it, so even if you only have one hand, if you wish you can intend the Reiki to flow in the area which would correspond with the 'missing' hand and the effect will be the same.

The Recipient's Dignity

As already stated, no intimate parts of the body ever need to be touched during a Reiki treatment, even if the recipient has a health problem in those areas. However, to ensure that someone feels at ease it is a good idea to let them know exactly where your hands are going to be placed, either by describing the hand positions, or by demonstrating them. It is unlikely, when given advance notice like this, that anyone will object to any of the standard hand positions. It also gives the recipient an opportunity to let you know if there are any specific areas where touch might be uncomfortable or unacceptable. You can then avoid those areas by placing your hands in the air above them, or on the body at nearby positions. Some religions or cultures have particular restrictions about touching others, which should always be respected.

Common Hand Positions

The most usual form of full Reiki treatment in the West is based on twelve hand positions on the head and body, each of which is normally held for about five minutes, with the option of leaving the hands on longer in any position where you can feel that there is still a lot of Reiki flowing, indicating that the area still needs more energy. Some Reiki Masters teach a slightly different structure for the treatment, with up to six hand positions on the head and neck, and up to ten hand positions on the front of the body, including the legs and feet, and another ten on the back of the body, again including the legs and feet. This gives a total of twenty-six hand positions, with those on the head and body being held for between three and five minutes, and those on the legs and feet being held for between one and three minutes.

When doing a 'hands-on' treatment, your hands are always used with the fingers close together, and the thumb close to the hand. When the hands are moved from one position to another, you should do this very gently, preferably lifting one hand at a time away from the body so that you have continuity of contact with the person. It is possible to let your hands glide along the body from one position to another, but this can be a little more disturbing to the recipient than lifting your hand off and placing it in the new position.

Alternative Positions

Most Reiki treatments are carried out with the recipient lying on a therapy couch or something similar, so the following section gives the standard hand positions for such a treatment. (The recipient is fully clothed, and will need at least one pillow under their head, and another under their knees.) Some people are unable to lie flat on their backs, or (for the second stage of the treatment) to lie on their stomach (e.g. a pregnant woman). In this case it is possible to get them to lie on their side, or to sit in a chair; the hand positions for those treatments are given on pages 58–60. The hand positions for self-treatment follow the same basic pattern, and are described in detail in Chapter 7.

Experiencing Sensations in Your Hands

Whenever you place your hands on yourself or on other people (or animals) the flow of Reiki may cause sensations in your hands. These can vary from warmth or heat, to coolness; or they could be feelings such as tingling, prickling, tickling, itchiness, or even numbness or a buzzing sensation, and these feelings may even travel up your arms. Any or all of these experiences are absolutely normal, but equally it is normal not to feel anything at all! Probably the most common sensations are warmth and tingling, but unfortunately it isn't possible to specify exactly what each feeling means, because they just indicate that the Reiki is reacting within the recipient's body and energy field, and this can be a different reaction in each hand position, or each time you treat that person. Sometimes the recipient experiences the same sensations as the practitioner, sometimes they feel the exact opposite – for example, your hands might feel hot, but the recipient might feel cold where you have placed your hands. Equally, the recipient might get lots of sensation during a treatment, but you haven't felt much at all in your hands. It might be a little frustrating, but all of these scenarios are perfectly natural! Yes, it would be nice to be able to explain what Reiki is doing, but realistically you just have to learn to trust that Reiki is doing what it needs to do, and leave it at that!

REIKI HAND POSITIONS FOR THE TREATMENT OF OTHERS

The hand positions used in a treatment are basically the same whether you are treating family members or friends or paying clients, so the following suggestions are appropriate whether you have just completed a Reiki 1 course, or are working as a professional practitioner. However, as you gain more experience, you may find you want to add an occasional extra hand position, depending upon the needs of the recipient, and of course that's fine. The basic structure of around twelve hand positions does allow Reiki to flow to the whole of a person's body, but it should be regarded as a sensible and effective guideline rather than an absolutely strict pattern that can never be altered! For more information about carrying out treatments, please see Chapters 8 and 12.

Hand Positions for the Head

The first four hand positions on the head and neck are usually carried out with the practitioner either standing or sitting behind the recipient's head. Make sure before the treatment starts that both you and the recipient are comfortable, and ensure that you have enough support for your arms to enable you to hold each of the four positions for up to five minutes each (or longer, if you intuitively feel this is needed), without having to press hard on the recipient's body.

1. **The Back of the Head** – Place both hands beneath the head, palms upwards, so that your little fingers are touching each other, and your fingertips are roughly level with the base of the skull.

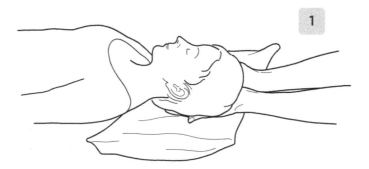

2. **The Eyes** – Place both hands slightly cupped over the eyes, resting the heel of each hand gently on the brow, but keeping your fingertips away

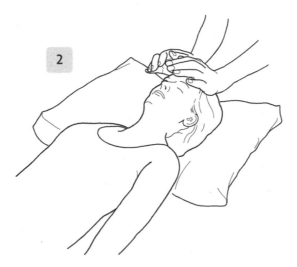

from the face (enclosing the eyes can make some people quite nervous or even feel claustrophobic).

3A. **The Ears/Temples** – *Either*, place one slightly cupped hand over each ear, with the heel of each hand resting gently against the side of the head so that the fingertips are roughly level with each earlobe.

3B. *Or*, place one slightly cupped hand over each side of the head, with the fingers at each temple.

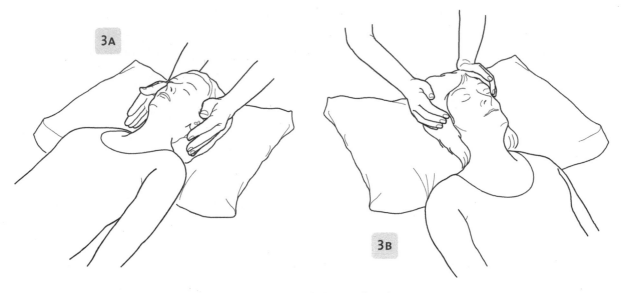

4. **The Neck** – Place one hand on each side of the neck, about 10 cm (4 inches) away, with the palms facing the neck and your little fingers resting gently on the recipient's shoulders. Your hands/fingers should not touch the neck, as this can make people feel very constricted and even unsafe.

Sometimes the order of the hand positions on the head is taught differently, starting with the hand position over the eyes, so please carry out the treatment in the way your Reiki Master suggests.

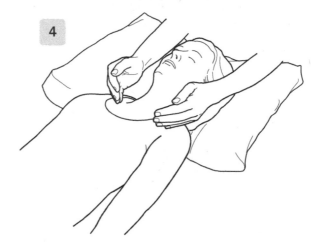

Hand Positions for the Front of the Body

The first hand position, on the upper chest, can be carried out whilst still seated behind the recipient's head, or, like the next three positions, with the practitioner standing or sitting on one side of the recipient (it doesn't matter which side). Please ensure that you can comfortably hold each hand position for between three and five minutes, without having to stretch too much, or press too hard on the recipient's body. Adjust your body appropriately, either by standing with your legs slightly apart with the knees softly bent (as in a Tai Chi or Qi Gong stance), or by sitting on a chair. (An office chair on wheels, but without arms, is excellent, as you can wheel yourself along between hand positions, rather than having to reposition the chair.)

5A. The Chest – *Either*, from behind the person's head, place your hands in a V shape at the top of the chest, with the heels of your hands roughly level with the person's collarbone, ensuring that they are not too close to the throat. (If you are treating a woman, be aware that it is neither appropriate nor necessary to have your hands directly on the breasts.)

5B. *Or*, from beside the person, place one hand in front of the other, flat on the upper chest (avoiding contact with the throat and the breasts). See illustrations 5A and 5B opposite.

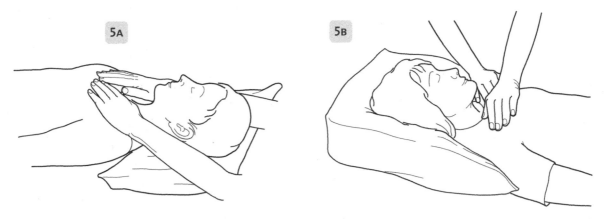

6. **The Solar Plexus** – Place one hand in front of the other, flat on the body, so that one hand is on the left side of the body and the other on the right side, on the solar plexus/midriff area, i.e. below the breasts and above the waist. See below.

7. **The Navel/Waist** – Place one hand in front of the other, flat on the body, so that one hand is on the left side of the body and the other on the right side, at waist level.

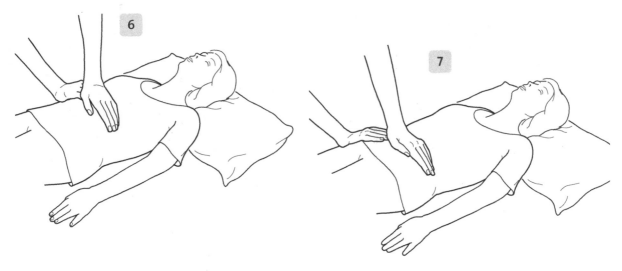

8A. **The Pelvic Area** – To show sensitivity about the genital area, the hand positions for male and female recipients can be different. For a *male recipient*, it is usual to place one hand on each hip bone.

8B. For a *female recipient*, you can either adopt the same position as above, i.e. on the hip bones, or place your hands in a V shape from the hip bones towards the pubic bone, ensuring that your hands are not too low down, which could be a bit intrusive. See illustrations overleaf.

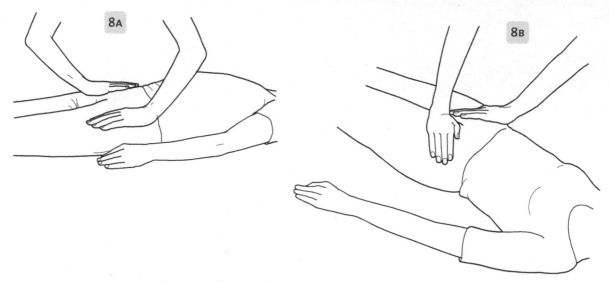

Getting the Recipient to Turn Over

When you have completed the first eight hand positions, covering the head and the front of the body, you will need to ask your recipient to turn over on to their stomach. The person will probably be very relaxed at this stage, and may even be asleep, so it is important to be kind and supportive. Very gently pat or stroke their shoulder, speak their name softly, and ask them to turn over. Assist them if they need this, and ensure that you reposition the pillow which was under their knees – move it so that it is under their ankles. The recipient's head can be held on one side, or it can rest on an arm – just let them find a position which suits them. When they are settled again, start the treatment of the back of the body. (Hand positions for treating someone who cannot lie on their stomach are given on pages 56–7.)

Hand Positions for Treating the Back of the Body

Hand position 9A can be done from behind the recipient's head, or from the side (9B), whichever you prefer. Positions 10, 11 and 12 are all done from beside the recipient's body (doesn't matter which side).

9A. The Shoulders – If you choose to sit or stand *behind* the recipient's head, place one hand on each shoulder so that the heels of your hands rest on the shoulders and the fingertips are pointing down the back

9B. If you choose to stand at the *side* of the recipient, place one hand on the left shoulder and the other hand on the right shoulder. See illustrations opposite.

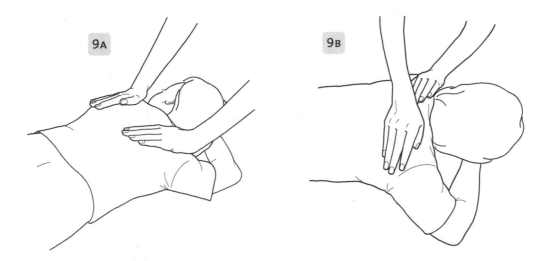

10. **The Back** – Stand beside the person and place one hand in front of the other on each side of the body, with a slight gap between (i.e. over the spine), palms flat against the back, roughly mid-way between the shoulders and the waist.

11. **The Waist/Adrenals** – From beside the person, place one hand in front of the other on each side of the body on the person's waist, with a slight gap between the hands, over the spine, with your palms flat.

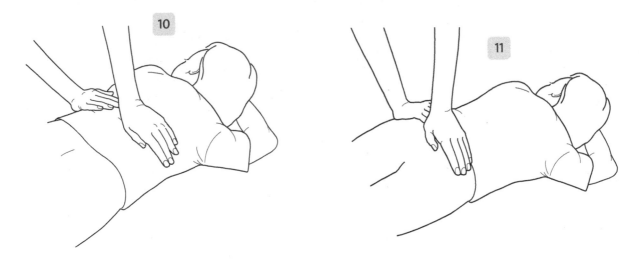

12A. **The Buttocks** – From beside the person, place one hand on each buttock, palms flat, leaving a slight gap between the hands over the spine.

12B. Some practitioners, and some recipients, prefer a hand position in the air above the coccyx. See illustrations overleaf.

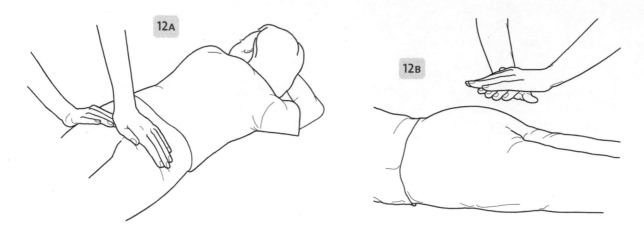

TREATING SOMEONE LYING ON THEIR SIDE

It is possible to carry out a full treatment with someone lying on their side, although the positions on the front of the body can be a little awkward. So if the person cannot lie on their back it is probably easiest to do their treatment whilst they are sitting in a chair – see the next section. However, if someone finds it difficult to lie on their stomach (for example, a pregnant woman), the four back positions can be done fairly easily if they lie on their side instead – particularly if the practitioner sits in a chair beside the therapy couch. Position your chair roughly opposite the space between the recipient's waist and the middle of their back, and then start at the shoulders, then move to the middle of their back, then the waist, and finally to the buttocks, as in the following illustrations. In each case, the most comfortable way to treat

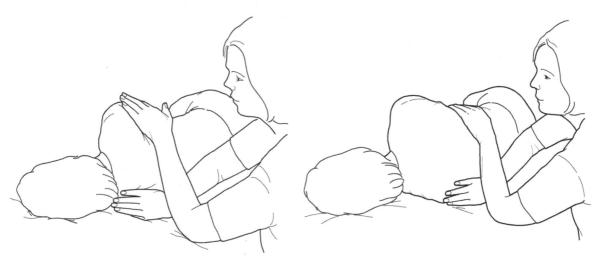

Shoulders from the side   Middle of the back from the side

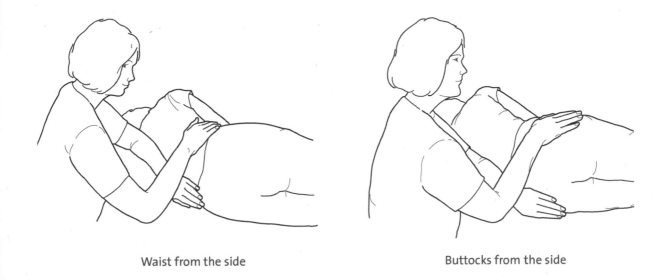

Waist from the side   Buttocks from the side

them is to lay one of your arms along the couch, with the elbow of the other arm resting on the couch, so that your arms are fully supported throughout.

TREATING SOMEONE IN A CHAIR

If the recipient is having their treatment whilst sitting on something like a dining chair, then you can stand beside them for the first position on the head, then move behind them for the hand positions over the eyes, ears, neck and shoulders, and then move back to the side. It is much easier and more comfortable for you to reduce the number of hand positions (from twelve to nine) by treating both the front and back of the body at the same time with a seated recipient. In other words, you would place one of your hands on the upper chest, and the other at about the same height on their back, then move down to the solar plexus with one hand, and place the other hand at a simi-lar height at the back, and so on. If the recipient can only sit in an armchair and is unable to lean forward a little, you can place your hands on the back of the chair in places which roughly correspond to the front-of-the-body hand positions. Yes, Reiki can easily go through the back of a chair!

Nine Hand Positions for a Seated Recipient

1. **The Back of the Head** – Stand beside the recipient, with one hand crad-ling the base of the skull, the other hand on the crown of the head. See illustration overleaf.

2. **The Eyes** – Move to stand behind the recipient with one hand cupped over each eye. Your fingertips do not touch the face, to avoid the recipient feeling claustrophobic.

3. **The Ears/Temples** – One hand is cupped over each ear, with the fingertips pointing towards the temples.

4. **The Neck** – Place the edge of your hands so that they rest on each shoulder, palms facing the neck, about 10 cm (4 inches) away from the neck itself, so the recipient does not feel threatened in any way.

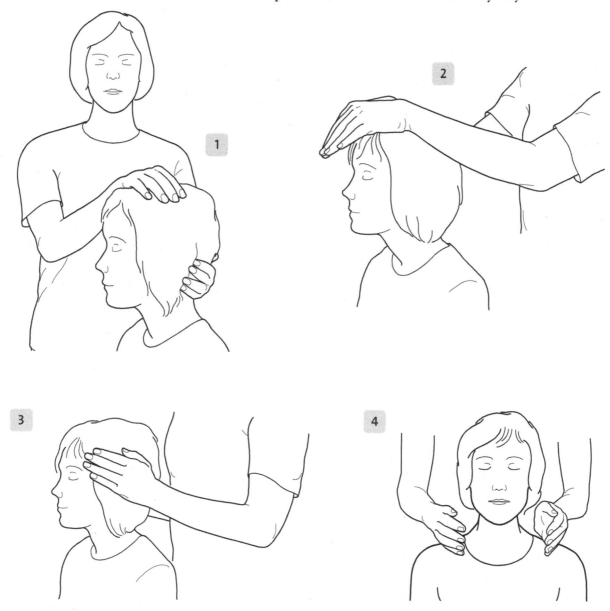

5. **The Shoulders** – One hand is placed on each shoulder, palms facing downwards.

6. **The Chest/Upper Back** – Move to the side of the recipient, and either standing or sitting, place one hand on the upper chest and one hand roughly level with it on the back.

7. **The Solar Plexus/Middle Back** – Place one hand on the solar plexus, the other hand roughly level with it on the back.

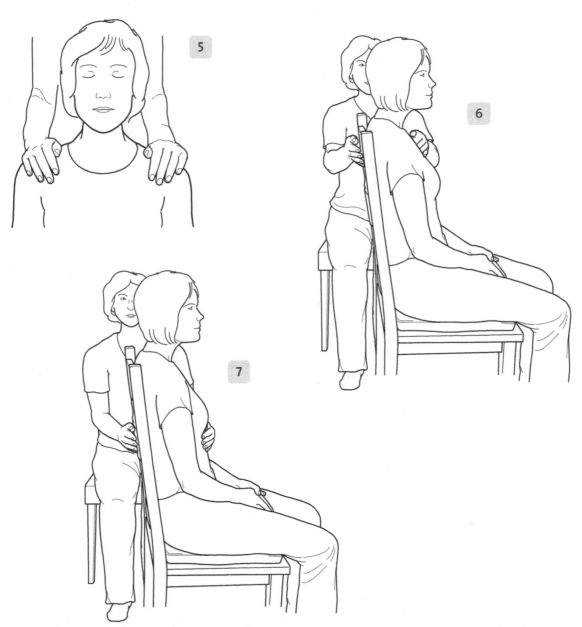

8. **The Waist/Adrenals** – Place one hand on the waist (near the navel) at the front, the other hand on the waist at the back (this is easiest to do from a seated or kneeling position).

9. **The Pelvic Area/Buttocks** – Hold one hand in the air with the palm focused towards the pelvic area (i.e. not placed on the body, which might be intrusive), with the other hand placed underneath the chair, focusing towards the buttocks.

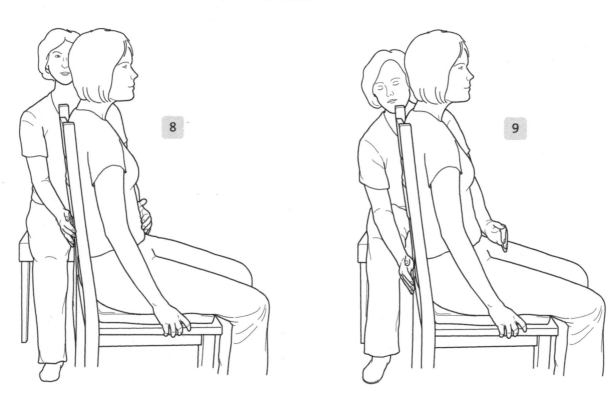

ADDITIONAL HAND POSITIONS

Reiki always flows to any areas of the whole person, physically or energetically, which need it, and because the classic twelve hand positions (or nine in the case of a seated recipient) enable the Reiki to flow easily and effectively into the whole body, other hand positions are not really necessary. For example, hand positions 8 (the pelvic area on the front of the body) and 12 (the buttocks) allow Reiki to flow into the legs and feet. However, over the years many other hand positions have been tried out, and the most common additional positions taught are those on the legs and feet, as given below. If you do use any additional hand positions such as these, they are usually held for between one and three minutes, but again, use your intuition: if your hands are still experiencing a lot of sensation in a particular position on a particular recipient, then continue for as long as seems appropriate.

Of course if the recipient has a health problem in any particular part of the body, it makes sense to give that area additional time, or to add an extra hand position if required. For instance, no specific hand positions are given for the upper arms, elbows, forearms, wrists, hands or fingers, because Reiki flows down the arms naturally – particularly when using the hand position 5 on the upper chest and hand position 9 on the shoulders. But if there is a health problem there, please treat it! Basically, use the twelve hand positions of the traditional full treatment as a framework. In most cases that will be all you need, but if you really feel it is necessary, add to them. Don't be afraid to be creative; Reiki is a dynamic energy and a living healing system, so use it in ways which feel right to you.

Hand Positions for Treatment on the Legs and Feet

The legs and feet can be treated both when the recipient is lying on their back, and again when they are lying on their front. The hand positions are virtually the same for both, except when the recipient is lying on their back, you treat the toes, and when lying on their front, you treat the soles of their feet.

1. One hand on each thigh.

2. One hand on each knee.

3. One hand on each shin (or calf).

4. One hand on each ankle.

5. One hand on the toes of each foot (or soles of each foot, when lying on their front). See illustrations overleaf.

Hand Positions for Treatment on the Arms and Hands

If you do treat the arms and hands, they have to be treated one at a time, as otherwise it would be too much of a stretch. So do all of one arm and hand, and then move to the other side of the body and repeat the hand positions, as shown in the illustration overleaf.

1. One hand on the upper arm, the other on the elbow.

2. One hand on the forearm, the other on the wrist.

3. One hand on top of the hand, the other underneath the palm.

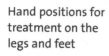

Hand positions for treatment on the legs and feet

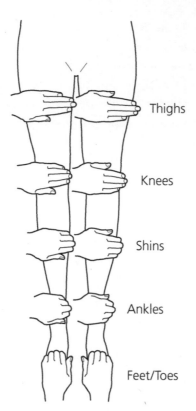

Thighs

Knees

Shins

Ankles

Feet/Toes

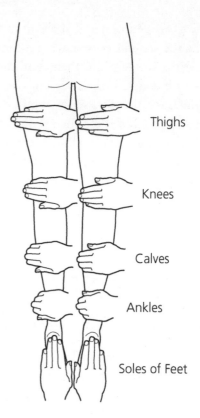

Thighs

Knees

Calves

Ankles

Soles of Feet

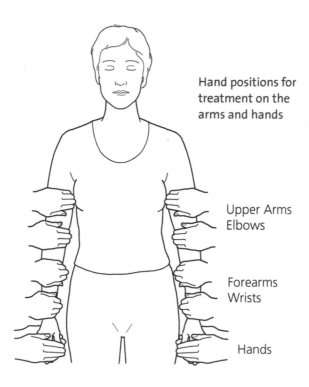

Hand positions for treatment on the arms and hands

Upper Arms
Elbows

Forearms
Wrists

Hands

REVISION QUESTIONS

1. How many classic hand positions are there when giving a Reiki treatment in the West?

2. For how much time is each hand position usually held?

3. How is the thumb held in each hand position?

4. How should you transfer your hands between hand positions?

5. What is the difference between the hand position in the pelvic area for a male and a female recipient?

6. How would the treatment differ if your recipient was heavily pregnant?

(Answers in Appendix 8)

REVISION ACTIVITIES

1. Put the following hand positions in order of treatment:

Ears	Back of Head
Chest	Eyes
Shoulders	Solar Plexus
Buttocks/Coccyx	Navel/Waist
Arms/Hands	Pelvic Area
Back	Waist/Adrenals
Neck	Legs/Feet

2. Prepare a set of hand positions on paper either by writing/printing them out, or by drawing around your hands in the correct 'hands-on' position.

   Mix up the hand positions so that they are in a random order.

   On a therapy couch (or a willing volunteer!) lay each of the paper hand positions in the correct place, and in the correct order for a traditional treatment (if you have learned a different set of hand positions from your Reiki Master use those instead).

Chapter Seven

USING REIKI FOR
SELF-HEALING

S elf-healing is one of the most important aspects of Reiki at any level –
Reiki 1, Reiki 2 or Master. It is an act of love to give yourself a Reiki treatment every day, to give yourself that priority, to find the time to just 'be' with
yourself, and because Reiki works holistically, it will support all aspects of
your self-healing programme – physically, emotionally, psychologically and
spiritually.

Bringing Reiki into yourself by doing regular self-treatments begins the
process of dislodging blocks and negativity within your energetic system –
the life-force energy (Ki) which flows within your physical body, and surrounds it as your aura (see Appendix 2). As these blocks are dislodged and
removed they come to the surface for review, which can mean that memories
of past events suddenly come into your mind, or you start to have very vivid
dreams. You don't need to become overly identified with them; simply
acknowledge them and let them go. (Imagining them in a pink bubble and
seeing that bubble rise up into the sky and beyond to the universe for healing is a good way to release them.) Occasionally you may find that old
situations recur, so you might feel that all those old problems have come back
to plague you! However, you need to understand that this can be a necessary
part of the process, and that you can use Reiki to heal, harmonise and balance these old feelings and fears simply by intending that this should happen
(there is more information on this in Chapter 10). Using Reiki regularly on
yourself can help you to feel better than you have ever felt before, as you
gradually rid yourself of years of blocked or stagnant energy.

TAKING RESPONSIBILITY FOR YOUR WELL-BEING

Reiki is not a cure-all, but it does involve you in your own healing, encouraging you to take responsibility for your own wholeness and health. That means treating your body and your whole self with love and respect, which often means you have to be willing to make changes in your life, perhaps eating a healthier diet, doing some regular exercise or getting more sleep. Other aspects of your life might also need to be examined. For example, are your major relationships healthy and loving? Are you happy with your job? Do you make time for hobbies and interests that add fun to your life? For ideas on how Reiki can help with these issues, please see Chapter 10.

A REIKI SELF-TREATMENT

One of the easiest and best ways of helping yourself with Reiki is to perform a Reiki self-treatment. This means placing your hands on yourself in the standard twelve hand positions (see pages 67–73) and intending that Reiki should flow into you for your greatest and highest good. Each hand position on the head, front and back of the body is normally held for between three and five minutes, and how you do the timing is up to you. Most people seem to prefer to close their eyes during a self-treatment, so you can count the seconds, which can be quite a meditative activity, as is listening to a ticking clock. Another possibility is to buy a CD on which gentle music is played in definite three or five minutes slots, with either silence or a soft gong sound played between each section, to let you know when to move your hands to a new position. These are available commercially but it is easy enough to record your own. That way you can tailor it specifically to the amount of time you prefer, and use music that you particularly like.

Alternatively, you can keep your hands in each position for as long as you feel is needed, using your intuition to let you know when to move on. The more practice you get in self-treatment, the easier it is to let the Reiki guide you. If any area appears to need longer (i.e. your hands are still reacting with heat or tingling, or you feel those sensations in the area of your body which is being treated), then it is fine to continue treatment for as long as seems appropriate. The actual number of minutes isn't what is crucial; it's the fact that you are giving yourself Reiki that matters!

Carrying Out a Self-treatment

Self-treatments can be carried out almost anywhere and at any time of day, but they are more comfortable if you are lying in bed or sitting in a comfy chair, so that your body and arms are well supported. Some people prefer to treat themselves first thing in the morning, whilst others like to do their self-treatment last thing at night to help them to drift off into a peaceful sleep, but don't force yourself to keep to a particular time. Any time that is convenient to you, that fits in with your lifestyle, is the best time, because that way you'll feel more relaxed so you'll enjoy the experience more.

Reiki doesn't need any complicated rituals before it will start to flow. All it takes is your intention to use Reiki, which can, if you wish, be accompanied by a simple invocation, such as: 'Let Reiki flow into me now for my highest and greatest good.' However, where and how Reiki flows is not up to you – you are merely a channel for this healing energy. It will go where it is needed, and not necessarily where you decide you would like it. Having the *intention* that it should flow for the highest and greatest good therefore helps to get rid of your ego, which might otherwise be involved.

For instance, you might really want to heal a particular illness, or get rid of some physical symptoms, but it might be for your greatest and highest good for those symptoms to remain until you are ready to face up to something about your life at the causative level. Therefore, because Reiki acts holistically it might flow first to the mental, emotional or spiritual aspects of your whole self. It may bring some temporary relief of physical symptoms, but you can never guarantee what Reiki will do because it is never under your control, even when you are treating yourself. This means that you need to get rid of any specific expectations as to the outcome of self-treatment. This can be difficult to come to terms with, but by treating yourself with Reiki you are helping yourself, even if that help doesn't manifest itself in exactly the way you hoped it would.

HAND POSITIONS FOR SELF-TREATMENT

The Reiki hand positions for a self-treatment follow the same pattern as for treating someone else, detailed in Chapter 6; i.e. four on the head, four on the front of the body and four on the back of the body. It is *optional* to give Reiki to the thighs, knees, calves, ankles and feet, or to the upper arms, elbows, forearms, wrists, hands or fingers. However, if you have a health problem in any of these areas it obviously makes sense to treat it.

If you have dexterity problems either through injury or disability, please adapt the hand positions as required, e.g. by using only one hand, or by positioning your hand(s) as near as you can to the following areas.

Hand Positions on the Head

There are normally four positions on the head, but some people like to start with an optional extra hand position (making the treatment consist of thirteen hand positions rather than the standard twelve), placing both of their hands on the crown of their head (1A), or one hand on the crown and one at the back of the head (1B). The order of the next three positions isn't vital – some people like to treat the eyes (2), then the ears (3) and then the back of the head (4) – but you can do them in whatever order feels right and comfortable for you, or the way in which your Reiki Master prefers them. The last position in this area is the neck, which can be done in two ways (5A or 5B).

1A. The Crown – *Either*, place both hands on the crown of the head.

1B. *Or*, place one hand on the crown of the head, and the other so it covers the back of the head.

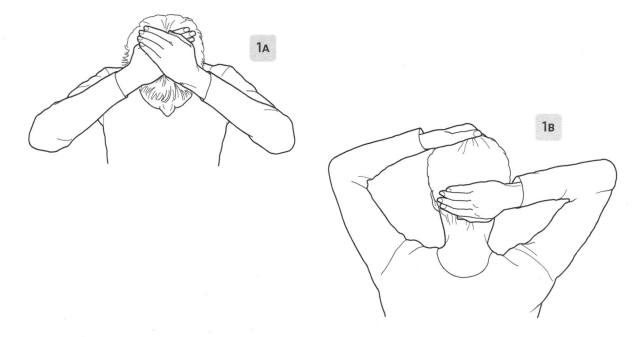

2. **The Eyes** – One hand should be held loosely over each eye, with the heel of each hand placed on your cheekbones, fingertips on your brow.

3. **The Ears/Temples** – One hand is held loosely cupped over each ear, with the heel of each hand placed roughly level with the earlobe and the fingertips pointing upwards towards the temples.

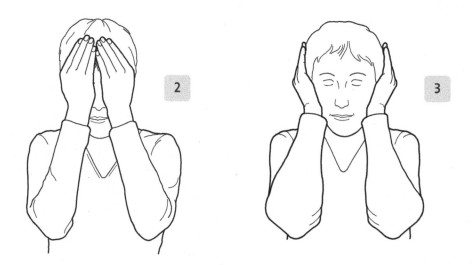

4. **The Back of the Head** – Place one hand so that it cradles the back of the skull, with the other hand just above it.

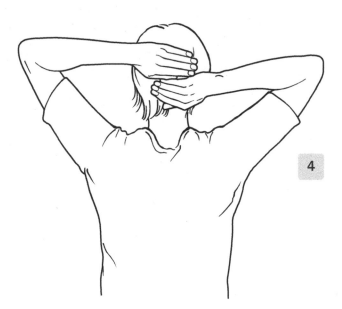

5A. **The Neck/Throat** – *Either*, place one hand on top of the other, covering the throat.

5B. *Or*, place one hand on each side of the neck. If you have quite large hands, the heels of each can touch in front of the throat; otherwise they can be slightly apart.

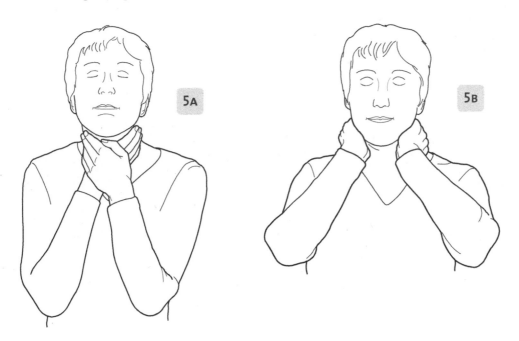

Hand Positions for the Front of the Body

It is usual to place your hands in four positions on the front of the body, starting with the chest, then moving to the solar plexus, then the navel area and finally the pelvic area. On the chest there are a couple of ways you can place your hands, as you will see below.

1A. **The Chest** – *Either*, place both hands crossed in the centre of the chest.

1B. *Or*, place one hand on each side of the chest. The fingertips can touch in the centre, or be slightly apart. See illustrations 1a and 1b overleaf.

2. **The Solar Plexus** – One hand is placed on each side of the body, covering the solar plexus (midriff). The fingertips can again touch in the centre or be slightly apart. See illustration overleaf.

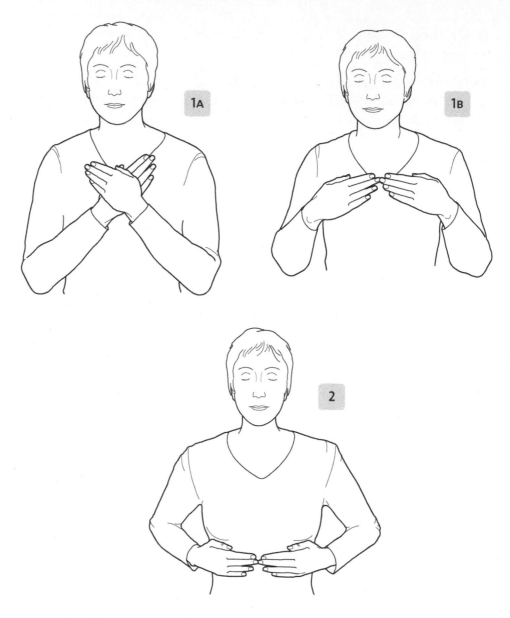

3. **The Waist/Navel** – Place one hand on each side of the body, with the fingers pointing towards each other (touching or slightly apart) at about the same level as your navel (either slightly above or below your natural waistline). See illustration opposite.

4. **The Pelvic Area** – Place one hand on each side of the body, fingers pointing diagonally downwards (as in a V shape) sloping towards the pelvic area. (The same hand position can be used whether you are male or female, as it is not intrusive when doing this hand position on yourself.) See illustration opposite.

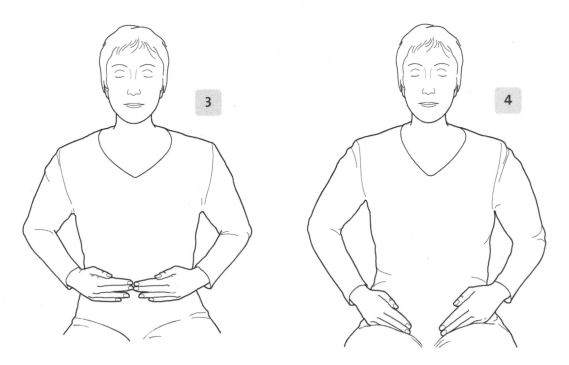

Hand Positions for the Back of the Body

There are usually four hand positions on the back, although some Reiki Masters encourage you to do more, especially if you have back problems or a particularly long back, so it is fine to add extra if that seems appropriate.

The standard four hand positions on the back of the body start with the shoulders, and there are a couple of ways you can do this, depending upon which you find most comfortable (1A or 1B). The positions down the rest of the back can be a little more difficult unless you are quite flexible, so feel free to place the backs of your hands against your body, rather than the palms, if that feels easier and more comfortable – Reiki can flow out of both sides of the hand, so you'll get the same benefits either way. Also, if your hands are reasonably near to a specific area, your intention to treat a particular part of your back will activate the Reiki to flow into that area.

1A. The Shoulders – *Either*, place one hand on top of each shoulder.

1B. *Or*, place one hand on top of each shoulder by crossing your arms in front of your chest.

2. The Upper Back – Place one hand on each side of your back, roughly midway between your shoulders and your waist (or as near to that position as you can comfortably reach).

See illustrations overleaf.

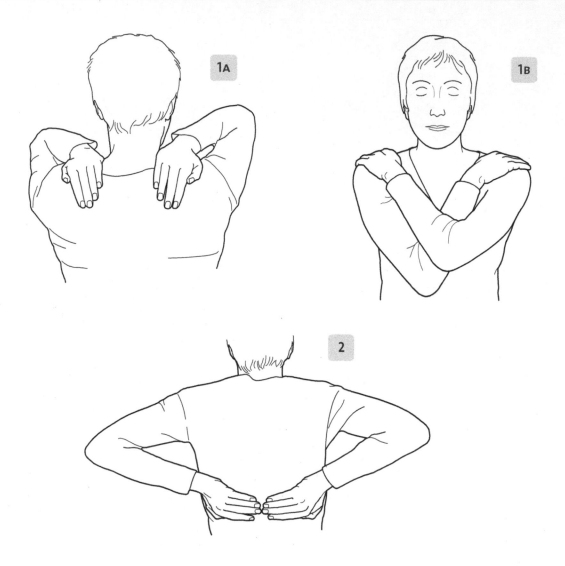

3. The Waist/Adrenals – Place one hand on each side of your back at roughly waist level.

4. The Buttocks – Place one hand on each buttock.

See illustrations opposite.

The above hand positions and timings are given as a framework, but as you get more practised using Reiki you will find yourself drawn to change things sometimes, and that's fine. Reiki will work with you to enhance your intuition and self-awareness, and you need to develop trust in your own responses to how you feel during the treatment, rather than just slavishly following a set of instructions every time. For example, the amount of time

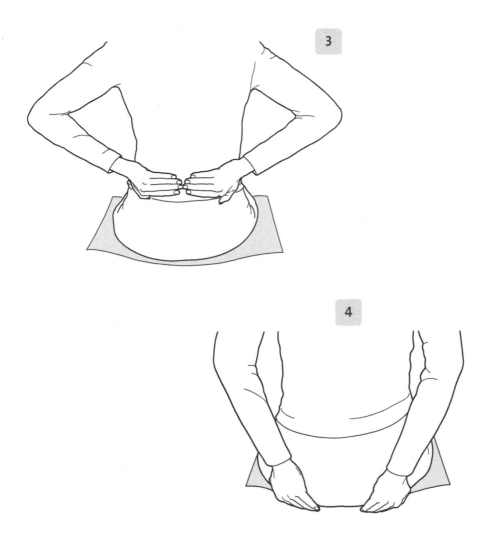

you spend in each hand position doesn't have to be exactly as suggested above. Three to five minutes on a head or body hand position is a good average to aim for, but if you feel a need for ten or fifteen minutes, then do it. Similarly, if you sense that part of you has received enough Reiki in less than three minutes, then simply move on to the next position.

Treating Your Legs and Arms

If you do want to treat your legs and/or arms as well, then the hand positions are as follows, and you can treat them for three to five minutes, as with the head and body positions, or for one or two minutes, which is more usual. When treating your legs, as overleaf, you will probably need to bend your knee to make it easier to reach your ankles and feet.

Legs

1. Place one hand on each thigh.

2. Place one hand on each knee.

3. Place one hand on each calf.

4. Place one hand on each ankle.

5. Place one hand on each foot.

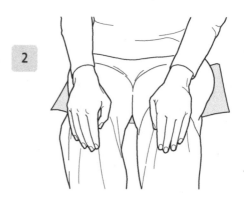

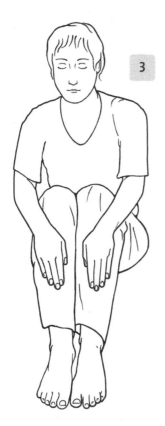

Arms

When treating your arms, you can either do one at a time, or cross your arms over your body to treat both at the same time, as in the illustrations.

1. Place one hand on each upper arm.

2. Place one hand on each elbow.

3. Place one hand on each forearm.

4. Place one hand to cup the other wrist and hand.

OTHER WAYS OF SELF-TREATING

Although doing a full self-treatment every day is an excellent practice to promote self-healing, please don't feel that it is the only way to give yourself Reiki! Reiki can be as flexible as you are; you can place your hands anywhere on your body and allow the energy to flow through you virtually anywhere, at any time. So you can Reiki yourself whilst watching TV, at the cinema, waiting for a bus or sitting in the car in a traffic jam, if safe to do so – the possibilities are endless. The point is, if you have some time to spare, give yourself Reiki. It will help to promote relaxation and a general feeling of well-being, and it doesn't require any conscious effort on your part. Simply put your hands on a convenient part of your body – your chest, solar plexus, stomach or thighs are usually the easiest – and *intend* that Reiki should flow.

Giving Yourself 'First Aid' Treatment

Whilst giving yourself a full Reiki self-treatment is always beneficial, it isn't always necessary. If you have a headache or a minor injury, you might just need to use Reiki as a bit of 'first aid'. So if you have a stiff neck or aching shoulders place your hands on those areas and treat them. If you have a headache or tired/sore eyes, treat them. If you fall and graze your knee, or trap your fingers in a door, treat them. All you need to do is intend that the Reiki should flow, and it will. Of course if your injury is more serious, it makes sense to seek medical help or advice, but you can give yourself Reiki whilst you wait for professional attention. (However, see the section on contraindications in Chapter 8.)

Using Reiki When You Feel Unwell

As well as giving yourself Reiki for minor injuries, remember to give yourself lots of Reiki if you are ill. You cannot 'overdose' on Reiki, so if you are feeling ill just place your hands on yourself anywhere that is comfortable, and let the Reiki keep flowing for as many hours as you like. It will accelerate your body's own healing processes, mobilising your immune system to heal wounds faster or fight off whatever 'bug' you have caught. Initially it may be a little uncomfortable, or it may even exacerbate your symptoms because many of the distressing symptoms we experience when we are ill or injured are actually the effects of the body's activities to fight off infection, release toxins or accelerate cell growth to close wounds, but it will shorten the length of time you feel ill, which has to be a good thing.

REVISION QUESTIONS

1. Why are self-treatments important?

2. What is Ki?

3. Fill in the blanks: when giving Reiki the intention is that it will always be used for the _____ and _____ good.

4. Can you specify what effect Reiki will have?

5. Give some examples of when you can give yourself Reiki.

(Answers in Appendix 8)

REVISION ACTIVITY

Give yourself a self-treatment!

Chapter Eight

USING REIKI TO TREAT FAMILY AND FRIENDS

Treating other people with Reiki is a very pleasurable experience, and in most cases it feels almost as good as receiving the Reiki yourself. There is a great deal of satisfaction to be gained in being able to help people, and the majority of Reiki students enjoy treating their friends and family, and find that it is very fulfilling. Some students, however, are keen to become professional Reiki practitioners, either to add to other therapies in which they are already qualified, or simply to offer Reiki treatments for a fee. If this is something you would like to do, then in addition to this chapter, you will need to read all of Part Four of this manual, which outlines not only the general things every practitioner needs to know, in any country, but also the changes in how to qualify for professional practitioner status in the UK. Even if you just want to treat family and friends, you might still find some useful information in Part Four as topics such as communicating with clients, and following professional standards and ethics, will help you become even better at giving treatments to your friends.

Carrying out a Reiki treatment is basically the same, whether you have Reiki 1, Reiki 2 or Reiki Master, and whether you are working with clients professionally, or just treating family and friends. Since the emphasis in this chapter is on treating friends and family at Reiki level 1, the terms 'practitioner' and 'recipient' are used, rather than 'practitioner' and 'client', to refer to any person using Reiki to treat anyone other than themselves and the person they are treating. It is important to remember that regardless of whether you are working as a professional practitioner or simply offering Reiki to a friend, it is always necessary to be respectful of your recipient's needs. Even when treating people you know well, you have a responsibility to ensure that they feel comfortable, safe and supported, and can rely on your confidentiality.

WHAT IS A REIKI TREATMENT?

A Reiki treatment takes about an hour, and is generally carried out with the recipient remaining fully clothed (except for shoes) and tucked up comfortably with pillows and a blanket on a therapy couch or other stable flat surface which is at a comfortable height for the practitioner to work at. The practitioner's hands are placed gently on or near the body and kept still for a few minutes in each place (see the hand position diagrams in Chapter 6). The recipient may feel heat or tingling where the practitioner's hands are placed, or may notice a flow of energy within their body, but usually the treatment helps them to feel calm and relaxed (although occasionally they might feel energised instead).

WHAT CAN BE TREATED?

The potential with Reiki is unlimited, so almost any physical condition can be treated, although it is important not to have specific expectations of what the Reiki will do, and how fast it will do it. Many physical symptoms that develop fairly quickly, such as a headache or a stiff neck, can be eased very quickly, whilst others which have developed over a long period, such as chronic conditions like arthritis, may need a lot of Reiki before starting to respond, and whilst some people report amazing results, remember that 'healing' is not always the same as 'curing'. Ten people with the same physical condition could have the same number of Reiki treatments from the same practitioner but there would be ten different results, because each person's healing depends not only on their physical state, but also on their mental, emotional and spiritual states. Another factor to consider is that there are some physical conditions where there are legal restrictions on treatment – details of these are given in Chapter 16.

Most people receiving a Reiki treatment want help with a specific physical problem – from frequent headaches or a frozen shoulder to more serious or potentially life-threatening complaints – although some simply want to be able to relax and cope better with the stresses of modern life. It certainly isn't necessary to feel ill in order to experience the benefits of Reiki! However, healing doesn't always happen on the physical level first. Reiki works holistically, so it may be that healing needs to happen first at the emotional level, releasing anger, guilt or hatred, or at the mental level, releasing negative thoughts, concepts or attitudes, before the physical symptom(s) can be addressed, so this is something you should discuss with the recipient before starting a treatment.

You may feel it necessary to advise someone to have further treatment(s) to maintain wellness – but please note that it is illegal to attempt to diagnose any illnesses unless you are medically qualified. If you feel there is a serious problem, you should gently advise the person to seek medical help in addition to Reiki, but always in a way which will not alarm them.

If you are giving Reiki to someone receiving conventional medical treatment, never advise them to stop taking any medicines or to stop seeing their doctor or other health professional, and if necessary advise them to check with their doctor, if they wish, that receiving Reiki healing is OK. As some doctors won't have heard of Reiki, it can be described as a form of spiritual healing. Also, always advise them to see a doctor if their health problem does not respond to treatment, or, as mentioned above, if you intuitively feel there may be some underlying serious problem. Please see below (page 83) and Chapter 20 for further information on ethics and codes of practice that are applicable regardless of whether you are a professional practitioner or just treating your friends and family.

Reiki for Terminal Conditions

It is particularly important to rid yourself of your expectations of the results of a Reiki treatment if you are dealing with people who have been diagnosed as being terminally ill. (It is actually illegal in the UK to offer or advertise a 'cure' for cancer.) Occasionally amazing things can happen with Reiki, and the person recovers completely or goes into substantial remission, but it is wrong to expect it. We are not in control of how Reiki will affect the person we are treating, and in the case of someone who is dying it may be that it will simply help them to make their transition more peacefully. Indeed, it can be a very beautiful and rewarding experience to help someone approaching their death, knowing that with Reiki we have helped to alleviate some of the pain and distress of that person's final days or weeks.

WHO CAN BE TREATED?

Reiki is suitable for virtually anyone of any age or gender. Babies and small children often love Reiki, although since they are so much smaller than an adult they don't need a full treatment. It is far easier to treat them casually, just allowing the Reiki to flow whilst you hold them or when they sit on your knee – there's no need to attempt specific hand positions. Older children and teenagers may sometimes be suspicious, but once they have the opportunity to receive some, they often like it.

Pregnant women usually find Reiki to be very soothing for themselves and their unborn child, and it can be really beneficial to both the mother and the baby to receive Reiki during labour, if the woman's husband, partner, or other 'birthing partner' is present and has been attuned to Reiki. Of course it is also possible for the woman giving birth to use Reiki on herself if she has been attuned, or for someone to send distant Reiki to her – see the end of this chapter, as well as Chapter 13, for more details about this process.

Elderly people often find receiving Reiki very helpful with the many aches and pains which old age can bring. However, unless you have qualifications and experience in dealing with people with serious psychological problems, it is best not to treat them unless you have medical supervision available, e.g. within a specialist clinic.

ARE THERE ANY CONTRAINDICATIONS TO REIKI TREATMENTS?

Reiki is very safe and gentle, yet there have been suggestions within the Reiki community that there are some occasions when you should not carry out a treatment. If it is used on its own (i.e. not in conjunction with any other therapy), there is no evidence that there are any possible contraindications to receiving Reiki. However, you may still hear that there are, so here are some of the most frequently cited contraindications, together with some suggestions for how to counter them.

- Someone who is receiving chemotherapy or radiotherapy should not be treated with Reiki, in case Reiki eliminates the toxins from the body that are part of the treatment. *Actually Reiki always works for the greatest good, so it can help to lessen the side effects of both types of treatment.*

- Someone with a heart pacemaker should not be treated, in case Reiki interferes with the timing. *Reiki isn't an electrical force, and its action is to bring things into balance, so it will probably just do the same job as the pacemaker, but if you or the recipient are concerned you can ask them to check with their doctor.*

- Someone under an anaesthetic (i.e. they should not receive a distant treatment, see Chapter 13), in case the Reiki eliminates toxins/the anaesthesia from the body and they might therefore recover consciousness during surgery. *As Reiki will only flow for the greatest good, this is not likely to be a problem!*

- A Reiki treatment shouldn't be given to someone with an unset broken bone, in case it accelerates the healing too soon. *Again, Reiki always works for the highest good. It can, however, be painful to treat the actual break, so give Reiki elsewhere on the body to help with the pain and shock, and then treat the area of the break frequently after it has been set, either with your hands on the plaster cast or above it.*

- Someone who has lost a finger or toe in an accident should not be treated with Reiki before it is reattached, again in case the Reiki accelerates the healing too soon. *It could be painful to treat the injury site, so give Reiki elsewhere to help with pain and shock, and then treat the area frequently after the finger or toe has been surgically reattached, either 'hands on', or 'hands off' if the area is still too painful.*

- Someone who has epilepsy should not be treated with Reiki in case the Reiki triggers an epileptic fit. *As Reiki usually relaxes people, this isn't likely to be a problem, but if either you or the recipient are concerned about this, then training in first aid would be helpful, so you know how to cope with such a situation, or you could ask them to bring a relative or friend with them who knows what to do if they have a fit.*

- Someone who is taking tablets or injecting insulin for diabetes should not receive Reiki, in case their blood glucose levels change because the Reiki helps to bring things into balance. *Most diabetics test their blood glucose levels regularly anyway, so it is just necessary to advise them to do so after any Reiki treatment(s); if they notice any significant change they should check with their doctor to see if they need to adjust their medication.*

- Someone taking tablets for high or low blood pressure shouldn't be treated with Reiki, in case Reiki brings their blood pressure back into its correct balance. *Similarly, people often have equipment to check their blood pressure, so advise them to check it regularly and then consult their doctor if they notice any significant change, to see if they need to adjust their medication.*

• Someone on medication for thyroid problems or adrenal insufficiency should not be treated. *As above, Reiki may affect their condition to bring the body back into better balance, so advise them to check with their doctor if they detect any changes, in case they need to adjust their medication.*

In all of the above scenarios, you need to communicate with the person receiving Reiki, use common sense and do what feels right. In the case of people on medication, Reiki may help their physical condition so their medication may need to be reassessed, but you must NEVER advise anyone to stop taking their medication! They should only reduce, change or stop their medication in consultation with a qualified medical practitioner.

CONFIDENTIALITY AND ETHICS

Even though you are not practising professionally, your family and friends should still be able to rely totally on your confidentiality. You are in a privileged position when treating them, so you must not discuss their condition or treatment with anyone else unless they give you permission to do so. (Although see Chapter 21 for some legal exceptions to this.) You may sometimes wish to encourage someone you're treating to examine their lifestyle and make positive, healthy modifications, but this should always be done with the utmost sensitivity, and in a positive, helpful manner, without criticism.

It is equally important not to promise any particular outcome from a treatment, because whatever healing takes place is not under your control. The Reiki flows through you into the recipient, but it is *pulled* by the recipient, not *pushed* by the practitioner (it is not possible to *force* healing into anyone), although this is not a conscious process. Reiki, as a spiritual energy, is guided by the recipient's Higher Self/Soul to go to those areas of greatest need, whether that is physical, mental, emotional or spiritual, so the recipient doesn't need to do anything consciously. Promising 'miracle cures' is both unethical and dangerous (and in some cases illegal – see Chapter 21), because you could be falsely raising hopes. Yes, wonderful things do sometimes happen, but no one knows when – or if – that will be. For further information on ethics and codes of practice, see Chapter 20.

HOW MANY TREATMENTS?

This clearly depends upon what is being treated. For minor health problems, or to alleviate stress and encourage relaxation, one or two treatments may be enough, whilst major illnesses are likely to require many treatments. For serious or chronic conditions it is generally accepted that to give four treatments, preferably on consecutive days, is an extremely effective way to start any treatment programme, and if it isn't possible to do the treatments on consecutive days, then at least two per week would be ideal. Another recommendation for dealing with serious illness is to give a full treatment to the affected person every day for at least twenty-one days. This is obviously easier to do if the recipient is a member of your own household, or a family member or friend who lives locally, but in other cases a combination of 'hands-on' and distant treatments can be given. The techniques taught at Reiki level 2 allow you to give a full treatment at a distance with exactly the same effect as if the person was with you – see Chapter 13. In all other instances, you simply need to follow your inner guidance and do what feels right.

WHAT IF PHYSICAL HEALING DOESN'T HAPPEN?

Each of us is a unique individual, experiencing life in a unique way, so it is hardly surprising that we should have complex and sometimes baffling responses to everything in our lives, including illness. Some people who try really hard to heal themselves, using all the self-help techniques and complementary therapies available, are often puzzled and upset when their efforts aren't immediately successful. Often this is because the causative levels (mental, emotional or spiritual) are very deeply buried, and need to come to the surface layer by layer to be understood, so the healing has to take time. (In Chapter 16 you will find details of what parts of the body each hand position is treating, as well as some ideas on the causative levels of healing.)

However, sometimes it is because the illness itself is a 'wake-up call' to the person. For example, something which affects the mobility of a person, bringing them literally to a full stop, might mean that they are forced to look at their lives and realise that changes are needed for their greater health and happiness. Whatever happens, it is important not to be critical or to blame the body for not co-operating, or Reiki for not doing what was hoped for. The person receiving Reiki may wish to stop having treatments, or may want to continue them, and it is important to respect their wishes and encourage them in any way you can. (You can use Reiki on the situation, and to seek guidance on what would be the best way to make progress – see Chapters 10 and 12 for appropriate methods.)

GIVING A REIKI TREATMENT

Equipment You Need to Treat Your Family and Friends

Reiki can be used without any equipment at all, because all you really need is your hands! However, if you want to carry out many Reiki treatments it is sensible to have a suitable 'therapy couch', together with several pillows and a soft blanket. There are various types of therapy couch on the market, some of which are portable and have adjustable-height legs, and these are usually not too expensive – you can find suppliers on the internet, or sometimes through beauty or health equipment suppliers local to you. However, you probably won't need to invest in a therapy couch unless you are planning to practise professionally, and there are various inexpensive alternatives:

- A dining table is often about the right height, and if it is sturdy enough and long enough, you could place some thick foam on top (the mattress from a folding Z-bed is ideal) and cover it with a sheet.

- A camp bed or sun lounger can be used if you are agile enough to sit on the floor with your legs underneath it.

- A chair is a good alternative, especially if someone finds it difficult to lie down – see the specific hand positions for treating seated recipients in Chapter 6.

It is possible to treat someone whilst they lie on a bed or on the floor, but whilst these might be reasonably comfortable for the recipient, they can be very uncomfortable for you after the first ten minutes or so, as you may have to kneel down and bend your back or stretch your arms too much.

Preparing to Give a Treatment

It is important that anyone choosing to receive Reiki from you should come into a comfortable, safe and supportive environment. They need you to behave in a professional manner, even if they know you really well. The room should be clean and tidy, and you can prepare it first by cleansing it with Reiki by sitting quietly for a few moments, and then allowing Reiki to flow through your hands and out into the room, intending that it should cleanse it of any negative energies (other methods are given in Chapter 12).

Set up your therapy couch or whatever alternative you want to use, place clean pillows and a blanket ready, and ensure that the room is at an appropriate temperature and that there will be no interruptions from telephones, children, pets or other distractions. You should also take off your watch and any intrusive metal jewellery (especially bracelets and large rings that might catch in the recipient's hair), and wash your hands before giving a treatment. (Other suggested preparations, such as cleansing yourself energetically, are given in Appendix 3.) You can also suggest that the recipient takes off their watch, spectacles and any large earrings.

Lots of people are quite nervous before having their first Reiki treatment, so always spend a little time talking to them beforehand. They usually find it reassuring when they realise that they can remain fully clothed, and you can also spend some time describing or demonstrating the hand positions you will be using, so that they know exactly what to expect (see Chapter 6). Tell them also what sort of experiences they may have, such as warmth or tingling where your hands are placed, the possibility of feeling rather emotional, or having their limbs jerk, or having vivid dreams, and reassure them that these reactions are all quite normal, and nothing to worry about. Also talk to the recipient about the reason they have come for a treatment, and give them a chance to ask questions.

Remember, regardless of whether the recipient is a paying client, a friend, or a member of your family, they are entitled to expect your complete confidentiality. So never talk to others – not even to their relatives – about their health or their treatments, unless you have their permission to do so (see also Chapters 20 and 21).

Getting Ready for the Reiki Treatment

You should help the recipient to get onto whatever treatment surface you have prepared, and a pillow should be placed under their head and neck, and another under their knees when the person is lying on their back. That second pillow should be moved to underneath the ankles when the recipient is lying on his or her front. Sometimes placing a soft blanket over the person makes them feel nurtured and more relaxed, and ensures they stay warm enough when their body cools down because they are lying still. It is important that both practitioner and recipient should relax and enjoy the treatment, so before you start make sure that both of you are comfortable, that the therapy surface is at a comfortable height for you, and the recipient is warm enough. Talking or asking questions during the treatment is an individual matter, although being quiet allows the recipient to relax more thoroughly, and usually he or she will feel sleepy, so simply playing soft, relaxing music in the background is often best, unless the recipient objects to that.

The Role of Intention

Whenever we want to start using Reiki, it is our *intention* to do so that allows the Reiki to begin flowing – there is no special ritual to follow. As an example of a contrast, when you put out your hand to pick up a cup of tea, the Reiki doesn't flow because you are not intending to use Reiki – you just want to drink your tea! But when you are giving someone a treatment, as you prepare to place your hands in the first position, just mentally *intend* the Reiki to flow into them for their highest and greatest good. You can, if you wish, silently say to yourself 'let Reiki flow into [recipient's name] for their greatest and highest good', although this isn't strictly necessary. Similarly, at the end of a treatment, as you take your hands away for the final time, it is your intention to stop, so the Reiki will usually stop flowing immediately, although occasionally it will continue to flow for a few minutes whilst you gently rouse the recipient, and even sometimes during the time you chat to them afterwards about their experience. This additional flow of Reiki can be helpful for the recipient, especially if they feel very emotional after a treatment, and the flow will stop when they no longer need this support. Remember, the Reiki is pulled by the recipient, not pushed by the practitioner, and all of this is at a subconscious level, so don't be concerned if this happens – just 'let go and let flow'!

When you're ready to begin, just spend a few moments quietly to centre yourself, and as you intend that the Reiki flows into the recipient for their greatest and highest good, place your hands in the first position on the recipient's head, as shown in Chapter 6. Hold them there (on or off the body, whichever you have been taught by your Reiki Master) for between three and five minutes. Continue the treatment by moving your hands gently, at roughly three- to five-minute intervals, to the rest of the positions on the head and body, and if necessary, also on the person's legs and/or arms.

After the Treatment

Your Reiki Master may recommend a variety of ways to end a Reiki treatment, but one suggestion is to smooth the recipient's aura (see Appendix 3 for information about auras) to remove any negative energy which may have risen from the body into their energy field during the treatment. Do this by intending that Reiki should flow out of your hands to clear and balance the recipient's aura, and then hold one or both of your hands about 15–20 cm (6–8 inches) above the recipient's body, and, starting above the crown of their head, allow your hands to flow gently in the air over their body (keeping at least 15–20 cm distance) right down to below the soles of the feet. Finish by throwing the energy downwards towards the floor to get rid of any negative energy, and repeat this action twice more.

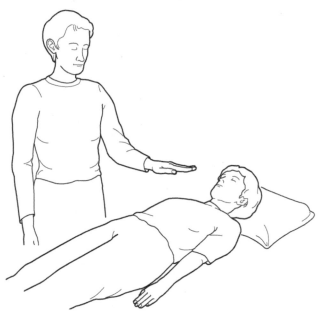

Finally, finish by brushing your own hands together a couple of times, to let go of any negative energy which might have clung to them, and then gently rouse the recipient by touching their shoulder and saying their name softly. If they are having difficulty in 'coming round', gently massage their feet to bring them back into a wakeful state. When they are ready, help them to sit up or get off the therapy couch, and offer them a glass of water, and do advise them to drink plenty of water for the next few days, to help the body to flush out any toxins which may have been dislodged by the Reiki. However, if they have any medical condition which might be exacerbated by drinking extra fluids, then please ask them to check with their doctor first.

Some people feel really energised immediately after a treatment, whilst others feel sleepy and very peaceful. If the person seems at all 'spaced out', then make sure you ground them before allowing them to leave. This is easily done by getting the person to sit with their feet flat on the floor, whilst you place one hand on each of their feet, and then you visualise any excess energy flowing out through the soles of their feet into the earth below. Alternatively, you can get them to stand and stamp their feet vigorously.

REIKI AS FIRST AID

Giving a full treatment is not the only way to give Reiki, so please don't feel constrained by the idea that you always need a therapy couch and time to do twelve or more hand positions! If anyone around you needs help, you have a tool available for which you only need your hands. Many minor problems or injuries can quickly be alleviated with Reiki, such as headaches, toothache, muscle strain, cramp, cuts and bruises and so on. Simply place your hands on or near the affected area and allow the Reiki to flow. Most such aches and pains will probably ease within a few minutes, and may be gone completely within a quarter of an hour. There's no specific amount of time for such events – just allow your inner guidance to let you know when the Reiki has stopped flowing. (Usually this will mean that you no longer feel any sensation in your hands, but for those people who get very little sensation anyway it may surprise you, but you will still 'know' when it is right to take your hands away.)

REIKI SHARING GROUPS

Getting together with other people who do Reiki is great fun, and the more confident and experienced members of a Reiki sharing group can help those who are new to Reiki, or who feel shy about trying it on their family or friends without getting some more practice first. The more Reiki you receive, the more you heal, and the more Reiki energy will flow through you so that you can help others to heal, so Reiki groups are an ideal place to 'swap' treatments with each other.

To have two, four, six or even more people treating you at once can be a delightful experience, producing an even deeper state of relaxation and well-being. The more people you have treating you, the less time it takes, as you simply share the hand positions out between you, usually with each person working on one side of the body only. If you have lots of people you can cover all of the head and body, and the legs, feet, arms and hands as well – and of course everyone can take it in turns to receive Reiki, as well as give it. However, when treating in a large group, don't feel constrained by the traditional hand positions, as it is often more comfortable to spread out a little.

If you like this idea, various Reiki organisations have lists of Reiki groups, so you could join one of those – there are some contact details at the back of this book. Alternatively, you could perhaps start a Reiki group yourself by contacting any people who trained at the same course as you, or any other Reiki people you know.

DISTANT HEALING

What do we mean by distant healing? It's something you can carry out when you are nowhere near the recipient, who could be in the next room, the next town, or in another country on the other side of the world. Sometimes this is called 'absent' healing, but it's basically the same thing. Sending distant healing – or rather, allowing the Reiki to flow to a person who isn't with you – is something which can be done at any level of Reiki, and in this chapter we cover how to do this at Reiki 1. However, when the Reiki 2 symbols are used, the Reiki healing received can be much stronger, so sending a distant Reiki treatment is usually only possible after Reiki 2, and so that is covered in Chapter 13.

One of the really nice things about Reiki for many of us is that we have a tool we can use to help other people, especially our family and friends, and we can 'send' healing and love to people we know are ill, or in distress, just as we can say prayers for them. There are a number of simple ways to do this at Reiki 1, but there are ethics to consider when sending distant Reiki. The person you are sending the Reiki to should usually know about it and have given you permission, unless they are unable to do this (if they are in a coma, for instance, or are too ill to be questioned). Also, whenever you send distant Reiki, you always intend that it flows for the recipient's highest and greatest good, so you are not presupposing any particular outcome – Reiki will flow to wherever it is needed, and you don't have any control over that.

1. Write the person's name on a piece of paper and hold it in your hands for five or ten minutes (or longer if you wish) and intend that Reiki flows to that person for their greatest and highest good.

2. *Or*, hold a photograph of the person in your hands and intend that Reiki flows to that person for their greatest good. See illustration opposite.

3. *Or*, visualise (imagine) the person small enough to be held within your hands, and, again, intend that Reiki flows to them for their greatest and highest good.

Any of the above methods can also be used to send Reiki to your pets or any other creature.

REVISION QUESTIONS

1. How long does a Reiki treatment normally last?

2. Can you offer guarantees to a Reiki recipient about the results it will bring?

3. Is healing the same as curing?

4. Can you attempt to diagnose illness?

5. Where should pillows be placed during a standard treatment?

(Answers in Appendix 8)

REVISION ACTIVITY

Arrange a Reiki sharing group with someone else who can give Reiki.

Chapter Nine

USING REIKI
WITH ANIMALS, PLANTS
AND OBJECTS

Reiki isn't only useful for treating people. It can also be used effectively on animals, birds and other creatures, as well as on plants, and even inanimate objects.

USING REIKI WITH ANIMALS

The way you treat a particular animal (or bird, fish, reptile or insect) will obviously depend upon its size and temperament, and whilst with some you can follow a similar format of hand positions to those you would use on humans, with others you may need to use different methods depending upon specific circumstances. However, the main methods are as follows:

1. Placing the hands directly on the animal, whenever it is safe and practicable to do so.

2. Holding a small animal or other type of creature in your hands, if this is safe to do (i.e. if it won't bite or scratch you) and it won't frighten the creature too much.

3. Placing the hands on or near the cage or tank in which the animal, bird, fish, reptile or insect is housed, where the creature is either too small or too dangerous to touch, or where direct touch would be disadvantageous to the creature (e.g. a fish).

4. Using distant healing techniques. At Reiki level 1 this can be by holding either a piece of paper with the animal's name on it, or a photograph of the animal, between your hands and intending that Reiki flows to it for its highest and greatest good; or alternatively, expanding your aura to encompass the animal and then allowing Reiki to flow out of your hands to fill your aura (this is sometimes called 'beaming' Reiki). See Appendix 2 for information about auras.

All animals, birds and other creatures can be treated using the Reiki symbols if you have Reiki 2 (see Chapter 12), including sending them distant treatments (see Chapter 13).

Treating Dogs and Cats

Dogs and cats are probably the most popular pets, and generally they are the easiest to treat with Reiki. Depending upon the animal's size, you might try one or two hand positions on the head, and two or three on either side of the body, for perhaps five minutes in each position, or less time (or longer) if you sense it is necessary – use the sensations in your hands and the animal's reactions to guide you. Any hand positions you choose will obviously depend upon where you can reach, and where the animal will allow you to touch, as well as where it is safe to touch. Even pets can be bad-tempered sometimes if they are in pain. If the animal has a specific injury it might be sensible to avoid direct contact with that area, but we know that Reiki will flow around the whole body, so wherever you place your hands the animal will draw sufficient Reiki into itself for its needs. See illustration overleaf.

The amount of time for treatment will obviously vary, depending upon the individual animal, from about ten minutes up to an hour or more. Some dogs or cats will happily sit or stand for a long time to receive Reiki. Generally, however, animals are much more intuitive about their health needs than humans, so they will sense when they have received enough. Sometimes they will move away quite quickly, and if this happens, please allow them to go.

Treating Small Mammals

If you are treating a much smaller pet like a rabbit, guinea pig, hamster or gerbil, you might be able to hold it in your hands to give it Reiki, and it will probably only need between five and twenty minutes. However, if the animal

is likely to bite or scratch you, you can hold your hands on or near its hutch or cage and just let the Reiki flow.

Pet Birds, Reptiles and Insects

For these categories of pets it is probably safest to treat them in their cage or tank if they are likely to peck, bite, scratch or sting. Just hold your hands on or near the container and intend that the Reiki should flow to the creature, and take your hands away when it feels appropriate to do so – it will probably only need a few minutes.

Fish

Cold water or tropical fish must obviously be treated in their normal environment, i.e. in water at the temperature they are used to. So hold your hands on or near to their tank and let the Reiki flow for a few minutes, or for as long as you feel it is necessary.

Treating Horses

It is possible to treat a horse with Reiki whilst sitting astride it, placing your hands on either side of the head, neck and flanks. Otherwise it is probably easiest to stand beside the animal and move along one side of it, placing your hands wherever you feel is appropriate, and then do roughly the same positions on the other side. Horses' legs and feet are often prone to injury, so these can be treated using both hands in much the same way as you would on a human leg – but please take particular care, as horses are prone to kick! Use your intuition, and the horse's reactions, to decide how long each hand position should be held.

Farm Animals

With animals such as cattle, sheep, pigs, goats, hens or geese, or more exotic species such as llamas and alpacas, unless you are very used to handling them it is often easiest to treat them through the aura from the edge of their field or beside the pen, sty or other enclosure, at Reiki level 1.

Treating Wild Animals or Birds

Wild birds or other small wild animals are probably best placed in a cardboard box with air holes before being treated, as contact with humans can be very frightening, and the shock can even cause some to die. Just place your hands on the box and let the Reiki flow. Of course if the injury is serious, it is best to transport it as quickly as you can to a veterinarian or an animal charity. However, please be aware that it is illegal for unauthorised people to handle some wild animals that are protected species, like bats and dormice, so in such cases please contact a wildlife sanctuary or other suitable organisation. If you should ever need to give Reiki to a wild animal that might prove dangerous (e.g. in a zoo), or which is too nervous to let you get near it, then it is perfectly acceptable to stand a safe distance away and send the Reiki through your own aura to the animal (or, at Reiki level 2, to use Reiki symbols and/or distant healing – see Chapters 12 and 13).

Using Reiki on Your Animal's Food and Medication

Another good way to help your pets, or any other animals you are caring for, is to Reiki their food and water to enhance its nutritional qualities and to offset any adverse effects of any chemicals or preservatives. This is simple to do. Hold the food or water bowl with one hand under it and one hand over it, and intend that Reiki should flow into the food or water. You can also do this with a box, packet or tin of food, placing your hands on either side of it and intending that Reiki should flow into it – a minute is usually enough, and thirty seconds will probably do. Any homeopathic remedies or medication dispensed by a veterinary surgeon can also be given Reiki in the same way.

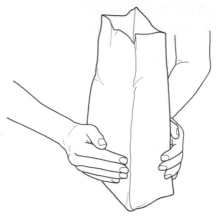

LEGAL ISSUES WHEN TREATING ANIMALS

According to the Royal College of Veterinary Surgeons, in the UK the Veterinary Surgeons Act of 1966 states that anyone treating animals must be a qualified veterinary surgeon, and that no one other than a qualified vet can diagnose problems, carry out tests for diagnostic purposes, advise or carry out medical or surgical treatment or prescribe medication.

However, it does appear to be legal for farm workers to treat their animals, and for anyone else to treat their own pets, or to treat an animal in an emergency. If you do decide to treat any animal other than your own with Reiki it is essential that you get the owner's permission, and advise him or her to register the animal with a qualified veterinary surgeon, and to take their animal to that vet for diagnosis and treatment (see Chapter 21 for more information). Regulations in other countries may be different, and I would advise you to find out exactly what they are before carrying out any work with animals – it is obviously best to stay within the law!

USING REIKI WITH PLANTS AND SEEDS

Seeds and plants respond very well to being treated with Reiki at any stage of their growth, so whether you're a keen gardener or just have a few houseplants, Reiki can be an important tool to help your plants to flourish.

Seeds and Seedlings

To give Reiki to seeds, simply hold the packet between your hands for between thirty seconds and one minute, and intend that Reiki should flow to the seeds. Alternatively, plant the seeds and then hold your hands over the seed trays. If you grow seedlings on your windowsill or in a greenhouse and wish to transplant them into your garden, then as well as giving them a good soaking beforehand, Reiki them before and after planting out, and daily for at least a week. You can either hold the seed tray in your hands, or hold your hands above the plants, and just let the Reiki flow.

Houseplants

For houseplants, the easiest way to treat them is to hold your hands on each side of the pot for about a minute, or you can hold your hands about 15 cm (6 inches) away from the plant, and allow Reiki to flow.

Other Plants, Bushes and Trees

You can Reiki your plants, bushes and trees at any stage, either as a regular thing, perhaps once a week, or occasionally – and especially if you can see them wilting or suffering from pests or disease, as this will help to strengthen their own defences. (Reiki will not kill pests, of course, so you will still need some conventional treatments!) If you have a lot of plants, a quick and easy method is to Reiki the water you use when giving them their regular watering. This is even possible when using a hosepipe, as you can intend that as the water passes through the section of the pipe you are holding, it will receive Reiki.

If you are moving plants from one part of the garden to another, then Reiki them before you dig them up, and again when they have been transplanted, as well as giving them plenty of water, and continue to Reiki them daily for about a week. Similarly, if you are pruning a plant, bush or tree, or cutting a hedge, Reiki it before and afterwards, to help it to recover.

USING REIKI WITH FOOD AND DRINK

It makes good sense to give Reiki to all the food you eat and to everything you drink. Not only does this enhance the nutritional value of the food, but it can also help to balance the ill effects of additives and chemicals and bring the food into harmony with your body. You don't have to hold your hands over your food in an overt act; you can be discreet and hold your hands at the sides of your plate, or around the cup or glass just for a brief time – a few seconds is all that is needed.

REIKI AND INANIMATE OBJECTS

You may find it difficult to believe, but Reiki can also work well on inanimate objects like cars, computers and washing machines. This isn't as strange as it sounds. Everything in the universe is energy (see Appendix 2), and all 'man-made' objects started out as natural materials such as iron ore, oil or wood. Those natural materials may have changed state, but they are still energy, and once energy has been created, it has to remain in some form, so it can only be transformed into some other state. Think of water, which can be changed into ice or steam.

We're not suggesting that Reiki should be used in place of regular maintenance; your car will still need a service and Reiki won't replace the need for diesel or petrol either, but it can be jolly useful when things go wrong! Place your hands on the object and intend that Reiki should flow into it for the highest and greatest good – you may feel your hands begin to tingle or get warm – and hold them there for as long as seems necessary, which could be ten minutes or longer.

REVISION QUESTIONS

1. How would you give Reiki to a cat or dog?

2. How would you give Reiki to a horse?

3. How would you give Reiki to a fish?

4. Other than giving Reiki directly, how else can Reiki help the animal?

5. What is the legal situation when treating animals?

6. How can you use Reiki to benefit plants and/or seeds?

7. Other than receiving Reiki directly, how else can Reiki benefit you?

(Answers in Appendix 8)

REVISION ACTIVITIES

1. Reiki the water next time you water your houseplants.

2. Reiki your animal's food next time you feed them.

Chapter Ten

USING REIKI
TO HEAL PERSONAL AND
GLOBAL SITUATIONS

Reiki is very versatile in the ways it can be used, so as well as treating people, animals and plants you can use it at any level – Reiki 1, 2 or Master – to help to heal personal problems or issues, and global situations. In Chapter 12 there are details about how to use the Reiki symbols on the various methods described here to make them even more effective, but all of the following can be used by people who have Reiki at First Degree level.

USING REIKI ON PERSONAL PROBLEMS AND ISSUES

Whatever kind of problems you are having, from strained relationships with your partner or family to difficulties at work or with studying, you can use Reiki to help to permeate the situation with healing. Simply write the situation down on paper – whether it needs a single sentence or several paragraphs to describe it – and then hold the paper between your hands, intending that Reiki should flow to the situation for the highest and greatest good of all. Do this for at least ten minutes a day for as long as the situation exists. However, you do need to detach yourself from specific expectations about the result, because Reiki will work towards what you *need*, for your highest good, and not necessarily what you *want*! Also, Reiki will only work ethically, so you cannot control anyone else using this method, for example, to persuade a particular person to fall in love with you.

Using Reiki on Your Hopes and Goals

You can use a similar method to work on your goals and dreams with Reiki. Write down what you really want – an interesting new job, a loving relationship (but not naming a particular person), a cottage in the country, a holiday in Greece, whatever – on a piece of paper, and be as specific as possible. Write down every aspect of what you are seeking, so if you want a cottage in the country, put down how many bedrooms and bathrooms you want, what kind of kitchen, whether you want central heating or open fires, a small garden or acres of farmland, etc. Then hold this piece of paper in your hands and give it Reiki for at least ten minutes a day until you achieve what you want – or until your circumstances change and you realise it isn't any longer what you really desire. If it is for your highest and greatest good to receive what you've asked for, then Reiki will work with your Higher Self to help you achieve it, although be aware that timing might still be an issue, or, in other words, you might have to wait for it!

Using Reiki with Affirmations

Affirmations are positive statements which can help to reprogramme your thinking, and they can be a really powerful method for change. You should make sure that your affirmations are always personal, really positive, and fully in the present, even if, right now, the statement isn't true. Examples of such positive affirmations are: 'I am healthy and vibrantly well', or 'I have an interesting job that pays well', or 'I am confident and assured'. If you use a statement founded in the future, such as 'I will have an interesting job', then it continues to be in the future, rather than potentially becoming a part of your reality now! You can make your affirmation even more effective by writing it down and holding the paper in your hands, saying it aloud over and over to yourself (at least twenty times a day, preferably more) whilst giving it Reiki. Again, do this daily until you notice changes happening, such as beginning to feel more confident.

Using Reiki for Personal Growth and Spiritual Development

Reiki is a spiritual energy, and part of each person's path with Reiki is personal growth and spiritual development. There are a number of ways in which you can use Reiki to help with this. You can write 'Let Reiki flow to help with my personal growth and spiritual development, for my greatest and highest good' on a piece of paper, and spend five or ten minutes each day giving it Reiki.

Alternatively, you can combine Reiki with a simple form of meditation. Sit comfortably and place your hands on your body wherever feels comfortable, for example your chest or solar plexus, and intend that Reiki should flow into you to help with your spiritual development. Then close your eyes and concentrate on your breathing – sometimes it helps to count your breaths – as you breathe slowly and deeply, and just let your body and mind relax. (You don't have to attempt to completely empty your mind – that can take many years of practice!) You should find that doing this for five or ten minutes a day, gradually building up to about twenty minutes, will bring feelings of calm, peace and contentment which will help you to cope with your daily life. You might also like to try the Hatsurei-ho meditation technique (from the Japanese traditions) which is described in Appendix 3.

USING REIKI ON WORLD SITUATIONS AND DISASTERS

To send Reiki healing to global situations, such as famines, ecological and environmental disasters or war zones, write down some details about the situation and hold the piece of paper in your hands, intending that Reiki should go to that situation for the highest possible good of all. In this way the Reiki is not being constrained to only go to one aspect of the situation, such as the people affected by the famine, but to the whole, so that it can also permeate the aid agencies, the governments, any warring factions, and so on. It is perfectly ethical to send Reiki in this way, as it is not intruding on anyone individually.

It is really rewarding to feel that you have a wonderful tool like Reiki and can therefore do something to help, because so often we are too far removed from such situations to either fully understand them or to offer practical assistance. Many thousands of people send Reiki to world situations every day, and if you have access to the internet you may find websites or online groups telling you about the latest healing 'target' so that you can join in, if you wish.

HEALING THE PLANET

Human intervention has caused, and continues to cause, considerable environmental problems for the earth, so you can use Reiki to help to heal the planet. There are many methods for earth healing, and all of them can be enhanced by using Reiki.

1. Go to a place of power, like an ancient stone circle such as Avebury in Wiltshire, or Castlerigg in Cumbria, and either sit in the middle or place your hands on one of the stones, and allow Reiki to flow into the stone, around the circle, and into the earth itself, intending that the Reiki flows for the greatest and highest good of the planet. It can be fun to also intend that the Reiki flows out of your feet as well, directly into the earth, and you will often find that your feet get really hot when you do this.

2 Sit or stand either outdoors or indoors with your palms facing downwards, and direct Reiki into the earth, intending that it be used by the planet for its greatest and highest good.

3. Imagine that you are holding a small version of the world between your hands, and send it Reiki, and intend that the Reiki flows to everything on and within the earth – rocks, minerals, metals, crystals, oceans, rivers, people, animals, birds, reptiles, fish, insects, trees, bushes, crops, grasses and all other plants, for the greatest and highest good.

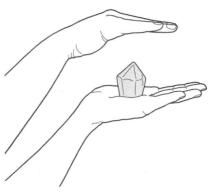

4. Hold something in your hands to represent the earth, such as a pebble or crystal, and fill it with Reiki, intending that the Reiki should fill the planet for the highest good.

REVISION QUESTIONS

1. Which of the these affirmations would be better to use, and why? 'I am in a fulfilling, loving relationship' or 'I will soon meet my ideal partner'.

2. How would you use Reiki to help environmental issues?

3. Can you use Reiki on a personal issue if you have only attained Reiki 1?

4. Can you use Reiki to change a situation in a specific way?

(Answers in Appendix 8)

REVISION ACTIVITY

Think of one personal situation, and one global situation, and send Reiki to them using one of the methods detailed in this chapter.

Part Three

REIKI THEORY
AND PRACTICE FOR
LEVEL 2/SECOND DEGREE

The Reiki Symbols and Their Mantras

·

Using the Power of the Reiki Symbols

·

Distant Treatments and Healing with the Reiki Symbols

Chapter Eleven

THE REIKI SYMBOLS

All of the theory and practice you learn at Reiki First Degree is still applicable at Reiki 2, but the major difference is that you have some additional tools – the Reiki symbols – to enhance your practice and make Reiki even more effective.

There are four symbols in the Usui System of Natural Healing, three of which are taught to Reiki 2 students, and one which is taught only to Master students, and each represents certain metaphysical energies. They are calligraphic shapes that come from a combination of Sanskrit and the Japanese kanji, the Japanese alphabet. The way your Reiki Master will probably show them to you will be flat, drawn on a piece of paper, but in reality they are three-dimensional, having height, width and depth, and their size is unlimited – they can be as small or as large as they need to be. Of course there are limits to the size the symbols can be drawn with your whole hand, which is how they are usually done, but it is possible to *imagine* any of the symbols large enough and deep enough to encompass a whole person, a whole building or even the whole planet, or small enough to fit on a postage stamp, or inside a single living cell.

Using any of the Reiki symbols adds power to the Reiki energy and enables it to work in different ways, depending upon which symbol (or combination of symbols) is being used. Despite their power and their spiritual nature, the symbols are easy to use, and they work automatically, every time they are used. They are like keys which open doors to higher levels of awareness or manifestation, or they can be likened to buttons – whenever you 'push' one, you automatically get specific results. In different combinations, the symbols can be used for a wide variety of purposes, both personal and global, from healing yourself, other people, animals and plants, to healing situations, empowering goals, healing and clearing your environment, healing the planet, healing past lives and possibly even more!

WHAT GIVES THE SYMBOLS THEIR POWER?

Some people have read about Reiki and seen the symbols in a book or on the internet and think they can use them for healing, but this isn't the case. It is the spiritual empowerment of the attunement process carried out by a Reiki Master which activates the symbols so that they can fulfil their intended purpose. Without that attunement, the symbols do not activate Reiki. During an attunement, the energies of each symbol come down and enter the student's mind and body, so that afterwards, whenever the student uses the symbol, the same energies they were connected to during the attunement are activated and begin flowing.

DRAWING THE SYMBOLS

The most usual way of drawing the shapes of the symbols is with the whole hand, or just with the fingers, in the air above or near to the person, animal or object you are treating. But they can also be drawn with the eyes (either by imagining the symbol being drawn, or by moving the eyes to follow the shape of the symbol), or, when someone is really familiar with them, each symbol can be fully visualised. When visualising them the symbols are often 'seen' in purple, white or gold, although they can appear in any colour.

Whilst it is important to draw the symbols correctly the way your Reiki Master shows you (which is being properly respectful to Reiki), some students get worried about this in case they make a 'mistake'. However, it is the *intention* to use them which activates the symbols, and brings in the specific energies associated with them; the *essence* of the symbol remains the same, although clearly you should always do your best to draw them as accurately as possible, rather than being careless or slapdash. If you do notice you've made a mistake whilst drawing any of the symbols, you can always 'rub it out' in the air with your hand, and start again!

SACREDNESS AND THE REIKI SYMBOLS

The Reiki symbols are regarded as sacred; up to the mid-1990s in the West they were not revealed to anyone who had not undertaken Reiki 2 training, or, for the Master symbol, Reiki 3 training. In this respect, they were viewed as being 'secret', although in the Japanese culture 'secret' and 'sacred' are interconnected, so it would be unnatural for them to openly discuss things that were part of a spiritual tradition. The symbols are in fact on view in the Saihoji Temple in Kyoto, which indicates their sacredness, so although they are not 'secret', they are special, and should be treated as such. In the West some people think that anything 'secret' should be viewed with suspicion, which is probably why over recent years the symbols have been openly printed in books or on the internet – although sometimes they have been reproduced inaccurately.

For this reason it seemed appropriate to include copies of the Reiki 2 symbols in this book, as accurately as possible, being copied from a document purported to have been written by Dr Hayashi, because this is a Reiki manual, to be used for Reiki training. This will support both Reiki 2 students, and their Reiki Masters. However, rather than reproduce them in the text of this chapter they are in Appendix 4, which gives your Reiki Master the opportunity to use them in class, or to provide you with copies they have drawn themselves, as they see fit.

Some Reiki Masters, when teaching Reiki 2, will hand out copies of the symbols and ask students to memorise them during the course and hand them back at the end, whilst some will allow their students to keep copies of the symbols; others prefer not to have them written on paper, and draw them in the air instead, instructing their students to copy their actions. It is just a matter of choice. However, the symbols do have to be memorised so that you can use them easily – it isn't very sensible to have to look at a piece of paper or a book every time you want to draw a symbol! Usually you are asked not to reveal the symbols (or their mantras) to anyone other than people who have already done Reiki 2, which means being careful not to allow people to see you drawing out the symbols, or hear you saying their mantras.

THE REIKI SYMBOLS' MANTRAS

A mantra traditionally is a word or sound that is repeated to aid concentration in meditation, particularly in Hinduism and Buddhism. In Sanskrit the word 'mantra' translates as 'an instrument of thought', from the word 'man' which means 'to think'. Each of the Reiki symbols has a corresponding mantra, sometimes referred to as 'kotodama', or 'jumon' – the word 'jumon' means 'spirit word', and 'kotodama' means 'the soul of language' – which some people mistakenly use as the symbol's name. For example, the first symbol has a three-syllable mantra (the syllables start with the letters CKR) but its *name* is the Power symbol (or the Focus symbol in the Japanese tradition). The second symbol, the Mental and Emotional symbol, or Harmony symbol, also has a three-syllable mantra (SHK), whilst the third symbol, the Distant or Connection symbol, has a five-syllable mantra, HSZSN. Each mantra works in conjunction with its related symbol, but the mantras themselves also have power, and chanting them can bring about states of energy, calm, connectedness and bliss.

THE THREE REIKI LEVEL 2 SYMBOLS

During a Reiki 2 course you are taught three of the four Reiki symbols to use during treatments on yourself, other people and animals, as well as for other creative uses such as clearing spaces, or working on problems and situations. In this chapter we give some simple examples of how each of the symbols can be used, but for more extensive and comprehensive uses, including using the symbols for distant healing and distant treatments, please see Chapters 12 and 13.

The First Symbol: The Power (or Focus) Symbol (CKR)

This symbol is probably the most versatile of the three given at this level; it can be used alone (it is the only symbol which can be used by itself), or in combination with either or both of the other two symbols (it turns the power on so that the others can work, hence its name). Its shape consists of three strokes, and it is usually drawn in a fluid motion with the hand (or visualised) and each time you draw the symbol once, you say its mantra (CKR) three times, either aloud if you are alone or silently in your head if you are with other people who haven't done Reiki 2 training.

   The main uses of the Power symbol are for empowering, cleansing and protecting, so whenever you use it, you think about, or intend, how you want it to work.

- It focuses and increases the power of Reiki onto or into whatever it is drawn over – for example, you can draw it on each of your palms, saying its mantra three times, before placing your hands on yourself, other people, animals, etc.

- It can be used to motivate yourself – draw it over your forehead and say its mantra three times – or to help your memory; draw it over the top of your head and say its mantra three times.

- It can be used to cleanse yourself after going to negative places such as hospitals or to funerals; for example, you could draw a large Power symbol in the air in front of you and step into it, saying its mantra three times and intending that it cleanses you.

- It can purify food and drink; draw the symbol discreetly over whatever you are about to eat or drink, saying its mantra three times and intending that it purifies and energises the food/liquid.

The Second Symbol: The Mental and Emotional (Harmony) Symbol (SHK)

In the West this symbol has traditionally been called the Mental and Emotional symbol, whereas the Japanese refer to it as the Harmony symbol. It has a very gentle energy, and is always used in conjunction with the Power symbol (draw the Harmony symbol first, followed by the Power symbol). Its shape consists of nine strokes, and its main functions are to help to restore psychological and emotional balance, to raise sensitivity and receptivity, and to bring peace and harmony. (When asking Reiki to flow, always do so 'for the greatest and highest good'.)

- It helps to balance the right and left sides of the brain, bringing feelings of harmony and peace. Draw the Harmony symbol (saying the mantra three times), then the Power symbol (saying its mantra three times) on each palm, and place one hand on your forehead and one on the back of your head for ten minutes or more, intending that Reiki flows to encourage harmony and peace.

- It can be used on relationship problems or difficulties with communications of any kind. Write the problem or difficulty on a piece of paper, and draw the Harmony symbol (saying its mantra three times) and the Power symbol (again, saying its mantra three times) over the paper, intending that Reiki flows into that problem, and hold it in your hands for about ten minutes each day until the problem is resolved.

- The Harmony symbol can free blocked feelings and bring calm to emotional or mental distress such as nervousness, fear, depression, anger, or sadness. Again, write down the problem or issue on a piece of paper, and draw the Harmony symbol (saying its mantra three times), followed by the Power symbol (repeating its mantra three times too) over the paper, intending that Reiki flows into that problem or issue, and hold the paper in your hands for about ten minutes each day until those feelings dissipate.

- To forgive yourself and others, to release attachments to past issues, cut energetic ties, and let go of the past, write down details of the situation, including the name(s) of anyone you wish to forgive, then draw the Harmony symbol (saying its mantra three times), followed by the Power symbol (saying its mantra three times) over the paper. Hold the paper in your hands for about ten minutes a day, intending that Reiki flows into the situation for the greatest and highest good of all.

The Third Symbol: The Distant (Connection) Symbol (HSZSN)

The Distant symbol, referred to in the Japanese tradition as the Connection symbol, cuts through, or goes beyond, time and space, bringing all time into the Now, and all space into the Here. The best analogy is that the Distant symbol is an energetic equivalent of a time machine, because it enables you to connect with anything, anywhere, at any time, allowing you to 'send' healing to anyone (or anything) anywhere in the world – in the next room, on the other side of town, or across continents to the other side of the planet – with exactly the same effectiveness as if the person (animal/thing) was right beside you, with your hands placed on the body. The Distant symbol can also be used to bridge time, connecting you with any time in the future, or in the past, as well as in the present.

Its shape consists of twenty-two strokes, and again, it is always used with the Power symbol (make the Distant symbol first and then the Power symbol), and sometimes also with the Harmony symbol (in the order Distant, then Harmony, then Power). It can be drawn with the hand, or visualised, and you always say its mantra (HSZSN) three times each time you draw it.

You can use the Distant symbol to:

- Send a full distant Reiki treatment to anyone, or anything, anywhere (see Chapter 13).

- Send Reiki into the future, including programming a Reiki treatment for a future time (see Chapters 12 and 13).

- Send Reiki to any point in the past, for example to heal past issues, trauma and hurtful relationships, as well as to heal the mental, emotional or spiritual effects of a past event (see Chapter 12).

The fourth symbol – the Master (Empowerment) symbol (DKM) is covered later in this manual, in Chapter 23.

REVISION QUESTIONS

1. How many symbols in the Usui System of Natural Healing are taught to Master level students?

2. Why are the Reiki symbols regarded as sacred? How does this differ from being secret?

3. What is a mantra?

4. If using all three of the Reiki 2 symbols, in which order should they be used?

5. What is the other name for the Power symbol?

6. Describe two uses for the Power symbol.

7. Describe two uses for the Harmony symbol.

8. Which symbol would be used to send Reiki to an event in the past?

(Answers in Appendix 8)

REVISION ACTIVITY

Using your hands, draw each of the symbols you have learned from your Reiki Master, and silently say the corresponding mantra.

Chapter Twelve

USING THE REIKI SYMBOLS FOR YOURSELF AND OTHERS

Each of the Reiki symbols can be used in many different ways. In this chapter we focus on how to use them in self-treatments and for healing others, as well as putting forward some ideas for using them creatively. Your Reiki Master may suggest some other techniques, as the symbols are very versatile. However, the way to use the symbols is always the same:

- Every time you draw any of the symbols, either in the air or actually on or over something, you always say its mantra three times – aloud if you are alone, or silently if you're with other people.

- If you are using two or more symbols, the order they are drawn in is always the same.

    a. First, the Distant symbol, to connect with a person or object or situation, if this is required.

    b. Second, the Harmony symbol, to bring peace and harmony to a person, object or situation, if this feels appropriate.

    c. Finally, the Power symbol, to bring in and focus the Reiki on the person, object or situation.

    The Power symbol can either be used alone, or when used in combination is always used last.

USING THE SYMBOLS FOR TREATMENTS

Reiki 2 equips you with increased potential for carrying out Reiki treatments, but this doesn't mean that your Reiki 1 skills are redundant. Using symbols when treating either yourself or other people simply adds to the standard treatment, so all the hand positions and the general methods of treatment remain the same – refer back to Chapters 6, 7 and 8 to remind yourself, if necessary.

Treatments on Yourself

At Reiki level 2, self-healing is *still* one of the most important aspects of Reiki. Not only is it an act of self-love to give yourself a Reiki treatment every day, it is a simple and sensible way to help your body to maintain good health. A full self-treatment of between thirty minutes and an hour or more can be made even more effective by using the Power symbol, and sometimes the Harmony symbol too.

1. Before you start, empower your whole energy field by drawing a Power symbol on each of your palms, and a large Power symbol in front of your whole body, each time saying its mantra three times.

2. Then before placing your hands in each of the twelve (or more) hand positions (see Chapter 7), either visualise a Power symbol in the air above, or draw it directly on your body in the area which is being treated, each time saying its mantra to yourself three times.

3. If you wish, you can also draw the Harmony symbol over any areas on your body that you feel need its gentle, harmonising energy, before drawing the Power symbol over that area. Remember to say each symbol's mantra three times as you draw it.

A Quick Self-treatment Using Symbols

This is an excellent treatment when you are short of time, or just wish to give yourself a 'top up' of energy. Using the symbols enhances the amount of Reiki you can receive in a short time, so doing this for about five minutes is probably equivalent to at least ten minutes in a traditional self-treatment.

1. Hold your hands out in front of you and visualise an image of yourself between them. (You can also use a piece of paper with your name on it, or a photograph of yourself.) Then, with your dominant hand, draw the

Distant symbol over your other hand, silently saying its mantra three times, and your own name three times.

2. Then draw the Harmony symbol over your hand/name/photo, silently saying its mantra three times, and your own name three times.

3. Then draw the Power symbol over your hand/name/photo, silently saying its mantra three times.

4. Next, hold your dominant hand over your other hand/name/photo, and intend that Reiki should flow to you for your greatest and highest good, and maintain this position for between five and ten minutes, or as long as you wish.

5. Finally, draw the Power symbol over your hand/name/photo again, saying its mantra three times and intending that this wonderful healing energy be sealed in, and intend that the treatment is over.

> For other treatment ideas using the symbols on yourself, please refer to *Self-healing with Reiki* by Penelope Quest.

Using Symbols When Treating Others

As with the self-treatment above, when you are treating someone else you can draw the Power symbol on each of your palms, and a large Power symbol in front of your whole body, and then before placing your hands in any of the twelve or more hand positions (see Chapter 6), draw a Power symbol over that position (discreetly, unless the recipient has his or her eyes closed), silently saying its mantra to yourself three times each time you draw the symbol. If there are any areas of the recipient's body that you feel would benefit from the Harmony symbol's gentle, harmonising energy, then you can draw that before the Power symbol over that area, too. When you have finished, you can seal in the healing by drawing a large Power symbol in the air, about 10–15 cm (4–6 inches) above the recipient's whole body, starting at the person's head, and ending around their pelvic area or their feet, whichever you prefer.

> For other treatment ideas using the symbols, please refer to *Reiki for Life* by Penelope Quest.

A Quick Reiki Treatment

Sometimes it isn't possible to do a full treatment, so here is a way in which you can perform a quick balancing treatment or energy boost which can be helpful. This can be done with the recipient either lying down or sitting upright in a chair, and it works on the areas of the main hand positions, which also correspond to the major energy centres, or chakras (see Appendix 2). Ask the recipient to close their eyes, and then quietly centre yourself, by breathing deeply and evenly, and intend that the Reiki should flow for your recipient's highest and greatest good.

1. When you feel ready, stand a little way away from the recipient and draw a Power symbol over each of your palms, and a large Power symbol down the front of your body, saying its mantra three times each time you do so. This empowers your whole energy field with Reiki, so that when you approach the recipient again, they will be encompassed in a field of Reiki.

2. Starting at their head, draw a Power symbol with your dominant hand in the air just above or beyond the crown of their head about 15–30 cm (6–12 inches) away, saying its mantra three times silently to yourself as you do so, and hold your hand there for approximately one minute.

3. Then move your hand to hold it above (or beside if they are seated) their brow, again about 15–30 cm (6–12 inches) away from their head. Draw the Power symbol in the air, silently saying the mantra three times, and hold your hand there for about one minute.

4. Repeat these actions in exactly the same way for each of the remaining main treatment positions – the throat, heart, solar plexus, navel area and pelvic area – holding your hand still about 15–30 cm (6–12 inches) above or beside each place for about one minute.

5. When you have finished, take your hand a little further away from the recipient's body and draw a large Power symbol in the air over the whole of their body, from their head down to their feet, intending that this seals in the Reiki.

6. Finally, move away from the recipient and click your fingers, or shake your hands vigorously, to end the energetic connection.

USING REIKI SYMBOLS ON PROBLEMS AND SITUATIONS

Whatever kind of problems you are having, you can use Reiki to infuse the situation with healing. Remember, the intention for Reiki should always be 'for the highest and greatest good', so it's fine to hope for a happy and harmonious result, but you need to develop trust in Reiki to always do what is best for you. It always works for your highest good, but we don't always know what is best for us – even if we think we do!

1. First, write down the details of any problem you are concerned about and hold the paper between your hands. Examples could be 'Allow Reiki to flow into my relationships, for the highest and greatest good' or 'Let Reiki flow into my money situation, for my highest and greatest good'.

2. Then draw the Distant symbol over the paper, silently saying its mantra three times, and intending that Reiki connect with the situation.

3. Next draw the Harmony symbol over the paper, saying its mantra three times, and asking that Reiki flow to harmonise and heal the situation in whatever way is for your highest and greatest good.

4. Then draw the Power symbol over the paper, repeating its mantra three times, and intending that Reiki flow for the highest and greatest good.

5. Hold the paper in your hands letting Reiki flow into it for five to ten minutes. When you have finished, thank Reiki for its help, draw another Power symbol (again, repeating the mantra three times) over the paper, intending that the healing is sealed in.

6. Do this each day, and continue until some resolution to the situation appears.

Empowering Goals with Reiki Symbols

Reiki can be used on your goals and dreams. Write down *all* the aspects of what you are seeking, so, for example, if you want a fulfilling new job, write down your preferred location, salary, whether you want to work alone or in a team, and so on. Then draw the Distant symbol, followed by the Harmony symbol and then the Power symbol over the paper, saying each symbol's mantra three times as you do so. Hold the paper in your hands and intend that Reiki should flow into that goal for the highest and greatest good.

Do this for about ten minutes every day until you achieve what you want, or your circumstances change and you decide that your goal isn't right for you after all.

Empowering Affirmations with Reiki Symbols

In the same way, you can use Reiki to empower affirmations. Make sure that your affirmations are always positive, have an intention for your highest and greatest good, and are focused fully in the present, rather than in a vague future. So, for example, use 'My body is healthy and full of vitality' rather than 'I will not be ill any more'. Write your affirmation down and then use all three symbols for this, together with their mantras, in the usual order – Distant, then Harmony, and finally Power. Repeat your affirmation aloud daily at least twenty times whilst holding the paper in your hands.

Using Symbols to Heal Unwanted Habits or Addictions

You can use Reiki to help you to change or eliminate habits or addictions that are no longer useful to you or are actually harmful, such as smoking cigarettes, drinking alcohol, taking non-prescription drugs, or even overeating, procrastinating or always being late. However, it is important that you should actually *want* to give up the habit that you're working on, because you recognise the benefits of stopping, and acknowledge those benefits as being more advantageous than whatever it is that the habit gives you. Reiki cannot force you to do something you don't want to do.

Write down a suitably positive statement, such as 'I am now choosing a healthier lifestyle, so I choose to heal and let go of my need to smoke/drink alcohol/overeat/take drugs'. Then in the air above the paper, draw first the Distant symbol, then the Harmony symbol and lastly the Power symbol, silently saying their mantras three times, and each time repeating aloud three times the statement you have written. Then hold the paper between your hands, treating it with Reiki for fifteen to twenty minutes. Do this daily until you feel that you have really let go of this unwanted habit.

Sending Reiki into Past Situations

You can send Reiki into the past, to allow it to heal past events or hurts. It won't necessarily physically alter what has happened, but it can allow healing and forgiveness to permeate that time which will gently alter the way you feel about it. For example, if you had a difficult or traumatic experience in the past and you know the approximate date, you can use the Distant symbol to send Reiki back to that time to bring healing to the situation. It often helps if you have a photograph of yourself taken close to the time of the event in question, but if you don't know the date, or don't have a photo, Reiki will still have an effect. Simply name the problem and ask that Reiki go to the cause and heal it.

1. Write down the situation and roughly the timing (e.g. a broken relationship when you were twenty years old) and draw or imagine the Distant symbol over the paper (and any photograph of you at that age, if you have one). Silently say its sacred mantra three times, sensing it connecting the you of today with the you of that time.

2. Next, draw or imagine the Harmony symbol over the paper/photo. Say its mantra three times, sensing its healing flowing to the hurt and upset, and to the root cause and the lessons you were meant to learn from the event.

3. Then draw or imagine the Power symbol over the paper/photo, and repeat that symbol's mantra three times, sensing a strong flow of Reiki moving into that time.

4. Allow the Reiki to flow for fifteen or twenty minutes or longer if it feels appropriate. Then draw the Power symbol again over the paper/photo and again say its mantra three times, intending that the healing be sealed in for the greatest and highest good. Clap your hands to break the connection, and let go of that event in your thoughts.

If in the days following this activity you get a sense that the healing is not complete – perhaps you've dreamed about the event, or it enters your thoughts quite a few times, unexpectedly – then repeat the above instructions, sending Reiki again to the same situation.

Sending Reiki into Future Situations

Sending Reiki into the future is just as simple. If you know you will be involved in an important or stressful event or activity in the future with which you feel you need Reiki's help, such as a job interview, or a visit to the dentist, or a potentially difficult business meeting, then again, write down the event or situation and the approximate date and time, and proceed in the same way as above, sensing the Reiki flowing into the future to wait for you there.

It is also possible to 'bank' Reiki so that you can draw on it as and when you need it, by imagining some sort of container – it could be a box, or a jug, or even a fun container like a big piggy bank. Draw the Distant symbol to connect to the imagined container, saying its sacred mantra three times. Then draw the Power symbol and say its mantra three times, and visualise the container filling up with Reiki. When it is used in this way, the Reiki energy stores up like a battery. When the time comes, you can call upon its healing energy to descend to surround you and help you.

OTHER USES FOR THE REIKI SYMBOLS

There are so many things you can do to enhance your life when using the Reiki symbols, in addition to treating yourself, other people, and personal problems or situations. The symbols are so versatile that the list is almost endless, and once you're really comfortable with using them, you may find other even more creative uses, so feel free to experiment a little and enjoy them!

Cleansing and Creating Sacred Space

Any space can become contaminated with negative energy, or negative energy can simply collect and stagnate in corners (see Appendix 3). The more you become involved in your spiritual path, the more important it is not to be surrounded by negativity, so use Reiki everywhere, frequently, to create positive space around you. The simplest and easiest way of clearing negative energy from your surroundings is to place Power symbols all around you – in all the corners and sides of any room, plus the ceiling and floor.

- Draw the Power symbol (as large as possible, if no one is watching, otherwise draw it discreetly) and say its mantra three times in each place, and intend that the Reiki should clear and cleanse the room and seal it in light, making it a sacred space.

This is good not only for any room in your home, but also in your workplace, in hotel bedrooms or hospital wards, or anywhere else you are staying – and of course for wherever you are carrying out Reiki treatments.

You can cleanse just about anything with Reiki, using the Power symbol and intending that the Reiki cleanse whatever you are directing it at – your bed, your car, your treatment couch in between treatments – in fact anything in your life which might attract or hold negative energy. You can also use the

Power symbol to cleanse yourself if you have been somewhere that you feel was energetically rather negative, such as after visiting people in hospital or after attending a funeral.

- Draw a Power symbol (discreetly) in the air above the top of your head, saying its mantra three times, and intending that the Reiki cleanse your whole energy field. Then imagine the Power symbol flowing over you and through you towards the ground, taking with it any negative energy, until the negativity flows into the earth, where Reiki can heal it and transmute it into useful energy for the planet.

Using the Symbols for Protection

The Power symbol can also be used for protection. Because Reiki works on all levels, the protection it provides is also on all levels and can include protection from physical harm, or verbal and emotional confrontations. It can be used to protect your car, your home, or anything else you value, and you can use it to protect you and your family when you are travelling, too.

- **Self-protection** – Draw a large Power symbol in front of you and step into it, silently saying its sacred mantra three times. Imagine it encompassing you and intend that it forms a protective barrier around you.

- **Your car, home, or other objects you care about** – Either physically draw, or imagine drawing, a large Power symbol over the object. Say its mantra three times, and then imagine the Power symbol expanding until it covers the object above, below and on all sides. Intend that the Power symbol protects that object for as long as is necessary. (If you are away from the object, then use the Distant symbol and its mantra to connect with it first.)

- **When travelling** – Draw a Distant symbol, saying its mantra silently to yourself three times and your destination three times, and imagine the symbol forming a bridge of light connecting you with your destination. Then imagine a large Power symbol over your car, or the bus, train, ship or plane you are travelling in. Say its mantra three times, and imagine the Power symbol spreading until it covers your means of transport above, below and on all sides. Intend that the Power symbol protects all the occupants of that means of transport for the duration of the journey. You can then imagine a Power symbol travelling ahead, clearing the way for you along the bridge of light formed by the Distant symbol.

Using Symbols When Treating Other Creatures

With the Reiki 2 symbols, you will find it even easier to treat animals, birds, reptiles and fish. You can use the Distant symbol to connect to any type of creature anywhere, at any time, and the Power symbol to bring the Reiki powerfully to it, and you can do this from any distance away. If an animal is particularly agitated or frightened, you can also use the Harmony symbol in the usual order – Distant, Harmony, Power.

Using the Symbols with Plants and Seeds

When you walk past any of your houseplants, occasionally draw the Power symbol over them, saying its mantra three times and intending that the Reiki flow for the plants' highest good. The same applies to plants in your garden, yard or patio, to the crops in your allotment or fields, to seeds or cuttings you are about to plant out, and to the water you are about to pour onto the plants. You can also treat plants using the Distant symbol before the Power symbol, if you're away on holiday, for instance.

Using the Symbols with Food and Drink

Adding the power of the Reiki symbols when you give Reiki to your own food and drink makes the energy even more beneficial. Use the Power symbol, and its mantra, over everything – over the food on your plate, and all your in-gredients when you're cooking, too. Food cooked with love always seems to taste better, and food treated with Reiki as well tastes best of all!

Using the Symbols with Inanimate Objects

Using the Reiki symbols, especially the Power symbol, enhances any Reiki you might give to machinery or equipment which isn't working. Either draw the Power symbol in front of or over the machine, or draw the Power symbol over each of your palms before placing your hands on it. For an object that's far away, simply connect with it using the Distant symbol, saying its mantra three times, and the name of the object three times (e.g. 'my son's car' – including the make, model and registration number if you wish, but these extra details probably aren't necessary because your intention sets up the correct connection). Then use the Power symbol, repeating its mantra three times, and intend that Reiki should flow into the object for the highest possible good.

Using the Symbols for Earth Healing or World Situations or Disasters

In Chapter 10 there are a number of methods described for healing the earth, or for bringing Reiki into world situations and disasters, and these can be made even more effective by using the Reiki symbols. For example:

- Sit or stand either outdoors or indoors, and draw or imagine a large Power symbol over the floor or earth; say its mantra three times and then, with your palms facing downwards, direct Reiki into the earth.

- Alternatively, you can 'walk' the shape of the Power symbol into the earth to send its healing properties into the planet.

- To send Reiki to global situations, such as famines, ecological disasters or war zones, write down the situation and hold the piece of paper in your hands. Draw the Distant symbol, then the Harmony symbol and then the Power symbol, saying each of their mantras three times in turn, and intend that Reiki should go to everyone and everything in that situation for the highest possible good.

Using Reiki with Crystals

Crystals and gems have been used throughout history for their healing qualities and beauty. Using Reiki with crystals is not a part of traditional Reiki, but many Masters and practitioners find crystals a useful and attractive addition to their healing work. There are many different types and shapes of crystal, traditionally the most commonly used for healing purposes are clear quartz, rose quartz and amethyst. When choosing your crystals, hold the intent or purpose of 'healing' in your mind, and when you first bring them home it is important to cleanse them thoroughly. This is because crystals absorb energy easily, and you don't know what kinds of energy they have been absorbing before you bought them, so cleansing them rids them of any negative energetic vibrations. There are various methods to do this, such as holding the crystals in clear running water (not salt water) and letting them dry naturally afterwards, leaving them in bright sunlight or moonlight to absorb a full charge of masculine (Sun) and feminine (Moon) energies. Alternatively you can use Reiki. Simply hold the crystal in your hands and draw the Power symbol over it (saying its mantra three times, of course) and intend that Reiki should cleanse it. If the crystal has multiple facets, then draw the Power symbol and repeat the mantra three times over each facet.

To empower and programme your crystal once it has been thoroughly cleansed, pick it up and draw all three Reiki symbols over it, saying their sacred mantras three times and intending that the crystal is filled with an unlimited supply of Reiki. You can then carry the crystal around with you to aid your own healing, or give it to someone else who needs healing energy. Some people use charged crystals (i.e. crystals filled with Reiki) placed near to or on a recipient during a treatment, although it would be important to find out if that person was happy with this before trying it.

You can also write down any problem you are experiencing on a piece of paper and place it under a charged crystal, intending that the Reiki flow constantly into the problem to promote healing for the highest and greatest good. However, if you do this it is best to cleanse the crystal and reprogramme it once a week to maintain the strength of the energy.

USING THE REIKI SYMBOLS AND MANTRAS FOR MEDITATION

The symbols and their mantras can be used as a focus for meditation, which helps you to still your mind and become calmer and more relaxed. However, it is not necessary, nor is it possible without many years of practice, to actually try to empty your mind of thoughts. Our minds are constantly busy, so just intend to 'let go' of any thoughts which come in, and refocus yourself on either the shape of the symbol, or the sounds of the mantra you are using.

Meditating on the Symbols

Choose any one of the symbols and either draw it on a piece of paper and focus your gaze on it, or close your eyes and visualise it, and spend a few minutes breathing slowly and deeply whilst concentrating on the symbol. Start with just two or three minutes each day, and gradually over a number of weeks build up to ten and then twenty minutes daily meditation, perhaps choosing a different symbol each week to meditate on.

Stepping into the Symbols

All of the Reiki symbols are three-dimensional, having height, width and depth, so experience each of them in turn by drawing them really large in the air, imagining that they stretch into the distance, and then step into them.

Let the essence of the symbol permeate your body and mind, and you may experience some insight or inspiration. This is particularly good to do in the open air, if you can find a nice private place.

Walking the Symbols

Imagine that one of the symbols is drawn out on the floor, and step into it. Wait for a short while, until you can feel the Reiki flowing, and then begin to walk the shape, slowly and steadily. Let yourself experience the beauty of the shape, whilst silently saying its mantra. If you use the Distant symbol, you can also imagine that it is connecting you to your future self, forming a bridge through time, which can be a particularly powerful and insightful experience!

Chanting Mantras

Sit quietly with your back straight, allowing yourself to become centred by breathing deeply and evenly, and begin to chant one of the symbol mantras. Chanting in this way is usually done in a monotone, and if you follow the Eastern traditions you would chant the mantra 180 times. However, just chant until you wish to stop.

Breathing Meditation with Mantras

If you are familiar with breathing meditation, then this will just be an adaptation to your practice. Sit quietly with your back straight, and concentrate on your breathing. As you breathe in, say one of the Reiki mantras, either silently or aloud. As you breathe out, silently say the mantra, allowing your breathing to become deeper and slower as you do so. You can follow this practice for as long as you like, but ten to fifteen minutes is good. You can use any of the symbols, or do five minutes of each, perhaps. To make this meditation even more powerful, visualise the symbol itself.

REVISION QUESTIONS

1. How many times should you say a symbol's mantra?

2. Which symbol would you use to 'seal in' the healing when treating others?

3. Which symbol is used to send Reiki into the past?

4. How can you use the symbols to 'cleanse' the room you're in?

(Answers in Appendix 8)

REVISION ACTIVITIES

1. Give yourself a self-treatment, using at least one of the Reiki symbols.

2. Use the Reiki symbols to send Reiki to a situation in the past or future.

Chapter Thirteen

DISTANT TREATMENTS AND HEALING WITH REIKI

Sending general distant healing into a situation or problem is something which can be done at any level of Reiki, and the simple methods you can use at Reiki 1 are outlined in Chapter 8. However, using the Reiki 2 symbols makes sending distant healing much stronger and more specific, and also enables you to send a full treatment to someone from a distance, with exactly the same effectiveness as if you were with the recipient and carrying out a hands-on treatment.

THE ETHICS OF DISTANT HEALING

It is a wonderful thing to be able to help other people, especially those we love, by sending Reiki to them, and our motives and intentions when sending healing to people or animals are laudable – we hope for the best for them, and of course that's a nice thing. But we need to realise that there is also something of a controlling element in these motivations: we want someone to 'get better' or 'be happy', which is *our* perception of what is right for them, *our* perception of what is for their highest and greatest good. We may *think* we know what that is, but most of the time we probably don't!

Sending healing with your Reiki 1 skills is very gentle, but sending healing with Reiki 2 skills – using the Reiki symbols – is much more powerful, so it just requires a little forethought. If you have a close friend or relative whom you think needs healing, please ask them first if they would like you to send them some Reiki. The same applies to colleagues and acquaintances, or friends of friends, and please ask them in such a way that they don't feel obliged to say 'yes'! However, there are occasions when it is definitely ethical to send healing without being asked, such as when natural disasters like earthquakes, floods, hurricanes or famines strike, or disasters caused by humans happen, such as acts of terrorism or war, which leave people (and animals) hurt and homeless, so please do send Reiki to such situations (see Chapter 12). There is no need to identify any individuals – just send Reiki to the relevant area, and to all of the people and animals involved, for the highest and greatest good.

USING THE REIKI SYMBOLS FOR GENERAL HEALING

There are lots of ways in which you can use the distant healing techniques of Reiki 2. The first, and simplest, is if you want to send healing and love to specific people. Bearing in mind the ethics above, just write their names and general location on a piece of paper and hold the paper in your hands. (You can also use a photograph of the person, holding it in your hands in the same way, or you can even imagine the person lying between a huge pair of hands, receiving Reiki to the whole of their body.)

1. Draw the Distant symbol (in the air) over the paper, saying its sacred mantra three times, then the name of the person three times, and the name of their location once. (The town, area or even country will be sufficient if you don't know exactly where they are – on an energetic level, your intention to connect with a specific person is enough.)

2. Then draw the Harmony symbol, say its mantra three times, the name of the person three times, and intend that its peaceful, harmonising energy should go to the person for their highest possible good.

3. Then draw the Power symbol, say its mantra three times, and intend that Reiki should go to the person for their highest possible good.

4. When you finish, draw the Power symbol again, say its mantra three times, with the intention of ending the healing. Clap your hands or shake them vigorously to end the connection.

Using the Symbols to Send Distant Healing to More Than One Person

You may sometimes wish to send distant healing on a regular basis to people, perhaps to quite a number at a time, such as friends or relatives who are ill or who are having difficulties of some kind, perhaps with their studies or jobs or relationships. Again, remember that it is best to have their permission.

1. Write all their names on a piece of paper, with the towns, counties or countries where they are situated, and hold this paper in your hands.

2. Draw the Distant symbol in the air above the paper and say its sacred mantra three times. Then say each person's name three times, with their location once.

3. If it feels appropriate, you can draw the Harmony symbol next in the air above the paper, saying its sacred mantra three times, and each person's name three times and their location once. It isn't necessary to always use the Harmony symbol though – just use your intuition to see if it feels right.

4. Then draw the Power symbol, say its mantra three times, and say that Reiki is sent with love and light to these people for their highest and greatest good. Hold the list between your hands for between ten and fifteen minutes, or longer if you wish.

5. When you finish, draw the Power symbol again, say its mantra three times, with the intention of ending the healing. To conclude, clap your hands, or shake them vigorously to end the connection.

SENDING DISTANT TREATMENTS TO PEOPLE

The techniques taught at Reiki 2 enable you send very powerful healing to anyone, anywhere, at any time (including the past and the future), using the Distant symbol. When you further empower the Reiki by using the Power symbol, this means that it is not only possible to send general healing as described above, i.e. simply allowing Reiki to flow to a person, animal or situation, but to carry out a complete Reiki treatment on a specific person (or animal) at a distance, with the same effectiveness as if they were with you, receiving a hands-on treatment.

However, there are a few points which need to be made clear before we discuss any of the specific techniques for distant treatments. The first is that although the term 'send' is used when referring to the Reiki flowing from you to the recipient, you cannot *force* healing into anyone, and that includes anyone who is far away. The person who is receiving the Reiki has to want it at least on a subconscious level, otherwise the Reiki either will not flow, or will simply come back to you. This leads on to the second point – the ethics of distant treatments.

The Ethics of Distant Treatments

If a person comes to you for a full hands-on Reiki treatment, or asks you to put your hands on their head for some Reiki to help get rid of a headache, for instance, then they obviously know what they are doing; by asking for the Reiki they are taking some responsibility for their own healing. So how might it be different in the case of distant treatments?

It is equally important that the person who is to receive the distant healing actually knows about it, other than in exceptional circumstances, because otherwise by sending Reiki to that person, you could be intruding on their personal space without permission. You wouldn't grab someone, throw them onto a therapy couch and start giving them Reiki without asking first, would you? Well, the same is true for a distant treatment. You have no right to 'send' a Reiki treatment to anyone, even if your motives are good and you just want to help, because it should really be their choice.

Sometimes a well-meaning relative or friend of a sick person will ask you to send that person a distant Reiki treatment, but they may not have asked that person whether they would like some Reiki, so do question them about this. It is much better to have the sick person's permission first, unless that person is in a coma, or too young or too ill to be able to make such a choice. Under those circumstances it is acceptable to attempt sending a Reiki treatment, and if the Reiki flows, then their Higher Self has given permission. If the Reiki doesn't seem to flow, however (i.e. you don't feel any reactions in your hands), you will know that it wasn't appropriate at that particular time, for whatever reason. It is important to remember that it isn't up to us to decide what is for any individual's highest good, so sometimes we just have to let go, without judgement.

The Distant Treatment Process

When you start 'sending' the Reiki – intending to allow it to flow would be a better description – it reaches its destination instantaneously, because the Distant symbol brings all time and all space into the here and now, so it is just as if you have placed your hands on the person and the Reiki has 'switched on' and started to flow into them. This ability to 'send' powerful and effective healing, where distance is no object, is one of the most fascinating features of Reiki. When this is compounded with the fact that time is also no object, so that healing can be sent into the past or into the future, and can even be 'programmed' (rather like a video or DVD recorder) to be delivered at a particular time, it is really quite amazing (see page 135).

CARRYING OUT A FULL DISTANT REIKI TREATMENT

Using the distant treatment technique detailed below enables you to send a full Reiki treatment with exactly the same effect as if you were carrying out a hands-on treatment on that person or animal. It is very simple to do, and takes much less time than a hands-on treatment, but it does require some concentration, so you need to be somewhere quiet where you won't be disturbed for twenty minutes or so. However, because this treatment works in the same way as if the person was with you, it is particularly important that you should have their permission before sending the treatment, and just as you would make an appointment for someone to receive a hands-on treatment, ideally you should arrange a convenient time when that person can be sitting comfortably or lying down somewhere quiet where they won't be disturbed for at least three-quarters of an hour. (This amount of time is to allow them some relaxation after the treatment.)

Using a 'Correspondence'

You can use a 'correspondence' to send a distant treatment, which is just something that you use to represent the person, and on which you can place your hands when you send a distant treatment, 'as if' they were on the person. The correspondence can be a pillow, or a soft toy such as a teddy bear.

Photographs and names written on pieces of paper also act as correspondences, as do images which you visualise. When visualising a person, you can imagine them to be life-size, so that when you move your hands to different parts of their (imaginary) body, your hands move as much as they would on the real body. When you use an object as a correspondence you are also visualising the person, of course, so the whole person seems the same size as the pillow or teddy bear, so you make fairly small movements of your hands to any new positions. Alternatively, you can visualise the person as really small, so they would fit onto your hand. Then you could use visualisation to imagine your hands in different positions on their body.

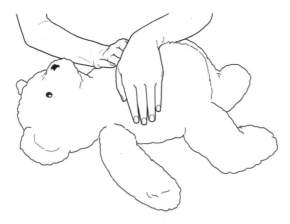

One word of caution: when using the Distant symbol you create a really powerful connection. When they are receiving a distant treatment, many people who are energetically quite sensitive actually feel as though the practitioner's hands are on their body, and can feel when the hands move to be placed elsewhere. Whilst this is excellent, it does mean that you must be as careful when doing a distant treatment as when doing a hands-on treatment, so make sure all your hand movements are gentle. This also means that when you are imagining the person turning over (or when you are physically turning over whatever you are using as a correspondence) to have their back treated, please do this *very slowly and gently* as the energetically sensitive person can become very disturbed by this, and can sometimes actually feel the need to turn over, so you must give them plenty of time to do this.

1. Prepare yourself for doing the treatment at whatever time you have agreed with the recipient. You should sit somewhere comfortable and quiet, where you will not be disturbed – switch the telephone off, ask the family to leave you alone for half an hour, etc.

2. Picture the person to whom you wish to send the distant Reiki treatment, using a photograph, teddy bear or pillow correspondence, or write their name and address on a piece of paper, or just visualise them.

3. Draw the Distant symbol over the photo, paper or body of the correspondence, say its mantra three times, the name of the person three times, and their location once (either their whole address, or just the town, area or country they are in, if you don't know exactly where they are). Imagine the Distant symbol forming a huge bridge between you and the person to whom you are sending the distant treatment.

4. At this stage you can draw the Harmony symbol over the photo, paper or body of the correspondence, and say its mantra three times and the person's name three times, if you feel it would be an advantage to the person because you know they are going through difficult times emotionally or psychologically. However, it isn't necessary to use the Harmony symbol every time you do a distant treatment.

5. Then draw the Power symbol over the photo, paper or body of the correspondence. Say its mantra three times, the name of the person once and their location once. Imagine a large Power symbol over the body of the person, and then let it descend, sensing that the person is completely encompassed by the symbol so that its healing energy can flow throughout the person during the treatment.

6. Then say to yourself that this Reiki is sent with love and light, for the highest and greatest good. You can also mention any parts of the body or illnesses or situations you know need special attention, and ask that they receive healing if this is possible at this time. (Remember, the person's Higher Self draws the energy into those areas most in need, so our expectations and wishes may be different, i.e. it is important to take our ego out of the healing process.)

7. You can then carry out a standard treatment by placing your hands as if they were in each of the twelve (or more) standard hand positions (see Chapter 6), either actually on the correspondence or in the air about 5 cm (2 inches) above any photo, etc. Start with hand position 1, and hold each hand position for between one and three minutes for those on the head and body, and for only about half a minute on any other part of the body you choose to do, such as the arms, legs and feet. However, if you feel that the Reiki is still flowing strongly in any of the hand positions, you can continue to treat that area for as long as necessary – the suggested timing is a guide, not a restriction!

8. When you have finished, close the whole treatment by smoothing down the person's energies with your hands, holding them in the air about 5 cm (2 inches) above the correspondence, moving them from their head down to their feet. Then draw a Power symbol in the air over whatever represents the whole of their body (starting at their head), saying its sacred mantra three times, with the intention of sealing in the healing and ending the treatment.

9. Finally, clap your hands together firmly a few times to break the energy connection.

You can use the same method to send a distant treatment to an animal, bird or any other creature too. At step 2 visualise the animal, and at step 3 say the animal's name (if you know it) and type of animal, plus its location, and carry on with the rest of the steps as before.

PROGRAMMING A DISTANT TREATMENT

When you and a potential recipient are discussing the arrangements for a distant treatment, it can sometimes be difficult to find a time which is convenient to both of you. If that is the case, then it is possible to 'programme' the treatment to go to the person either at a specific time suitable to them, or whilst they are asleep, rather like setting a video or DVD recorder to record a TV programme at a particular time. This is fairly simple to do.

Follow the instructions above for carrying out a distant treatment until you have reached step 3. Then after specifying the person's name and location, say: 'This Reiki is to be received by [name of person] at [date and time agreed] (or when they are asleep tonight).'

Programming for Multiple Treatments

If there is a requirement to give a person a lot of distant treatments – say, for example, someone needs several consecutive treatments (traditionally over twenty-one days) to help with some chronic or life-threatening condition – then it is perfectly reasonable to spend the twenty minutes or so each day required for these treatments. However, there may be times when you have quite a few distant treatments to do on a daily basis, or perhaps you have some serious commitments and are unsure of being available to carry out the treatments at the right time. In these instances it is possible to arrange a suitable daily time with the recipient when they can be sitting or lying down somewhere quiet and comfortable, and 'programme' a treatment to be received regularly at the same time each day – again, rather like programming a video recorder to record the same TV programme at the same time each day.

Carry out the distant treatment in exactly the same way as above, but when you get to step 3, after you have specified the name and location of the recipient, say: 'This Reiki is to be received by [name of person] at [time agreed] (or when they are asleep tonight) and for the following six days (or nights).' Then, after a week you can either get back to doing the distant treatment on a daily basis, or if the same conditions exist for you, you can reprogramme the treatment for another seven days.

It is advisable not to programme a number of treatments, for example one each night for a week, until you have already carried out one or two distant treatments on that person and got some feedback from them to discover how they react to them. Once a Reiki treatment has been sent, it can't be cancelled, so if the client experiences difficult reactions or discomfort – which is rare, but does sometimes happen – it would be unpleasant for them to know they're going to experience that reaction potentially another five or six times!

Sending a Distant Treatment to Yourself

It might sound a bit strange, but you can also carry out a distant self-treatment, which can be a lovely 'gift' to yourself. Follow the steps detailed on page 133; at step 2, picture yourself, and then at step 3, say your own name and location, and state a time when you know you can sit or lie down to receive the treatment. Continue all the steps, and then at whatever time you've specified, go and sit or lie down somewhere quiet and comfortable to receive the treatment when you're ready. This is a very relaxing, peaceful and pleasant way of doing a self-treatment!

REVISION QUESTIONS

1. What is the difference between general distant healing and a distant treatment?

2. How can you 'send' Reiki?

3. Can you carry out a distant treatment on an animal?

4. What important considerations are there when programming a treatment?

(Answers in Appendix 8)

REVISION ACTIVITY

Ask a friend or a member of the family for permission to send them a distant treatment; then at a prearranged time, send them Reiki.

Part Four

SETTING UP
AS A PROFESSIONAL
PRACTITIONER

The Regulation of the Reiki Profession in the UK
·
National Occupational Standards
·
Expected Levels of Reiki Knowledge for Professional Registration
·
Common Illnesses, Notifiable Diseases and 'Red Flag' Symptoms
·
Communicating with Clients
·
The Process of Providing Reiki to Clients
·
Running a Professional Reiki Practice
·
The Legal Requirements of Running a Practice
·
Continuing Professional Development (CPD)

Chapter Fourteen

REGULATING THE PRACTICE OF REIKI

Whether you are just setting up as a professional Reiki practitioner, or have already been practising for some time, and wherever in the world you are working, the whole of Part Four is designed to give you a comprehensive understanding of what is 'best practice' in the provision of Reiki to the general public.

Reiki treatments are now available in most countries in the world, and in the past the training of Reiki practitioners has mostly been by attending a Reiki 1 course, and in some cases a Reiki 2 course as well. However, standards of training and practice vary enormously, and this makes it very difficult for the public to identify who is, and who is not, an appropriately trained professional Reiki practitioner. Wherever they live, members of the public have the right to expect healthcare services to be provided by well-trained, safe, competent practitioners, and some countries address this problem by putting restrictions on who can practise Reiki. For example, in some states in the USA it is illegal to use hands-on healing (including Reiki) unless you are a qualified priest or minister of religion, and the legal position of Reiki in some European countries means that you have to be medically qualified before practising Reiki professionally.

Chapters 15 to 22 in Part Four deal with different aspects of professional practice, to help you provide the best possible service to your clients, whilst this chapter concentrates particularly on the regulation process for practitioners in the UK. If you work in another part of the world you might prefer to go straight to Chapter 15, unless you are interested in how Britain has decided to deal with this situation in case it is replicated in a similar way in your country.

REGULATING REIKI IN THE UK

In the UK various complementary and alternative therapies have gone down the route of becoming regulated in recent years, so that training standards are formalised. Examples include osteopathy, chiropractic and acupuncture, all of which are now available in most areas of the country through the National Health Service (NHS). However, a House of Lords report in 2000 accepted that voluntary self-regulation was sufficient for the vast majority of complementary healthcare professions, and in 2003 a number of Reiki organisations in the UK met to discuss the possibility of voluntary self-regulation for Reiki, rather than potentially having regulation imposed upon the Reiki community by government at some time in the future. They agreed to work together so that progress could be made on identifying consistent, high professional standards, and in the development of a single UK Register for professional Reiki practitioners, and a single regulatory body. The initial meeting led to the establishment of the Reiki Regulatory Working Group (RRWG), now called the Reiki Council, which was made up of representatives from:

- The Complementary Therapists Association

- The Federation of Holistic Therapists (FHT)

- Independent Professional Therapists International (IPTI UK)

- The Open Reiki Group

- The Reiki Healers and Teachers Society (RHATS)

- The Reiki Alliance

- The Reiki Association

- The Tera-Mai™ Association (Tera-Mai is a style of Reiki)

- The UK Reiki Federation

The wider Reiki community was also consulted through each of the above organisations, as well as through downloadable consultation documents and road shows in nine cities throughout the UK.

The RRWG was totally committed to the preservation of Reiki as a spiritual practice and healing art, and they respected and honoured all styles and traditions of Reiki. Their remit was to develop a definition of minimum standards that could be applied to all Reiki groups, allowing for variations in styles; to prepare a code of professional practice for Reiki, including disciplinary and complaints procedures; and to set up a national register of Reiki practitioners. This work was initially funded by the Prince's Foundation for Integrated Health, which also offered support and funding (provided by the Department of Health) for the next step in the regulation programme.

This regulatory process was about looking after clients' needs, not about regulating the practitioners' individual style of practice, to ensure the safety of the public who receive Reiki from a registrant (a registered Reiki practitioner). The RRWG believed that as healthcare professionals, it is vital to protect the health and well-being of those who use or need professional Reiki practitioners in any circumstance, so the important benefits of having an effective voluntary self-regulatory body are that it:

- Maintains a register of individual members

- Sets educational standards and runs an accreditation system

- Maintains professional competence among its members with an adequate programme of Continuing Professional Development (CPD)

- Provides a code of conduct, ethics and practice

- Has in place a complaints mechanism for members of the public

- Has in place a disciplinary procedure that is accessible to the public

- Requires members to have adequate professional indemnity insurance

- Has the capacity to represent the whole profession

- Includes external representatives (i.e. people not involved in Reiki) to represent patients or clients and the wider public interest

The RRWG recognised that many people undertake Reiki training for self-development and personal use, and may also wish to continue to use it informally to help friends or family. The proposed requirements for registration do not apply to those whose wish is to use it in this way. For others, offering Reiki becomes their profession or vocation, so they may work more formally in a paid or voluntary capacity with the public in venues such as their own treatment room, or in clinics, health or community facilities; these are the people who will have to meet the criteria for registration.

Students will be able to learn Reiki from one or more Reiki Masters who feel right for them, and some aspects of professional practice, such as health and safety training, first aid, effective communication, running a business and marketing, etc., could be learned from other appropriate sources, and not necessarily from a Reiki Master. The aim is that Masters who wish to concentrate on Reiki will not be affected, whilst those who also want to teach aspects of professional practice will be able to do so. This will provide some flexibility and there is therefore less risk of losing teachers who regard Reiki primarily as a pursuit of spiritual/self-development. Some potential registrants will meet the practice requirements from experience in other work, especially if they have already trained in other therapies. Most importantly, practitioners will be able to find their own path.

Through their discussions the RRWG identified that:

- The route to meeting the required standards should be the choice and the responsibility of the practitioner.

- Self-healing and informal sharing of Reiki are fundamental practices.

- The learning of Reiki as a spiritual pursuit will remain unaffected.

- The creation of a two-tiered system, where a particular route to registration may be considered superior, is to be avoided.

- The experience of those already in practice will be acknowledged, whilst identifying any need for further training or development.

NATIONAL OCCUPATIONAL STANDARDS

The conclusions of the RRWG led to the creation of National Occupational Standards (NOS) for Reiki practitioners who are offering Reiki treatments to the public. NOS give guidance on the minimum levels of knowledge, understanding and training for a professional Reiki practitioner. The Reiki National Occupational Standards were developed through a process of discussion and consultation between the RRWG and Skills for Health, and are based on agreed good practice. They are appropriate for all styles of Reiki and are specifically about practitioner skills, not about Reiki itself. Skills for Health is the Sector Skills Council for the UK health sector. Its purpose is to help the whole sector develop solutions that deliver a skilled and flexible UK workforce in order to improve health and healthcare, hence its involvement in setting up professional standards for Reiki.

The Reiki NOS include the performance criteria – i.e. what practitioners must be able to do – and the essential underpinning knowledge and understanding – i.e. what practitioners must know. At the time of writing there are currently three NOS which are relevant to the practice of Reiki: CNH1, CNH2 and CNH12 (see below). CNH stands for Complementary and Natural Healthcare, and CNH1 and CNH2 are generic standards, applying to most complementary therapies, whilst CNH12 is specific to Reiki. They can be downloaded in full from the Skills for Health website at www.skillsforhealth.org.uk, although at some point in the future they may change so please check with this and other websites given in the Resources section at the end of this manual for any up-to-date information.

CNH1: Explore and establish the client's needs for complementary and natural healthcare

All forms of complementary and natural healthcare rely on exploring and establishing the client's needs and expectations. This may take place at the outset, but also during the delivery of complementary and natural healthcare. This allows the practitioner to consider whether it is appropriate to offer the service to the client, the type of service that should be offered, and any required modifications to that service.

CNH2: Develop and agree plans for complementary and natural healthcare with clients

It is important that the planning of complementary and natural healthcare takes place through discussion and agreement with the client and relevant others (e.g. carers). Competence in this is about developing and agreeing plans that meet the client's needs, and such plans may be subject to change as the service proceeds.

CNH12: Provide Reiki to clients

This competence is about the provision of Reiki to clients. Reiki is described as being non-invasive and used holistically to restore balance in body, mind and spirit. Practitioners will need to ensure that their practice reflects up-to-date information and policies.

The rest of Part Four deals with the basics of all aspects of these National Occupation Standards. As you read through the following chapters what you need to know, where to find that information, and how to provide evidence of your knowledge and experience will become clearer!

THE ROLES WITHIN THE REGULATORY PROCESS

There are basically four roles within this regulatory process, and you will find contact details for each organisation in the Resources section.

The Regulator

The regulator regulates the practice of Reiki (and other therapies/disciplines). Currently in the UK we have voluntary self-regulation for complementary therapies, i.e. it is not compulsory, and it is the person doing the Reiki who is regulated, not the Reiki itself, meaning it is how the practitioner works and their interaction with the public that is subject to standards. The role of the regulatory body is primarily to protect the public, in that it gives the public and employers quality assurance that the practitioner's qualifications and/or experience is such that he or she meets the minimum standard required for professional practice. It also gives the same quality assurance to doctors and all other healthcare professionals who may use a National Register. Practitioners applying to be on the National Register will have to be insured and sign up to a CPD policy, disciplinary procedures and a code of professional conduct and ethics.

At the time of writing the only regulator for Reiki is the General Regulatory Council for Complementary Therapies (GRCCT).

Professional Associations

A professional association's role is to represent its membership, looking after the needs of the professional therapist. A professional body will offer insurance, CPD opportunities, journals or newsletters, support groups, advertising leaflets, conferences, etc. The UK Reiki Federation (UKRF) is one of many such professional associations. In addition the UKRF deals with innumerable enquiries from the public about Reiki, and requests for names of practitioners and teachers. It helps to promote these through its website, advertising and attendance at exhibitions and conferences.

Lead Body

The Reiki Council (formerly the RRWG) is the lead advisory body for the profession of Reiki in the UK. It provides advice and guidance on training and all aspects of the professional practice of Reiki. It has no allegiance to any one regulator (although at the time of writing there is only one regulator – the GRCCT – for Reiki in the UK).

Awarding Bodies

An awarding body sets up and gets approval to run accredited training courses, e.g. colleges, businesses or private training establishments. Approval for accreditation is given through Ofqual, which is part of the QCA (Qualifications Curriculum Authority). Ofqual is not an awarding body itself, but is the regulator for qualifications, examinations and assessments in the UK; it assesses organisations that wish to offer qualifications, to ensure they can attain the right standards.

CORE CURRICULUM

A Core Curriculum is a framework on which courses can be developed, but it is not prescriptive regarding the order of training – in other words, Reiki Masters can decide how they teach Reiki. It should be read in conjunction with the National Occupational Standards, and it can be expanded and developed by teachers if they wish to include additional topics. The main recommendations for the Core Curriculum for professional Reiki practitioner training are:

- The potential registrants should carry out seventy-five full treatments (in person) which should be properly recorded on each client's treatment record card or sheet; five of these need to be supervised by someone occupationally competent in Reiki, e.g. a Reiki Master or a registered Reiki practitioner.

- The training period for potential registrants, from beginning to completion of the required elements, should be a minimum of nine months.

- The training should include at least forty-five hours' in-person learning.

- The total training hours should be a minimum of 145.

The recommended breakdown of training is as follows, showing in-person training (i.e. face-to-face contact), distance learning (e.g. manuals, emails, DVDs, etc.) and total hours:

	In-person	Distance	Total
Reiki – theory and practical	15	35	50
Practitioner skills	20	40	60
Practice management	10	20	30
Total	45	95	140

Reading all the chapters in Part Four will give you a good understanding of what knowledge of practitioner skills and practice management you will require, and of course Parts Two and Three deal with the theory and practice of Reiki.

There are also recommendations regarding the qualifications of tutors.

- Teachers of the Reiki aspects of the training should hold a Master Teacher certificate in Reiki, and be qualified practitioners with not less than two years' experience post-qualification as a Reiki Master.

- Teachers of non-Reiki or specialist subjects (e.g. health and safety, first aid) should be qualified in their subjects or have experience relevant to the subject they are teaching.

The recommendations for CPD after completing the training required for registration are twelve hours per year, six hours of which should be Reiki specific (see Chapter 22).

ACCREDITATION

In England qualifications are formally accredited by the Qualifications and Curriculum Development Agency (QCDA). Their role is to develop the curriculum, improve and deliver assessments, and review and reform qualifications. They don't, however, work only with schools and colleges; they also work with businesses to develop qualifications that ensure people get the right skills for their jobs, and that those qualifications can become part of the new Qualifications and Credit Framework (QCF), which is a system that allows people to build up their qualifications in small stages. In Scotland qualifications are accredited by the Scottish Qualifications Authority (SQA), which works with slightly different criteria regarding accreditation, and there are similar organisations in Wales and in Northern Ireland.

At the time of writing many, if not most, people who have trained in Reiki have probably done so with an individual independent Reiki Master, and these individual courses or workshops are not accredited – although most Reiki Masters do issue their students with a certificate to indicate what level of training they have achieved. However, there is no standardisation of what is taught at any of the levels, and the certificates are usually produced by each individual Master, rather than by any central organisation.

For those people who just wish to learn Reiki for their own self-healing, or to treat family and friends, it has not mattered whether their qualification has been accredited or not, and for them this situation will not change. However, for those who are not members of a professional organisation but who want to become registered practitioners, their training will need to cover the National Occupational Standards and match the Core Curriculum guidelines. If it does not, they will have to provide evidence that they have updated their training to that level, and professional organisations might also wish to insist on the same standards for their membership. If this is something you want to find out more about, you can refer to the Reiki Council's information on 'Grandparenting' (see below, page 149), which is on their website – www.reikicouncil.org.uk.

There are some Reiki courses which have been accredited and which are offered through awarding bodies such as ITEC (International Therapy Examination Council) and VTCT (Vocational Training Charitable Trust), mostly in colleges or privately owned educational establishments, but there are currently no accredited qualifications that incorporate either the new National Occupational Standards or the recommended Core Curriculum for Reiki. However, it is anticipated that in the near future awarding bodies will be applying for accreditation of Reiki courses based on these new standards. (Individuals cannot apply to accredit a course.)

THE NATIONAL REGISTER OF REIKI PRACTITIONERS

The National Register of Reiki Practitioners will be maintained by the GRCCT as an electronic up-to-date database, containing the names of all those who have met the agreed criteria for entry onto the register. The primary function of regulation is to protect the public from practitioners who have not trained, or have trained on a course below the profession-determined standard, and perhaps have no insurance to practise and therefore a member of the public has no means of redress if something goes wrong. The public therefore need to check that their practitioner is on the National Register. All registrants will be required to apply individually, to sign up to a code of ethics and practice, to commit to CPD and agree to abide by the Reiki NOS as an integral part of initial and continuing registration.

Basically there are two routes to register with the GRCCT, and they depend upon whether or not you are a member of one of the listed professional associations – the list is available on the GRCCT website, www.grcct.org.uk.

If you are a member of a listed professional association you will need:

1. The title of your qualifications or award

2. The year in which you qualified

3. The name of the professional organisation to which you belong

4. The registration number issued to you by the professional association

If you are not a member of a listed professional association, you will need:

1. Details of previous courses studied, these should be supported by certificates and diplomas

2. Copies of work experience details, supported by witness statements confirming your ability

3. Statements of work experience, supported by employers' statements confirming your ability

4. Voluntary work can also be included, if this has resulted in additional competences

5. A portfolio of evidence. This portfolio should be suitably organised and indexed to show the link between your competences and those required by the GRCCT Regulatory Group for the therapy or therapies for which you seek admission to the National Register

Basically, it will be up to the individual pre-registered practitioner to take responsibility for their own learning and development, but it is empowering for the practitioner to be responsible for their own research into professional practice standards. Registration – and the process of gathering knowledge and understanding and fulfilling the requirements of the National Occupation Standards which lead to it – should be seen as a dynamic process, and the start of lifelong learning, rather than an end in itself.

GRANDPARENTING

'Grandparenting' is the term used to denote Accreditation of Prior Learning (APL), which is a familiar aspect of training in the commercial world. It is a process that allows Reiki practitioners who have already been working professionally for a number of years to apply for registration without having to undertake further training, provided they meet certain criteria – see the Reiki Council's website for more information. Such things as experience, number of years working and CPD may be taken into consideration, and would need to be evidenced. There are four routes to registration available to existing Reiki practitioners who wish to take advantage of the 'grandparenting' option.

Route 1

An application may be submitted by a practitioner who:

1. Is a full member of a professional association which, after vetting prospective members, accepts Reiki practitioners onto its register, and the practitioner has been a member of that professional association for a minimum period of two years prior to their application to go on the National Register

2. Has personally received 'face-to-face' attunement by a Reiki Master Teacher

3. Provides a Reiki lineage traceable back to Mikao Usui

4. Holds current professional indemnity and public liability insurance.

Route 2

An application may be submitted by a practitioner who:

1. Is able to provide evidence of having worked (full or part-time, paid or unpaid, e.g. voluntary work) as a professional Reiki practitioner, for a period of not less than two years within the last five years

2. Provides a copy of their Reiki certificate(s) signed by a Reiki Master Teacher

3. Has personally received 'face-to-face' attunement by a Reiki Master Teacher

4. Provides a Reiki lineage traceable back to Mikao Usui

5. Holds current professional indemnity and public liability insurance.

Route 3

An application may be submitted by a practitioner who may not have been practising for the required period of time as specified in Route 2, provided that the practitioner:

1. Provides evidence to confirm that their training matches the standards set within the Reiki NOS and the recommendations of the Core Curriculum for Reiki.

2. Holds current professional indemnity and public liability insurance.

Route 4

An application may be submitted by a practitioner who may not have been practising for the required period of time as specified in Route 2, provided that:

1. Their existing training is mapped against the Reiki NOS and recommendations of the Core Curriculum for Reiki, and areas not covered are identified by an appropriately qualified person.

2. They agree to complete training identified to supplement the training already received in order to fully meet the standards set within the Reiki NOS and recommendations within the Core Curriculum for Reiki. Such training must be completed within twelve months of application.

3. They hold current professional indemnity and public liability insurance.

Full details of all of the NOS can be found on the Reiki Council's website, at www.reikicouncil.org.uk, and on the Skills for Health website, www.skillsforhealth.org.uk, and you will probably also be able to access them on the websites of the twelve Reiki organisations who contributed to the voluntary registration consultation process – their contact details are given in the Resources section at the back of this manual.

ASSESSMENT

In order to become registered, a Reiki practitioner will need to prove that their training complies with the National Occupational Standards, the Performance Criteria and the Core Curriculum. In order to do this they will have to provide evidence such as records of training and treatments, and this evidence will have to be assessed. There is a range of methods that can be used for assessment.

Observation

This could be through:

- Direct observation of practice by a qualified/approved assessor.

- Observation of competences specific to Reiki by an expert witness/ mentor/ sponsor, e.g. another Reiki practitioner or Master.

- Inference of knowledge from direct observation of practice.

- Direct questioning and assignments.

Receiving Reiki

The receipt of Reiki by a qualified assessor could be essential to establish whether a practitioner does have a connection to the Reiki energy. It would also demonstrate how the practitioner handles the client/practitioner relationship.

Review of Documentary Evidence

This could be an examination by a suitably qualified assessor of documentary evidence provided by the potential registrant. Such evidence could include records of treatments, leaflets and other publicity materials, the practitioner's journal, case studies, witness statements, certificates and evidence of prior learning where relevant.

Examinations/Assignments

Some aspects of essential knowledge are not observable or provable by regular documentation. These include aspects of understanding such as legal requirements, health and safety regulations, confidentiality and relationships with organisations such as the NHS. To assess these aspects an assignment or an oral or written examination might be considered necessary.

Simulations

Again, some aspects of essential knowledge which are not normally observable or demonstrated by documentation could be assessed by simulation or role-play. These could include situations where the safety of a practitioner might be at risk from a drunken or aggressive client, or where the practitioner needs to be able to deal competently with an emergency, such as a client having a severe asthma attack.

At the time of writing the assessor training and assessment process are still in the early stages of development, but information will become available through your professional association or the GRCCT.

FURTHER INFORMATION

The whole of Part Four is fundamentally about the National Occupational Standards and the Performance Criteria. However, although as much information as possible has been included to help you to fulfil the requirements, simply reading about what you need to know will not be enough! You will need to put the ideas and information into practice during treatments, keep records of everything you do, research topics more fully to give you a better understanding of them, perhaps attend courses or workshops on areas of theory or practice you don't feel fully confident about, and make sure you keep up to date. Remember, the responsibility for ensuring that you meet the registration criteria is up to you, so check, check and check again! But do try to enjoy the process – learning can be fun!

Chapter Fifteen

KNOWLEDGE OF REIKI

As a professional practitioner you will naturally be expected to have a thorough knowledge of Reiki theory and practice up to the level of training you have achieved, which means all of Part Two of this manual, and probably Part Three as well – Chapters 3 through to 13. This chapter is intended as a summary of the basics of good Reiki practice you need to understand before we go into more specific things in later chapters, such as how best to communicate with your clients, what legal restrictions there might be to treatment, and so on. The information here does relate particularly to the knowledge of Reiki required by those wishing to become registered practitioners in the UK, but it is also valid for anyone practising Reiki professionally in other countries.

STYLES AND SYSTEMS OF REIKI

There are a variety of different styles and systems of Reiki (see Appendix 1), which do have differing teachings. So you will need to know and identify these differences, and comply with what you have been taught. For example, some styles of Reiki advocate that hands should be placed on the body during a treatment, whilst others advocate that hands should be placed near to, but not directly on, the body, so you should know which of these practices is appropriate for you. Also, of course, a Reiki treatment can be carried out from a distance, and if this has been included in your training – usually at Reiki level 2 – then you will need to know how to do this as well.

In addition you should know about the history and development of Reiki in accordance with your particular Reiki style or system. Some Reiki Masters like to tell the traditional Reiki story as it was told by Mrs Takata, whilst others prefer to incorporate the information which began to come out of Japan in the late 1990s (see Chapter 4), and either is appropriate.

REIKI LINEAGE

It is important, especially if you wish to become a registered practitioner in the UK, that you know your Reiki Master's lineage, as you will be required to submit a copy of this when registering. The lineage shows your Master's connection through a number of other Reiki Masters to the founder of Reiki, Mikao Usui, and helps to provide evidence of the system of Reiki and type of training you have undergone. However, you will not be able to become a registered practitioner if you have not received an in-person attunement, i.e. if you have only received what is referred to as a 'distant attunement', meaning that you and the Reiki Master were in different places at that time, rather than actually being with your Reiki Master during a course or workshop. This distinction is made because when you have a personal relationship with your Reiki Master you will not only be attuned to Reiki, but will also be taught how to use it, for example to perform treatments on yourself and other people, or on animals and other creatures. In addition, you will be able to receive support from your initiating Master after your Reiki course, either in person (perhaps at a Reiki sharing group, where a group of Reiki students get together to share treatments, usually supervised by the Master who trained them), or by email or telephone. This is a really valuable aspect of the Master–student relationship.

PHYSICAL, EMOTIONAL, MENTAL AND SPIRITUAL HEALTH

You should also have a basic understanding of what 'healing' is, and how Reiki impacts on people's health. According to the World Health Organization, the definition of health is 'a state of complete physical, mental and social well-being, not merely the absence of disease'. Working to create a sense of well-being and health on all levels is what underlies our practice of Reiki. Reiki aids the body, mind and spirit to heal, but something which seems to confuse people is what healing really means. Unfortunately many people use the words 'healing' and 'curing' interchangeably, yet they don't necessarily mean the same thing. *Curing* means to completely eradicate an illness or disease, usually in the physical body, whereas *healing* can occur on many different levels, and doesn't have to be linked with a physical illness at all:

- **Healing on the *physical* level** – This might mean eradicating an illness completely, or it could simply mean limiting or alleviating the symptoms for a time whilst a person learns about and tackles any causative issues on the emotional, mental or spiritual levels – aspects of their life or lifestyle which are having a negative impact on their health.

- **Healing on the *emotional* level** – This could allow someone to calm any fears and to reach an acceptance of the effects of the illness, so that they can move on with the rest of their life, rather than just 'getting back to the way things were'. Or it might help them to come to terms with loss or bereavement, or allow them to let go of destructive emotions such as anger, jealousy and resentment.

- **Healing on the *mental* (psychological) level** – This could enable a recipient to relax and let go of stress and anxiety, as well as letting go of destructive, negative thought patterns, attitudes or prejudices that are holding them back and preventing them from getting the most out of life.

- **Healing on the *spiritual* level** – This could enable someone to develop a more loving and forgiving relationship with themselves, helping them to achieve greater self-esteem; or it could help them to let go of belief systems which are restricting them, allowing them greater self-expression and creativity; or perhaps even help them at the end of their life to make a peaceful transition into death.

You don't need to become an expert, but in order to help your clients it is useful for you to have at least a basic understanding of physical, mental, emotional and spiritual health so that you can discuss this before commencing a treatment. Some aspects of these might have been covered during one of the Reiki courses you attended, but otherwise there are many books in the Resources section which can help with this.

SELF-HEALING

As a Reiki practitioner you have a responsibility to use Reiki for self-healing as well as for treating other people. You will probably have heard the expression 'healer, heal thyself', and it is important for you to create good health and a sense of well-being in yourself so that you will be better able to help others – and also, of course, so that you are a good example to your clients.

YOUR RESPONSIBILITY AS A PRACTITIONER

Whatever Reiki system you use, and however you carry out treatments on your clients, it is the flow of Reiki energy through you which has beneficial effects. As mentioned above, Reiki works on four levels – physical, emotional, mental and spiritual – and as it flows out of your hands you will need to decide what the best way of treatment is to meet the needs of your client. Do they need a full Reiki treatment of about an hour, where you place your hands on or above the body in the twelve or more hand positions (see Chapter 6)? Do they need to be lying on a therapy couch, or would they be more comfortable seated in a chair (see Chapter 8)? Would they benefit from a partial treatment which would perhaps take only twenty or thirty minutes? Do they perhaps just require some 'first aid' treatment for a headache which might take only ten minutes? Are they seeking relief from stress, so would placing your hands on their shoulders, which often store a lot of tension, be the best way forward? You may have a range of alternatives at your fingertips, literally, but it is your responsibility, in consultation with your client, to decide which would be the best to use for specific conditions and under particular circumstances.

You should, of course, reassure your client that Reiki always works for the greatest good, so it is not harmful in any way, and that there are no known contraindications to Reiki when it is used on its own. However, as detailed in Chapter 16, there may be occasions when it is not appropriate to use Reiki, for example if the client is exhibiting any of what are known as 'red flag symptoms', or you suspect they may have an illness which is classed as a notifiable disease, or if you are concerned that they may not be fully aware of what Reiki is, despite your explanations, so that you do not have their informed consent (see Chapter 20). Alternatively, you might decide that it would be better to refer the client to some other practitioner, because whereas Reiki is helpful in almost all circumstances, there are occasions when it is sensible to direct a client to another form of therapy. For example, someone who is suffering with back problems may need to visit a chiropractor or an osteopath; or someone with considerable tension and stiffness in their muscles may need to have a remedial massage. Make it your business to find out about other therapists in your area, so that if need be you can recommend someone – your client will thank you for it!

Of course Reiki works very well in conjunction with many other therapies, especially those where physical touch is required, such as reflexology, aromatherapy massage and shiatsu, so if you offer any of these as well you may find that alternating treatments is useful for some clients. Moreover, if it is appropriate for that person you will probably find that Reiki flows out of your hands even when you are carrying out some other therapy, so it is a good idea to discuss this possibility with your client before you start their treatment, because ideally you should have their permission for this!

Chapter Sixteen

ANATOMY AND PHYSIOLOGY

As Reiki does not involve any massage or manipulation, you are unlikely to need an extensive knowledge of anatomy and physiology as a Reiki practitioner when treating your clients, so you won't need to memorise the names of lots of bones, muscle groups or nerves unless you also practise other therapies which do require such knowledge. However, you will need a basic knowledge of the skeletal structure of the body, as well as the functions and locations of the major organs. You will also need to have sufficient awareness of physical conditions to be able to communicate effectively with a client, and be able to identify whether Reiki is appropriate for him or her. Please do remember that you cannot diagnose any conditions unless you are medically qualified. In addition, you should also be able to identify 'red flag symptoms', meaning symptoms of conditions which require immediate medical attention, or are symptoms of notifiable diseases.

The basic information you need as a professional practitioner is covered in this chapter. However, you may decide it is beneficial to do further study, perhaps taking a qualification in anatomy and physiology, and you should certainly have a good anatomy and physiology book you can refer to – there are some recommended in the Resources section at the back of this manual.

LINKING HAND POSITIONS WITH PARTS OF THE BODY

A Reiki treatment requires you to place your hands on various parts of the body (see Chapter 6), and most people doing informal treatments on family and friends probably don't need to know exactly what each hand position is treating. However, as a practitioner this is valuable to know so that you can be better able to help your clients with specific health problems. So let's first look at what each of the hand positions is treating in terms of body parts.

The Head

The first hand positions, on the back of the head, over the eyes, over the ears, and the throat, work together to treat the head and the brain, including all of its functions and control mechanisms for the whole body, from memory to movement, the nervous system and the endocrine system. The following illustration may be helpful, as it shows the areas of the brain and what each area controls. (The illustration overleaf shows the location of the glands in the head and neck, as well as the rest of the body.)

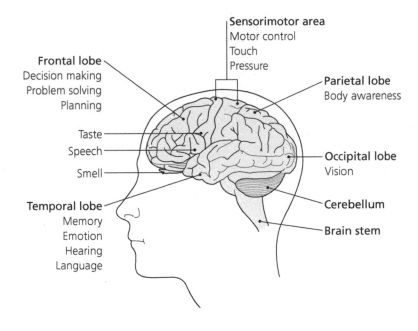

1. **Back of the Head** – From this position Reiki flows into the whole head and brain, nervous system, endocrine system, pituitary and pineal glands, as well as into the visual cortex.

2. **Brow/Eyes** – This position also treats the whole head and brain, nervous system, endocrine system, pituitary and pineal glands, as well as the eyes and face.

3. **Ears/Temples** – Once again, this position treats the head, brain, nervous system, endocrine system, pituitary and pineal glands, as well as the ears, sinuses, nose and face.

4. **Neck/Throat** – This position treats the neck, throat, tonsils, adenoids and vocal chords, as well as the jaw, mouth, teeth, gums, nose, sinuses and ears, plus the thyroid and parathyroid glands which control metabolism and growth.

The Front of the Body

The hand positions on the front of the body treat the major organs and their associated body systems, including the heart, lungs, liver, kidneys and reproductive organs. See below for the locations of the major organs and glands.

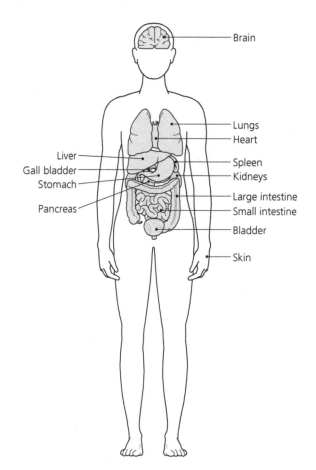

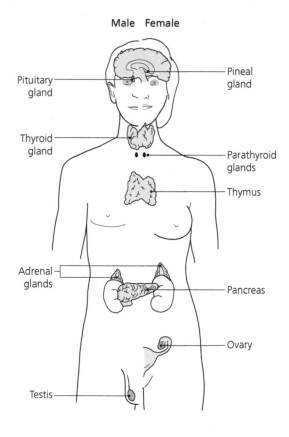

5. **Chest** – This position treats the heart and the whole cardiovascular system, the lymphatic system, the immune system, the lungs and respiration system, and the thymus gland, as well as allowing Reiki to flow into the arms and hands.

6. **Solar Plexus** – From here Reiki flows into the liver, spleen, pancreas, gall bladder, stomach and the whole of the digestive system.

7. **Waist/Navel** – This position treats the kidneys and adrenal glands, the lower digestive organs, the prostate, bladder and urinary tract, and the female reproductive system: the uterus and ovaries.

8. **Pelvic Area** – From here Reiki flows into the body's structure, including the whole skeleton, the muscles, tendons, and the body's largest organ, the skin, as well as the bladder, bowels and urinary/elimination system, the genitals and the male reproductive organs (testes), and the pelvis, hips, legs and feet.

The Back of the Body

Although all the hand positions on the front of the body enable Reiki to flow around the whole body, and therefore into the back as well, treating the back separately allows Reiki to flow even more effectively into some particular parts of the body. The spine, for example, is a very important part of our skeleton and nervous system. The four hand positions on the back treat the whole of the spine from the base of the neck down to the coccyx, as well as treating other vital areas again, such as the heart, lungs, liver and kidneys.

9. **Shoulders** – Reiki flows into the shoulders, especially into the muscles which often hold a lot of tension, and also into the top of the spine at the base of the neck, and down into the arms and hands.

10. **Middle Back** – This position treats the upper part of the spine, as well as the heart and lungs.

11. **Waist** – From here Reiki flows into the middle part of the spine, as well as into the pancreas, digestive system, liver, kidneys, spleen and adrenal glands, and the female reproductive system.

12. **Buttocks** – This position treats the lower portion of the spine, including the lumbar region and the coccyx, and also allows Reiki to flow around the whole skeleton, as well as the skin, blood and urinary/elimination system, and the genitals, male reproductive system, hips, legs and feet.

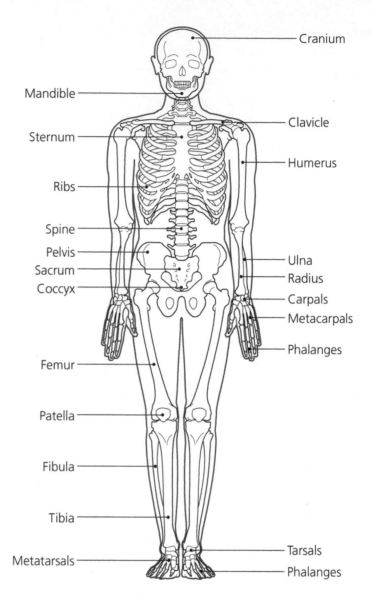

Cranium

Mandible

Sternum

Ribs

Spine

Pelvis

Sacrum

Coccyx

Femur

Patella

Fibula

Tibia

Metatarsals

Clavicle

Humerus

Ulna

Radius

Carpals

Metacarpals

Phalanges

Tarsals

Phalanges

(In effect each hand position treats parts of the skeleton and skin, but Reiki seems to flow into the whole of the skeleton and skin particularly when treating the pelvic area and buttocks.)

Of course Reiki doesn't only treat the physical body, as we know, so if you find your hands reacting a lot in one or more areas, for example your hands feel particularly warm or tingly, don't necessarily assume that there is a physical problem in that area. Each part of the body can also relate to emotional, psychological or spiritual issues: remember that Reiki works holistically, so sometimes it is these issues which Reiki will address first. It is not regarded as essential to know or understand what are referred to as 'causative issues', as many clients might not be prepared to listen to these ideas, but there are various books in the Resources section which can help if this is something that particularly interests you, especially *Your Body Speaks Your Mind* by Debbie Shapiro. However, as a very brief introduction here are some ideas:

- **Left side of body** – Represents our feminine side and our inner journey, as well as creativity, imagination, and spiritual issues.

- **Right side of body** – Represents our masculine side and our outer journey, as well as money or job issues, and other practical, physical and material concerns.

- **Eyes** – Show how we 'see' the world. What are you not prepared to see? Are you looking at things from an unhelpful perspective?

- **Ears** – What is it you are unwilling to hear? Are you avoiding listening to your inner guidance?

- **Throat** – Communication issues. Have you swallowed your anger and hurt? Are you expressing your feelings? Are you telling the truth?

- **Shoulders** – Are you carrying too many burdens? Do you always put yourself last in your list of priorities? Is your life too stressful?

- **Arms** – What or who are you holding on to? Are you afraid to let go? Who or what would you like to embrace?

- **Hands** – Associated with giving (right hand) and receiving (left hand), and the details of life. What issues or situations can't you handle?

- **Chest (Heart/Lungs)** – Relationship issues, self-esteem and feelings of worthlessness, suppressed emotions and feeling smothered or controlled by others.

- **Back** – Associated with stored anger and resentment, feeling unsupported and trying to be perfect, as well as money issues and indefinable fears.

- **Legs** – Associated with progress through life, fear of change, fear of the future, and family or parental issues. Who or what is holding you back?

- **Knees** – Linked with stubbornness, inflexibility and indecision. What decision are you afraid to make? Are you being obstinate over something?

- **Ankles** – Do you need to change direction? Is your life unbalanced?

- **Feet** – Associated with security and survival, reaching our goals or completing tasks, fear of taking the next step, of being 'grounded'.

COMMON ILLNESSES

As a professional Reiki practitioner you cannot be expected to know about every illness or disease that exists – unless you are also medically qualified, of course. However, you should have enough knowledge about some of the more common illnesses so that you can talk to your clients in an informed way – although please do remember that it is illegal to diagnose any illnesses unless you are medically qualified.

For instance, you have probably heard of sinusitis, and would correctly assume that the client would need treatment on the head, especially over the ears and temples, and the throat. But if your client told you they were suffering from rhinitis, would you recognise the term and realise that it was also a condition affecting the nose? It is also important to know whether Reiki is an appropriate way to treat a client's condition, or whether they should be directed to seek medical help, or be referred to some other practitioner. For example, for serious back pain Reiki may indeed be very helpful in reducing the level of pain, but this condition could also benefit from treatment from either a chiropractor or an osteopath.

It is obviously not possible to give in-depth information in this book about all of the common illnesses; that amount of detail would need an entire book to itself! And of course you are unlikely to come across many of these conditions as a Reiki practitioner, but although the following list is not exhaustive, it will give you the names of most of the common illnesses or ailments, some of which will be familiar to you, whilst others you may not have heard of but which you can then find out more about by researching in other books. If you come across anything which is not on this list, please do look that up too!

> There are some sources of information about anatomy and physiology in the Resources section, and I would particularly recommend the *Ross and Wilson Anatomy and Physiology in Health and Illness*, by Anne Waugh and Allison Grant as a good all-round text.

Conditions Affecting the Musculoskeletal System
(Bones, Joints, Muscles, Ligaments, Tendons)

Ankylosing Spondylitis, Bunions, Bursitis, Carpal Tunnel Syndrome, Cramp, Crush Syndrome, Dislocation, Fibrositis, Fractures, Frozen Shoulder, Gout,

Muscle Fatigue/Strain, Muscle/Tendon Tears, Muscular Dystrophy, Osteoarthritis, Osteomyelitis, Osteoporosis, Paget's Disease, Psoriatic Arthritis, Reiter's Syndrome, Repetitive Strain Injury (RSI), Rheumatoid Arthritis (RA), Rheumatic Fever, Rickets, Scoliosis, Slipped Disc, Sprain, Tennis Elbow

Conditions Affecting the Skin
(Hair, Nails and Membranes)

Acne, Allergies, Alopecia, Athlete's Foot, Blackheads, Boils, Burns, Cold Sores, Conjunctivitis, Corns, Styes, Dermatitis, Eczema, Folliculitis, Herpes Viruses, Impetigo, Fungal Nail Infection, Hair Lice, Ingrowing Toenails, Malignant Melanoma, Pigmentation Disorders, Pressure Ulcers, Psoriasis, Ringworm, Rosacea, Scabies, Shingles, Skin Cancer, Urticaria, Verrucas, Warts

Conditions of the Respiratory and Olfactory Systems
(Nose, Pharynx, Larynx, Trachea, Bronchi, Bronchioles, Alveoli, Lungs, Diaphragm)

Asthma, Bronchitis, Bronchopneumonia, Collapsed Lung, Cystic Fibrosis, Diphtheria, Emphysema, Hay Fever, Influenza, Laryngitis, Occupational Lung Diseases (Asbestosis, Byssinosis, Pneumoconiosis, Silicosis), Pharyngitis, Pleurisy, Pneumonia, Rhinitis, Sinusitis, Tonsillitis, Tuberculosis, Whooping Cough

Conditions of the Circulatory System
(Blood, Heart, Arteries, Veins, Capillaries)

Anaemia, Anaphylactic Shock, Aneurysm, Arteriosclerosis, Blood Pressure Problems (Hypertension, Hypotension), Cardiac Arrhythmia, Deep Vein Thrombosis (DVT), Embolism, Haemophilia, Haemorrhage, Heart Disease (Ischaemic and Rheumatic), Hepatitis A, B and C, HIV/AIDS, Leukaemia, Myocardial Infarction (Heart Attack), Oedema, Phlebitis, Septic Shock, Septicaemia, Thrombosis, Varicose Veins, Venous Thrombosis

Conditions Affecting the Lymphatic System
(Lymph Capillaries, Lymph Vessels, Lymph Nodes, Spleen, Thymus Gland)

Lymphadenitis, Lymphangitis, Lymphatic Obstruction, Malignant Neoplastic Metastases, Lymphomas (Hodgkin's Disease and Non-Hodgkin

Lymphoma), Spleen Problems (Splenomegaly), Thymus Gland Problems, Tonsil or Adenoid Problems

Problems of the Digestive System
(Mouth, Salivary Glands, Oesophagus, Stomach, Appendix, Small Intestine, Pancreas, Large Intestine, Rectum, Liver)

Anorexia Nervosa, Appendicitis, Bulimia Nervosa, Cholecystitis, Cholera, Cirrhosis, Cleft Palate/Lip, Coeliac Disease, Constipation, Crohn's Disease, Diarrhoea, Diphtheria, Diverticulitis, Duodenal Ulcers, Dysentery, Food Poisoning, Gall Stones, Gastritis, Heartburn, Hepatitis, Hernia, Irritable Bowel Syndrome (IBS), Jaundice, Mumps, Pancreatitis, Paratyphoid Fever, Peptic Ulcers, Peritonitis, Oesophagitis, Salmonella Infections, Thrush, Tonsillitis, Typhoid Fever

Conditions Affecting the Urinary/Elimination System
(Kidneys, Bladder, Bowel, Ureter, Urethra)

Bowel Cancer, Cystitis, Diabetic Nephropathy, Glomerulonephritis, Incontinence, Kidney Stones, Nephrotic Syndrome, Pyelonephritis, Renal Failure, Stress Incontinence, Ureteritis, Urethritis

Conditions of the Reproductive System
(Female: Vulva, Vagina, Uterus, Fallopian Tubes, Ovaries; Male: Scrotum, Testes, Prostate Gland, Urethra, Penis)

AIDS, Breast Cancer, Candidiasis, Cervical Carcinoma, Chlamydia, Ectopic Pregnancy, Endometriosis, Female Infertility, Gonorrhoea, Hepatitis B, Mastitis, Menopause Problems, Pelvic Inflammatory Disease (PID), Penis Infection, Polycystic Ovarian Syndrome, Prostate Cancer, Syphilis, Testicular Cancer, Urethra Infection, Vaginismus

Diseases of the Nervous System
(Brain, Spinal Cord, Neurones, Central Nervous System, Peripheral Nervous System, Autonomic Nervous System)

Alzheimer's Disease, Anxiety Attack, Bell's Palsy, Cerebral Hypoxia, Cerebral Oedema, Cerebral Palsy, Chronic Fatigue Syndrome, Creutzfeldt-Jakob Disease, Dementia, Epilepsy, Guillain-Barre Syndrome, Head Injuries,

Hydrocephalus, Huntington's Disease, Meningitis, Motor Neurone Disease, Multiple Sclerosis (MS), Myalgic Encephalitis (ME), Neuralgia, Neuritis, Parkinson's Disease, Peripheral Neuropathy, Poliomyelitis, Rabies, Raynaud's Disease, Shingles (Herpes Zoster), Spina Bifida, Stroke

Conditions Affecting the Senses
(Hearing, Balance, Sight, Smell, Taste)

Cataract, Conjunctivitis, Ear Infections, Glaucoma, Hearing Loss, Keratomalacia, Meniere's Disease, Labyrinthitis, Motion Sickness, Presbyopia, Retinal Detachment, Retinitis Pigmentosa, Retinopathy, Squint, Stye, Trachoma, Tumours

Diseases Affecting the Endocrine System
(Pituitary, Pineal, Thyroid, Parathyroid, Thymus and Adrenal Glands, Pancreas, Ovaries, Testes)

Addison's Disease, Cushing's Syndrome, Diabetes Insipidus, Diabetes Mellitus (Type 1 and Type 2), Dwarfism, Gestational Diabetes, Giantism, Goitre, Gynocemastia, Hirsutism, Parathyroid Problems (Hyperparathyroidsm, Hypoparathyroidism), Thyroid Problems (Graves' Disease, Hyperthyroidism, Hypothyroidism), Adrenal Problems (Hypersecretion, Hyposecretion), Menopause Problems, Virilism

RED FLAG SYMPTOMS

A 'red flag' symptom is something which indicates that your client should be referred immediately to their doctor. However, it is important not to frighten your client, so this should be done in a sensitive and tactful way – unless, of course, you believe their life is in imminent danger. For example, if your client is exhibiting symptoms of a heart attack, you should keep calm yourself, call for an ambulance, and do your best to keep your client relaxed and comfortable. In such instances it is helpful to have undertaken first aid training so that you know exactly what to do in a variety of circumstances. This might be something you should consider. Training courses are available worldwide, so check the internet for courses in your country; in the UK they are offered particularly by St John Ambulance and the Red Cross, and their websites are listed in the Resources section.

There are six major red flag sets of symptoms which call for immediate medical attention:

1. **Paralysis in the arms or legs, tingling, numbness, confusion, dizziness, double vision, slurred speech, trouble finding words, or weakness, especially on one side of the face or body.** These are potentially signs of a stroke.

2. **Chest pain or discomfort; pain in the arm, jaw or neck; breaking out in a cold sweat; extreme weakness; nausea; vomiting; feeling faint or dizzy; or being very short of breath.** These are all potentially signs of heart attack.

3. **Tenderness and pain in the back of the lower leg, chest pain, shortness of breath, or coughing up blood.** These are symptoms of a potentially dangerous blood clot in your leg, especially after someone has been sitting for a long time, or has been bedridden.

4. **Blood in the urine, even without accompanying pain.** This could be symptomatic of kidney stones, or bladder or prostate infection. Lack of pain doesn't necessarily mean lack of seriousness.

5. **Asthma attacks – severe wheezing or difficulties in breathing.** If symptoms don't improve, or get worse, then left untreated this can lead to severe chest muscle fatigue and is potentially fatal.

6. **Depression and suicidal thoughts.** Symptoms of depression include sadness, fatigue, apathy, anxiety, changes in sleep habits, and loss of appetite.

Apart from the six mentioned above, there are other symptoms which could also be classified as 'red flag':

- Abnormal bleeding – from the rectum, from the vagina outside the normal menstrual cycle, blood in the urine or in vomit, or coughing up blood

- Sudden changes in bowel habit, or unusual stools

- Severe constipation or failure to produce adequate urine

- Unexplained vomiting or difficulty in swallowing

- Unexplained exhaustion or tiredness, or changes in sleeping patterns

- Persistent cough or breathing difficulties

- Severe headache which doesn't respond fairly quickly to analgesics

- Sudden weight loss without dieting, or weight gain when dieting

- Unexplained loss of appetite or increased appetite

If a client mentions any of the above symptoms, even if they are not immediately apparent, then you should advise them to see a doctor or other medical professional as soon as possible – but again, try to do so in such a way that you do not alarm them, but that they realise you are serious in your suggestion.

NOTIFIABLE DISEASES

The spread of disease is an international concern, and for further information please see the websites for the Health Protection Agency (www.hpa. org.uk) if you are practising in the UK, or the World Health Organization (www.who.int) for other countries. Other websites are provided in the Resources section.

Notifiable Diseases in the UK

In the UK there are currently about thirty infectious diseases which are classified as 'notifiable', in other words, they must be reported immediately to a medical practitioner. As a Reiki practitioner you have neither the knowledge, nor the legal right to diagnose any illness unless you are also medically qualified, but if you suspect a client has any of the following diseases, or your client reports that they suspect they have, then you must act promptly – and clearly must not treat the client in case you also become infected! (You may need to see a doctor yourself, after exposure to an infected person.)

Their doctor must be informed immediately, and after seeing the patient he or she then has a statutory duty to inform the Health Protection Agency's Centre for Infections (CFI). Diseases which are notifiable under the Public Health (Infectious Diseases) Regulations 1988 include:

- Acute encephalitis

- Acute poliomyelitis

- Anthrax

- Cholera

- Diphtheria

- Dysentery
- Food poisoning
- Leprosy
- Leptospirosis
- Malaria
- Measles
- Meningitis (meningococcal, pneumococcal, haemophilus influenzae, viral, other specified or unspecified)
- Meningococcal septicaemia (without meningitis)
- Mumps
- Ophthalmia neonatorum
- Paratyphoid fever
- Plague
- Rabies
- Relapsing fever
- Rubella
- Scarlet fever
- Smallpox
- Tetanus
- Tuberculosis
- Typhoid fever
- Typhus fever
- Viral haemorrhagic fever
- Viral hepatitis (Hepatitis A, Hepatitis B, Hepatitis C, other)
- Whooping cough
- Yellow fever

Notifiable Diseases and the World Health Organization (WHO)

The UK is not the only country to have issues regarding notifiable diseases, so if you are practising Reiki in other countries you need to ensure that you find out the current regulations in your area. There is understandably international concern over potentially dangerous infectious diseases, since worldwide travel is now so prevalent, and the International Health Regulations (IHR), which came into force in June 2007, require countries to report certain disease outbreaks and public health events. The regulations are binding on 194 countries around the world, including all the member states of the WHO. Their aim is to help the international community to prevent and respond to acute public health risks that have the potential to cross borders and threaten people worldwide. There are a number of classifications of diseases, dependent upon the potential seriousness in terms of public health impact, where the WHO must be informed.

1. Where notification to the WHO is required immediately for a single case, irrespective of context:
   - Influenza
   - Poliomyelitis
   - Severe Acute Respiratory Syndrome (SARS)
   - Smallpox

2. Where a disease has the ability to cause serious health impact and spread rapidly across borders:
   - Vector-borne viral infections (i.e. transmitted to humans by insects, e.g. mosquitoes and ticks)
   - Cholera and other epidemic diarrhoeal diseases
   - Meningococcal meningitis
   - Plague
   - Viral haemorrhagic fevers
   - Yellow fever

3. Where a disease has epidemic potential:
   - Anthrax
   - Anti-microbial resistance (i.e. resistance to antibiotics or other medicines)
   - Chemical safety (e.g. toxicology, ecotoxicology, ensuring safety of human health and/or environment)
   - Dengue fever
   - Food safety
   - HIV/AIDS

- Malaria
- Measles and other vaccine-preventable diseases
- Ionising radiation
- Non-ionising radiation
- Tuberculosis
- Zoonoses (infectious diseases which can transfer from animals to humans)

It is important to take all of the above information in context. You are very unlikely to come into contact with clients who have any of the above diseases. Most of them make patients very ill, so they are much more likely to contact their doctor for help rather than make an appointment with any practitioner of a complementary or alternative therapy! But in order to practise responsibly, you should ensure that you keep up to date with current regulations, and have sufficient knowledge to identify dangerous symptoms, for your own safety as well as for the well-being of your clients.

Except in cases of sudden or urgent necessity, it is an offence for anyone other than a certified midwife to attend a woman in childbirth without medical supervision, or for anyone other than a registered nurse to attend for reward as nurse on a woman in childbirth or during a period of ten days thereafter. This doesn't mean that you cannot treat women with Reiki during or after their pregnancy, with their permission, or that a suitable birthing partner cannot give Reiki during a woman's labour, providing the attending medical staff are happy with that situation.

Chapter Seventeen

COMMUNICATING
WITH CLIENTS

Apart from being able to perform Reiki treatments properly, one of the most essential skills you can have is to be able to communicate effectively with your clients. This is a wide-ranging subject, covering written, verbal and non-verbal communication. Just a few examples of communication with your client might be:

- Explaining what Reiki is, how long a treatment might last and how much it will cost

- Discussing your client's needs and expectations

- Asking relevant questions about your client's current and past health

- Encouraging the client to ask questions

- Establishing whether both you and the client have understood everything and that you have the client's consent before starting the treatment

- Assessing verbally and through body language whether your client is happy or unhappy about anything to do with the treatment

- Writing information in your client records

- Listening effectively to what your client does, and doesn't, say!

On a client's first visit you need to greet them and make them feel comfortable before you explain what Reiki is, what a Reiki treatment is, how long a treatment takes, and how much you charge. You then need to discuss your client's needs and expectations in a way that encourages the client to be open and honest with you, and makes them feel able to ask questions or express any concerns. You can then explain the available options (e.g. a full Reiki treatment on a couch, or in a chair, etc.) and what responses they may have to Reiki, such as feeling relaxed and sleepy, or a bit emotional, and you can also advise on realistic expectations, perhaps by explaining the difference between 'healing' and 'curing', and discussing the way Reiki works holistically.

You will need to write down their personal details – name, address, telephone number, date of birth and the name and contact details of someone who can be contacted in case of emergency – a relative, a carer, or their family doctor (see Appendix 6 for an example of a Client Treatment Record). You will also need to establish why they've come for a Reiki treatment, whether they're currently receiving medical treatment or taking regular medication, and whether they are also receiving other complementary treatments. It may be necessary to explain any interactions between Reiki and those treatments, and that there are no known contraindications to Reiki when it is used on its own. You could also suggest that they inform their doctor or other health practitioner that they are receiving Reiki as well, and a note of this advice should be made on their records. In addition, you should ascertain whether they have any specific physical problems which would make it uncomfortable for them to lie on their back and/or their front, or whether they need to lie on their side or be treated in a chair. Finally, ask them if there is anything else they feel it is important to tell you.

By this time you will probably have sufficient information to decide whether a Reiki treatment is appropriate for them, or whether they should be referred to some other therapist. If it is appropriate to treat them with Reiki, obtain their consent, and then write all of this information on their client record sheet in accordance with legal requirements (see Chapter 21), and so that you can refer to it again at any future appointment.

Communication Difficulties

As a Reiki practitioner you are likely to attract many different types of people as clients. Because of this it is possible that you may encounter difficulties communicating with some clients, possibly because of cultural or language differences, the age of the client, speech or sensory impairment or some other form of disability. In these cases you will have to adapt your way of communicating with the client, using appropriate eye contact and body language, and methods of listening that will encourage the client to communicate as best they can. Of course it may be necessary to communicate through someone else, which could be a carer, a family member, or anyone else in a position of responsibility for the client in situations where the client is too young, or has reduced capacity for comprehension and decision making, or where the client does not speak your language.

In such cases it is important to explain your role and responsibilities, what information you need and why you need it, and that any information given will be written down but will be kept confidential. In all cases, you should ensure that you understand the legal requirements on equality, diversity, discrimination, confidentiality, and the rights of the client to be treated as an individual in a dignified way (see Chapter 21).

Effective Communication

Communication is the art of successfully sharing meaningful information with people by means of an interchange of experience. Whether you are communicating in writing, verbally or non-verbally, to be effective your communication should be:

- Clear – ensure that the information is presented in a manner which is easy to understand

- Concise – don't give long-winded explanations

- Correct – be accurate and avoid giving misleading information

- Complete – give all the information, not just part of it

- Courteous – be polite and non-threatening

- Constructive – be positive, and avoid being critical or negative

WRITTEN COMMUNICATION

As a Reiki practitioner you are required to document information about your client, about any treatments you carry out, and any advice you give. Details of what information is required are given above. However, something to bear in mind when writing client notes is that, in legal terms, *if it's not documented, it didn't happen*!

The main characteristics of documentation are that, depending upon what amount of detail is required, it should be concise but comprehensive, factual and objective but descriptive where necessary, as well as being relevant/appropriate and legally prudent (see Chapter 21 for information about data protection legislation). That may sound challenging, but if you follow the guidelines above in terms of what information is required about your client, it won't seem so difficult. You should always write legibly in ink – if you don't have tidy handwriting, you could type up your notes afterwards – and you should ensure that words are spelled correctly (so use a dictionary or the spell-check facility on a computer).

VERBAL COMMUNICATION

Verbal communication is probably the most common way of communicating your thoughts through words. Such thoughts may be ideas, opinions, directions, dissatisfactions, objections, emotions and pleasure. Verbal or oral communication is something that many of us need to do well; the basic requirement is to be able to talk and be understood. However, beyond that, we have to consider the underlying purpose of oral communication. Very often we talk too much and with too little structure. Whatever you are doing, the way you communicate sets the emotional tone to any encounter and builds relationships that will colour the success of your professional Reiki practice. Your choice of words should reflect the age, education, development, level of self-esteem, and the culture of your client. You therefore need to adapt your vocabulary, pace and tone of speaking to meet their needs.

Communication Blocks

Difficulties in communicating with a client may be due to a number of issues, such as:

- The client's perception of something may be different from yours

- The client may jump to a conclusion instead of working through the process of hearing, understanding and accepting

- The client may lack the knowledge needed to understand what you are trying to communicate

- You may have difficulty in expressing what you wish to say to the client

- Emotions may interfere in the communication process

- There may be a clash of personalities between you and the client

You should ask yourself the following questions:

- Do I have the client's attention?

- Am I explaining myself in an easily understood manner?

- Has the client understood?

- Does the client believe what I am telling him/her?

- Does the client accept what I am saying?

If you're happy that the answers to the above questions are 'yes', that's fine, but if not you will need to think how to rephrase or re-explain what you're trying to communicate.

HOW PEOPLE PROCESS INFORMATION

The way in which people process information has a great impact on whether or not you have successful communication. You may not have thought about it before, but we all have a preferred 'style' of language which is linked to one or more of our five senses: visual (seeing), auditory (hearing), kinaesthetic (feeling), olfactory (smelling), and gustatory (tasting). Of course most of us have all five senses, but we will have one or two which predominate, and if you listen to these language cues you can often discover what your client's preferred way of experiencing life is – although we all move from one to another at times. If you then mirror the types of words or phrases they use, it will help your communication to flow more easily and will make your client feel more at ease.

The majority of us use visual, auditory or kinaesthetic words, but occasionally you will come across someone who uses a lot of non-sensory words, and less often there will be people whose words are often olfactory or gustatory based. See if you can recognise which category you prefer in the table overleaf.

If both you and your client share the same predominant sense you should find it fairly easy to communicate well with each other, but if you have different predominant senses this might mean you'll talk at cross purposes and find it difficult to understand one another. You can make the communication flow easily by listening carefully to the type of words and phrases your client is using and changing your language to match or mirror theirs, which creates greater rapport.

SENSE	WORD CUES
Visual Seeing	picture, watch, show, glance, stare, glare, perspective, vision, viewpoint, illuminate, look, gaze, insight, vivid, illustrate, visible, regard, examine, see, look
	Predominantly visual people often speak fairly quickly, because they think in pictures. Favourite phrases might be: 'nice to see you', 'looks to me like...', 'appears to me', 'see eye to eye'.
Auditory Hearing	hear, listen, talk, groan, cry, whine, chatter, shout, moan, harmony, noisy, accent, rhythm, hearsay, tone, call, loud, told, resounding, voice, silence, quiet, silent, note
	Predominantly auditory people often speak quite slowly, using words carefully and selectively. Favourite phrases might be: 'I hear what you're saying', 'word for word', 'loud and clear', 'unheard of'.
Kinaesthetic Feeling	feel, warm, touch, soft, firm, hard, clumsy, concrete, rough, relaxed, pressure, handle, shake, grasp, itch, creeps, texture, sticky, cold, smooth, sharp, atmosphere
	Predominantly kinaesthetic people generally speak quite slowly, because they are reacting to their feelings and may have trouble finding the right words to match those feelings. Favourite phrases might be: 'get to grips with', 'hand in hand', 'this feels right', 'how are you feeling?'.
Olfactory Smelling	aroma, scent, nose, odour, stink, fragrant, fresh, stench, smell, sniff, perfume, foul, rotten, stale, noxious, musty
Gustatory Tasting	flavour, sour, sweet, appetite, juicy, bitter, taste, relish, feed, swallow, bland, spicy, succulent, hungry, thirsty
Non-sensory based	think, know, understand, decide, explain, arrange, recognise, consider, attend, remember, believe, reflect, accept, follow, conceive, comprehend, study, respect
	Predominantly non-sensory based people generally think before they speak, but are usually very eloquent. Favourite phrases might be: 'I know what you mean', 'let's think about this', 'I find that hard to believe'.

QUESTIONING TECHNIQUES

One important skill when communicating is using the right kind of questioning technique. The most frequently used forms of questions are referred to as 'open' questions and 'closed' questions, but other types include probing questions, leading questions and rhetorical questions.

Closed questions usually get answered with a single word or with a very short, factual answer. Take, for example, the question 'Are you warm enough?' The answer is going to be either 'yes' or 'no'. Closed questions are good for testing your understanding or making a decision: 'Are we agreed that this is the right course of action?'

Open questions elicit longer answers, and they usually begin with the words 'what', 'where', 'when', 'who', 'how' or 'why'. An open question asks the respondent for his or her knowledge, opinion or feelings, so they are good for finding out more detail, or discovering the other person's opinions. 'Tell me' and 'describe' can also be used in the same way as open questions. Here are some examples:

- When did you begin to have this problem?

- How does the illness affect you?

- Describe the symptoms in more detail.

- What medication are you taking?

- Tell me what happened during the treatment.

Probing questions are another way of finding out more detail. Sometimes it's as simple as asking your client for an example, to help you understand something they have said. At other times they can be used when you need additional information for clarification: 'Where do you experience that pain?'

Leading questions try to lead the respondent to your way of thinking, such as 'Getting a second option is better, isn't it?' Note that leading questions tend also to be closed questions, but they can sometimes be helpful if your client seems shy about expressing their opinion.

Rhetorical questions aren't really questions at all, in that they don't actually need an answer. They're really just statements phrased in question form, such as, 'Isn't this blanket a pretty colour?' They might be useful when trying to put your client at ease.

COMMUNICATION STYLES

Whenever we speak we choose and use one of four basic communication styles: assertive, aggressive, passive or passive-aggressive. Clearly if, when you are talking to your client, you seem aggressive, this might make them feel at the very least uncomfortable, and possibly even a bit frightened of you! On the other hand, their communication may seem passive, which could mean they are just accepting what you say to avoid any conflict or bad feeling. Understanding the four styles is therefore helpful in creating good communication and a good relationship between yourself and your client.

Assertive Communication

The most effective and healthiest form of communication is the assertive style. It's how we naturally express ourselves when our self-esteem is intact, giving us the confidence to communicate without games and manipulation. When we are being assertive, we work hard to create mutually satisfying solutions. We communicate our needs clearly and forthrightly. We care about the relationship and know our limits and refuse to be pushed beyond them just because someone else wants or needs something from us. Surprisingly, the assertive style of communication is the one most people use least, but it is the preferred style when working with a client.

Aggressive Communication

Aggressive communication always involves manipulation. We may attempt to make people do what we want by inducing guilt (hurt) or by using intimidation and control tactics (anger). Covert or overt, we simply want our needs met – right now! Although there are a few arenas where aggressive behaviour is called for, such as in sport, it will always be a disadvantage in a relationship, and is quite wrong in the practitioner/client relationship.

Passive Communication

Passive communication is based on compliance and hopes to avoid confrontation at all costs. In this mode we don't talk much, question even less, and actually do very little. We just don't want to rock the boat. Passive communicators have learned that it is safer not to react and better to disappear than to stand up and be noticed. If this is how your client is communicating you need to encourage them to ask questions, and reassure them by explaining that you won't take exception to anything they say, you just want their experience of a Reiki treatment to be a good one.

Passive-Aggressive Communication

A combination of styles, passive-aggressive communication avoids direct confrontation (passive), but attempts to get even through manipulation (aggressive). If you've ever thought about making that certain someone who needs to be 'taught a thing or two' suffer (even just a teeny bit), you've stepped pretty close to (if not into) the devious and sneaky world of the passive-aggressive! It's unlikely that you would use this style of communication when talking to a client, but it is just possible your client could try it with you, perhaps trying to make you charge less for the treatment by giving you a sob story about how hard up they are!

LISTENING SKILLS

Even if you are excellent at communicating verbally, if you don't listen effectively to your client you are likely to create misunderstandings which could result in the experience not being as good as it could be for either of you. A person who is listening attentively keeps a comfortable level of eye contact with the other person and has an open and relaxed but alert pose. You should face your client and respond to what he or she is saying with appropriate facial expressions, offering encouragement with a nod or a smile.

Adopting the behaviour of a good listener will help you establish good rapport with your client. It requires a degree of self-discipline and a genuine desire to take on board the message the speaker is trying to convey. You need to be able to suspend judgement and avoid contradicting or interrupting him or her. Postpone saying your bit until you are sure they have finished and you have understood their point. Reflecting and summarising – repeating back a key word or phrase the speaker has used – shows you have listened and understood. Summarising also gives the client a chance to add to or amend your understanding.

BODY LANGUAGE AND NON-VERBAL COMMUNICATION

You may think that face-to-face communication consists of just taking it in turns to speak. While the practitioner is speaking, the client is expected to listen and wait patiently until the practitioner finishes. In reality, people resort to a variety of verbal and non-verbal behaviour in order to maintain a smooth flow of communication. Such behaviour includes head-nods, smiles, frowns, bodily contact such as touching someone's arm, eye movements, laughter, adopting certain body postures and many other actions. The facial expressions of clients can provide feedback to the practitioner. Glazed or down-turned eyes could indicate boredom or disinterest, as does fidgeting. Fully raised eyebrows signal disbelief, and half-raised eyebrows indicate puzzlement. Postures such as sitting with crossed arms and legs could indicate shyness, embarrassment or even anger.

It is said that when we communicate we take in only 7 per cent of what is meant from the actual words, whereas 38 per cent of meaning is conveyed by the tone of voice used, and 55 per cent from a person's non-verbal signals – their body language.

What is Body Language?

Body language is all the communication signals you give by voluntary or involuntary body movements, such as:

- Head movements – nodding, shaking, holding the head on one side, etc.

- Facial expressions through facial muscle movements of the eyebrows (e.g. raised, furrowed), eyes (e.g. dilation of pupils), nose, lips (e.g. smiling), tongue (e.g. licking the lips) and jaw

- Overall body posture, including proximity, leaning backwards or forwards, shoulder movements (e.g. shrugging), arm placements (e.g. folded in front of the body), hand and finger gestures, leg and feet placement (e.g. crossed legs), handling and placement of objects (e.g. pens, papers, etc.)

Body language can also include appearance, as how you look and what you wear can have quite a big impact on your client's impression of you, so you need to look clean, tidy and professional.

Sometimes a person will say one thing, but their body language is demonstrating the opposite, so it is important to notice whether the verbal and non-verbal message has congruency, i.e. whether they match up. It is also important to realise what your body language is saying! Are you focusing on the individual and keeping a good level of eye contact? Are you giving the impression that you are more important than your client by standing when they are sitting? Are you giving them enough time to communicate their wants and needs, or are you 'tutting' or showing other signs of impatience such as tapping your foot?

A practitioner needs to be sensitive to the body language being demonstrated by their clients, so a good working knowledge of the meaning behind non-verbal signals will prove invaluable. Clearly non-verbal communication is a big subject, but one which is well worth learning more about. It is too extensive a topic to explain fully in this manual, but you can learn a lot from well-illustrated books which show facial expressions, postures and so on, and what they are likely to mean – there are some recommended in the Resources section.

Developing effective communication skills is of paramount importance for a professional Reiki practitioner in order to have successful relationships with clients. The better the communication, the better the experience for both you and your client – and the more likely it will be that your client comes back for more treatments! There are a variety of courses on communication which are available at many colleges, and some may even be arranged by your local business network. It would be a good idea to investigate these, because communication is such a vital tool for anyone involved in therapeutic relationships.

Chapter Eighteen

PROVIDING REIKI
TO CLIENTS

So far in Part Four we have looked at what knowledge you need to practise professionally, including of Reiki itself, of anatomy and physiology and how to communicate effectively with your clients. Also, in Chapters 6 and 8 we covered the hand positions used in Reiki and how to carry out a Reiki treatment, which is virtually the same whether you are treating family and friends or working as a practitioner. Now we move on to the actual provision of Reiki to a client. Although some of the ideas in this chapter have been covered briefly before, when you are working professionally it is important to demonstrate to your clients that you are well trained, well organised and skilled in what you do. Providing everything in a logical order will help your clients to feel reassured, so here we will cover the whole process from start to finish:

- Making an appointment

- Preparations you need to make before the client's arrival

- Initial discussion with your client

- Carrying out the Reiki treatment

- When to refuse to carry out a treatment

- After the Reiki treatment

MAKING AN APPOINTMENT

When someone contacts you to enquire about Reiki you may at that stage be required to tell them about it, explaining what Reiki is, what a Reiki treatment is, how long a treatment lasts, and so on. You may also need to explain that the client can remain fully clothed throughout the treatment – this is often very reassuring for them – and you can tell them that you will be placing your hands gently on (or above) various parts of the head and body, but that no intimate parts of the body will be touched, which is also comforting for them.

You may have a leaflet about yourself, giving details about your qualifications and experience, as well as about Reiki, so it may be possible to give one of these to your potential client, as often they feel more relaxed if they know more about what to expect. Your leaflet will probably explain how much you charge for treatments, and it will also have details of the location of your practice and how the client can contact you – it is important to show the full address and telephone number.

You may have to give all of this information over the telephone, or perhaps even by email, before actually making an appointment. When you do make the appointment, it is a good idea to have an appointments diary which has one or two pages per day, with the times in the margin, so that you can see when you are available for treatments. Do remember to strike out any times when you will be busy with other activities, such as dental appointments, collecting children from school and so on!

When you make the appointment with the client, write down their name, address and telephone number in the appointments diary against the time they are due to arrive, and make sure you leave enough time before making the next appointment. Remember that you will need some time for greeting and settling your client, as well as for carrying out the treatment, and time afterwards for the client to 'come round', and for some discussion of their experience, so you will probably need an absolute minimum of an hour for each client, and more likely an hour and a half.

If it is the first appointment with a particular client you will need an extra half an hour to discuss why they want a Reiki treatment, what their expectations are, and to write down their medical history and any other details they want to give you. Without this information you will not be able to guide and support the client to make informed choices about receiving a Reiki treatment.

Please note that even if you are planning to give the client any distant treatments, you will still need to make an appointment with them, agreeing dates and times and their location, and you will still need to talk to them about Reiki, about their expectations, and about what to expect during and after the treatment. Using the Reiki Distant symbol to send a distant treatment creates a very profound connection, and a distant treatment is as effective as a hands-on treatment: the same informed consent is needed as for face-to-face treatment.

Giving your client your contact details, and obtaining theirs, is vital in case either of you has to change the date or time of the appointment for any reason. In order to be professional it is important that you only cancel or postpone an appointment with a client under exceptional circumstances, or if you are ill. Clearly if you have any infectious illness it is inappropriate to treat clients, as it would be most unethical to pass on the infection, even if it is 'just' a cold. Some people have reduced immune function and for them catching a cold can be much worse than for most other people, and this isn't necessarily something they would discuss with you.

If your client contacts you to postpone or cancel a treatment it might be a little annoying, although that will depend upon the reason they give. But that is still better than them not getting in touch and just not turning up! However, basically you just have to shrug your shoulders and accept it, whichever way it happens.

PREPARATIONS BEFORE THE CLIENT ARRIVES

There are suggestions about this in Chapter 8, but in brief, you should check that the environment for your treatment meets your client's needs, so ensure that your treatment room is clean and tidy and that you have sufficient clean pillows, pillowcases and blankets for your therapy couch. You also need some fresh water and a glass on hand for your client after the treatment, and your client record sheets and appointment book should be available (with a pen, of course!). You should also make sure you are personally well prepared to carry out the treatment. This might just be making sure you are clean and tidy, and washing your hands, but if you are comfortable with the idea you might do some energy cleansing work on yourself and your treatment space (see Appendix 3), and perhaps some meditation before your client arrives.

INITIAL DISCUSSION WITH THE CLIENT

When a client arrives for their appointment you obviously need to greet them and make them feel welcome. It might be a good idea to get them to sit down first of all, so that they have a chance to relax – and they will probably find it much easier to talk to you when seated, rather than lying down on a therapy couch! Lots of people are quite nervous before having their first Reiki treatment, so always spend a little time talking to them beforehand, and if you haven't already explained what Reiki is and what a treatment is when they booked their appointment, do this now. You will also need to write down all of the client's details (see Appendix 6 for a sample client record sheet), which should include not only their medical history and any medical or complementary treatment they are having, but also their emotional, mental and spiritual well-being – you can explain that Reiki works on all these levels – and their expectations of how they think Reiki can help them.

You may have to explain that they (and possibly any significant others in their lives) will need to take an active role in their healing, perhaps by changing some behaviours that are not helpful to their physical, mental or emotional health because this will make the Reiki more effective. This idea can be quite a challenging thing to present to a client, so it must be done as sensitively as possible; essentially it is up to the client what they do, or don't do, to improve their health and well-being, and you must respect this. During your discussions it may become apparent that whilst Reiki may well be beneficial for them, it might not be sufficient to deal totally with their problem, so they may have to seek advice from other sources. These sources might be medical – e.g. a doctor, acupuncturist, chiropractor, osteopath or some other therapist – or it might be non-medical, such as a counsellor, the Citizens' Advice Bureau, or even a financial adviser. (The types of problems clients bring to practitioners can be very varied!)

Clients usually find it reassuring when they realise that they can remain fully clothed except for their coat and shoes, although removing their watch, spectacles and any intrusive jewellery such as large earrings can be a good idea. You can also spend some time describing or demonstrating the hand positions you will be using, and whether your hands will be placed directly on their body, or held slightly above, so that they know exactly what to expect.

Tell them also what sort of experiences they may have, such as feeling warmth or tingling where your hands are placed, or that they might 'see' colours, or have vivid dreams. Usually the client feels very relaxed and peaceful as the Reiki flows through their body, although occasionally they might feel emotional as old energy patterns surface. They may even shed some tears (or laugh!), or their arms or legs might suddenly jerk even if they are asleep, but all of these reactions are perfectly normal – it is just energy releasing in different ways from the body and you should always reassure your client about this. Occasionally there may be a 'healing crisis', some temporary physical symptoms such as a sudden cold, in the days immediately following a treatment, as the energy works through the blockages and the body does its best to get rid of them. You should mention this briefly, but without alarming them – it only happens sometimes, so you don't want to turn it into a self-fulfilling prophecy!

It is important to discuss with your client the possible effects of a Reiki treatment in terms not only of any potential physical healing, but also potential changes in your client's emotional, psychological and spiritual well-being. They may experience a shift in consciousness, a realisation about the causes of some problem(s). This is an important part of healing, and if the client wants to talk about it after the treatment they should be encouraged to do so. However, remember that your client is entitled to expect your complete confidentiality, so never talk to others – even their relatives – about particular clients or their treatments, unless you have your client's permission to do so.

You should also warn clients that for some conditions, such as diabetes, thyroid problems and high blood pressure, the Reiki may help to bring the body into better balance, so it may be necessary for them to monitor their condition (if they have suitable self-monitoring equipment), and certainly to check with their doctor, in case their health condition changes and they need their medication reassessed. However, you do need to emphasise that with Reiki it is important not to become too attached to any specific outcomes. Reiki flows where it is needed, which is not always where it is expected to go, so whilst someone may come with the expectation that they will receive some particular result for a physical condition, this may happen, but equally it may be that Reiki will flow first into emotional, psychological or spiritual issues. They should feel these benefits too, of course, perhaps becoming much calmer and more relaxed, or having insights into some worries or concerns they have had. It would certainly make practitioners' lives easier if we could guarantee certain results each time we treated a client, but this just isn't the case!

Talk to the client about the reason they have come for a treatment, and give them a chance to ask questions and express any concerns, so that you can set their mind at rest. Of course you will also need to find out at this stage whether, because of any health difficulties or advanced pregnancy, they might find it difficult to lie on a therapy couch on their back or on their front, and whether they would prefer to lie on their side, or be treated sitting in a chair instead.

CARRYING OUT THE REIKI TREATMENT

You can then help them onto the couch (or chair) and make sure they are comfortable, placing pillows wherever needed. For most clients, when lying on their back one pillow under their head and one under their knees is sufficient, but some people like more in either or both positions, so make sure you have enough in reserve. The pillow(s) under their knees should be moved to underneath their ankles when the client is lying on his/her front, to help to take pressure off the back. Sometimes a soft blanket over the client makes them feel nurtured and more relaxed, and it ensures they stay warm enough when their body cools down because they are lying still.

It is important to tailor the treatment appropriately for the needs of each client, so be aware of this when talking to them before the treatment as well as when actually giving them Reiki. It may be necessary to just do a few hand positions rather than a full treatment, or to give more Reiki to some parts of the body, or even to treat just one part, such as one shoulder if they have the condition of 'frozen shoulder' which can make it very painful to lie down.

It is essential that both practitioner and client should relax and enjoy the treatment, so before you start make sure that both of you are comfortable, that the therapy couch, if you are using one, is at a comfortable height for you, and that the client is warm enough. Talking or asking questions during the treatment is an individual matter, although being quiet allows the client to relax more thoroughly. Usually he or she will feel sleepy, so simply playing soft, relaxing music is often best, although do check with the client first in case they prefer silence. However, please do tell the client before you start that if at any time they are uncomfortable, or they need something (such as a tissue), or if they would prefer you to stop the treatment, they must tell you at once. Even when told this, some clients are too shy to mention their discomfort, so look out for non-verbal signs such as fidgeting, or visible tension, in which case you can ask the client directly if there is anything wrong, or if they perhaps need to go to the toilet (people can be embarrassed by this, but often Reiki does seem to have a strong effect on the bladder!), or need a glass of water or a tissue, or if they want you to stop the treatment.

WHEN TO REFUSE A TREATMENT

There may be occasions when, as a professional practitioner, you might choose not to accept a client. Obviously if you realise that the client doesn't want Reiki, that would be a good reason to refuse to treat them! However, you might also realise that a Reiki treatment would not be appropriate, perhaps because the client is exhibiting 'red flag' symptoms (detailed in Chapter 16) where medical referral is essential, or because they have a medical condition that you do not feel you have the right amount of experience or expertise to deal with. This highlights the necessity for you to have a basic knowledge of physical conditions so that you can communicate effectively with your client, and there is a list of many common illnesses given in Chapter 16. As you are unlikely to be familiar with all of them – it is quite a long list! – it is recommended that you find out a little about each (there are suitable reference books recommended in the Resources section) so that you can recognise any conditions which might require immediate medical attention, or which might indicate that the client has a notifiable disease (again, see Chapter 16).

Other reasons why you might not wish to provide Reiki are because the client appears drunk or is abusive, or makes you feel physically or sexually vulnerable. In these cases you are within your rights to refuse to treat the client, although you do need to employ sensitivity, tact and diplomacy in dealing with awkward clients. If in doubt, call for assistance from someone you trust. If you work within a holistic health centre or other similar establishment, ask another therapist or other member of staff to help you; if you practice from home, then if there is another person in the property, ask them for help, or phone a neighbour or friend. However, if the situation becomes in any way dangerous, call the police, or in the case of medical emergency, call for an ambulance.

AFTER A REIKI TREATMENT

You will need to allow your client time to 'come round' after the treatment, and it is a good idea to hand them a glass of fresh water, and to advise them to drink plenty of water for a few days after the treatment, as this will help the Reiki to eliminate any negativity or toxins from the body. You can say that they may feel a need to rest and relax more for a while, and also mention that sometimes they might experience an increase in any symptoms for a short time, but that this shouldn't last very long and they should then feel some improvement. If your client has been attuned to Reiki, you can suggest that doing a daily self-treatment would be an advantage, as this will obviously also aid the healing process.

Many clients will want to talk about their experience during the Reiki treatment, and this should be encouraged. Take care to listen carefully, and also to assess any non-verbal signals (see Chapter 17), because this will help you to evaluate how effective the treatment has been and whether it would be beneficial for the client to have further treatments, or whether you need to refer them to some other therapist for additional help. If they don't seem particularly forthcoming, you can prompt them by asking questions, perhaps based on your earlier discussion before the treatment. For example, if they mentioned they had a headache, or an aching hip or knee, you might ask if those areas felt any better. It is advantageous to elicit some information because this will inform any future treatments you do, not just on this client, but potentially on other people too. However, obviously you mustn't turn this into an interrogation! Take your cues from the client, and if they seem reluctant, then don't continue and perhaps just have a general friendly chat about how they're feeling now.

Help them down from the couch, and if they seem at all 'spaced out', and especially if they are about to drive home, make sure you 'ground' them. This is easily achieved, either by getting them to stamp their feet fairly vigorously or to do the 'cross-crawl' – raising their left knee and touching it with their right hand, then raising the right knee and touching it with their left hand, for about fifteen seconds. This not only helps to ground them but also to balance both sides of the body and both hemispheres of the brain, so they should feel more alert afterwards.

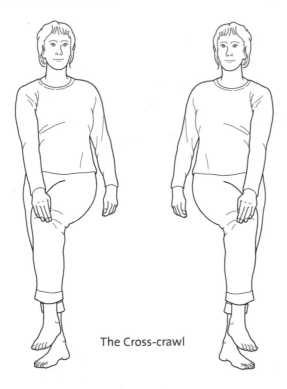

The Cross-crawl

Ask them if they would like to make another appointment, but don't hassle them. If they seem reluctant, you can just give them your business card or a leaflet with your telephone number on it, and say that you would be pleased to hear from them if they would like another Reiki treatment. When your client has gone, make sure that you write down details of the treatment, including any results and advice you've given them, on their client record sheet as soon as possible, so that you don't forget any salient points.

Chapter Nineteen

PRACTICE MANAGEMENT

Knowing how to carry out Reiki treatments and how to communicate effectively with your clients are both obviously necessary, but that isn't all you need to know to be a successful Reiki practitioner. You also have to run your practice professionally, because that is also essential in giving your clients the best possible service. This chapter gives details of all the necessary organisational aspects of running your practice.

YOUR PREMISES

As a professional practitioner it is important that you provide an appropriate and safe environment for your practice, so you will need to decide on a suitable location for your business. And it's important to remember that if you want to work full-time as a practitioner, you should always first do some market research in the locality where you want to set up, to find out if there is a large enough market there for you to be able to make a worthwhile profit.

When you first start it might be sensible to use your own home. In this case it is best if you have a room you can set aside for the purpose, so that it can always be kept clean and tidy. Of course you can set up a treatment couch in your living room, but it tends not to give such a professional feel, and if you share your living space with other people or pets this could be difficult. But you will need to check the legal position regarding working from home, or regarding a change of use of one of the rooms. This varies depending upon where you live, even in the UK, and obviously will be different in other countries, but you may need planning permission, or have to comply with certain trading regulations, or pay local taxes – check with www.hmrc.gov.uk for guidelines on premises and tax in the UK. Your household insurance may have to change too, or there may be clauses in your mortgage or rental agreements which have to be complied with; do check with your insurance company, mortgage holder or landlord. You should also consider accessibility, as you may get clients with disabilities. A room on the ground floor with level access is far preferable to one that can only be reached up a flight of stairs.

An alternative is to take your therapy couch to clients' homes, and treat them there. This does have the advantage that the client will probably feel comfortable within their own environment, but you need to check whether the space is suitable. Cramped conditions, children or pets running around, telephones ringing or babies crying whilst you are trying to perform a soothing, relaxing Reiki treatment would be a great disadvantage.

Another option is to hire a room, perhaps in a nearby complementary health clinic, but you would need plenty of clients to make this financially worthwhile. Wherever you decide to practise you will no doubt want to create the right atmosphere in your treatment space – an attractive blend of comfort and professionalism. To create a calm, relaxing space make sure you clear any clutter, and always keep everything clean and tidy.

EQUIPMENT

As a Reiki practitioner there are relatively few things you need, but you should certainly have a proper therapy couch. There are various types on the market, from reasonably priced portable couches to more expensive static or even hydraulically operated couches, and a search on the internet, or recommendations from other therapists, are probably the best sources of information.

It is probably sensible to start with a portable couch, which will give you the most flexibility in providing your service as they can be placed in your own therapy room, or taken to a client's home. These come in various widths and are made of various materials, the most common being wood and aluminium with a washable padded surface, and some can be made to the height you request, whilst others have adjustable legs. One thing to bear in mind about the height of the couch is that whilst your height obviously doesn't change, the depth of your clients does! Your first client might be quite thin, whilst your next one might be quite large, or perhaps might be a woman who is heavily pregnant, so the height of their bodies on the couch can vary considerably, which can impact on your comfort when placing your hands during the treatment. Therefore a couch with adjustable legs can be quite an advantage – although clearly you have to make the adjustments before the client climbs on!

Remember also that some clients might be very tall, and the width and weight of their bodies will vary a lot, so you need your therapy couch to be strong, sturdy, reasonably wide and as long as possible. Most couches are about 185 cm (6 feet) long, and some also come with extra head rests to extend the length. However, you do need to consider your short clients too, who may find it difficult to climb up onto the couch, so having a sturdy footstool on which they can stand is useful.

You will also need several pillows – some clients will need a couple of pillows under their head, and maybe two or three under their knees when lying on their back. In addition you'll need plenty of clean pillowcases, because these will need to be changed between each client, plus a few stretchy towelling sheets to cover the couch. These don't need to be changed between clients, as the clients will be fully clothed, but you do need to wash them regularly, and of course you will also need one or two soft blankets to place on the client to keep them warm (these should also be made of washable material). Be aware, however, that some clients may have allergies to certain materials, so it would be advisable to purchase anti-allergy pillows, blankets, etc., if possible.

Apart from that, you might like to have a CD player or similar equipment in order to play gentle, relaxing music during the treatment, but this isn't essential, and sometimes clients actually prefer silence. Some practitioners like to burn incense or essential oils such as lavender in their treatment room, but this may also impact on clients who have allergies or breathing difficulties, so it isn't recommended.

HEALTH AND SAFETY

You will be responsible for the health and safety both of your clients and yourself, and if you work within an organisation such as a spa or holistic health centre you may find that they have specific policies on health and safety which you should learn and make sure you adhere to. However, if you work in your own premises, whether in your own home or in rooms you rent, you should ensure that you consider health and safety in all aspects of your work.

Most health and safety is actually common sense. You should make sure that any equipment you use is safe, and that you keep it clean and in good condition. Flooring should be non-slip, and there should be no trailing wires or other trip hazards, and if you do use a footstool to enable your shorter clients to climb onto the therapy couch, this should also be sturdy and non-slip. Reiki doesn't require you to have any hazardous substances around, but if there are any in the room you use (for example, if you rent space in a hair and beauty salon there may be some chemicals stored in the room) then ensure that they are safely locked away.

Make sure you know the exits and evacuation procedures in the case of fire or some other emergency, and that you have access to first aid equipment in the case of minor injury.

Taking a first aid course would be very useful, and should be seriously considered. You would then feel fully prepared if either you or your client suffered an injury or exhibited any 'red flag' symptoms where immediate medical aid was necessary – such as cardiac arrest, fainting or loss of consciousness, epileptic seizure, choking or difficulty with breathing, or severe bleeding (see Chapter 16 for more information). Even in the safest environments a client may have a fall and could potentially suffer a fracture or other injury.

In the UK St John Ambulance (www.sja.org.uk) and the British Red Cross (www.redcrossfirstaidtraining.co.uk) are the leading suppliers of first aid training. If you practise in another country a search on the internet should help you to find suitable local courses.

You also need to consider how a correct level of cleanliness can be achieved to ensure that there is little possibility of cross-infection. When cleaning the room and any equipment, use some form of disinfectant (there are lots of non-toxic products on the market now) and wash any reusable materials at a temperature of at least 60 degrees. Also, of course, ensure that your own health and hygiene does not pose a threat to others, so do not treat anyone if you have a cold, flu or other infectious illness, and wash your hands thoroughly before and after treating a client, or use an alcohol-based hand rub to remove or destroy any bacteria. (You may also like to cleanse yourself and your room energetically, if you are comfortable with that idea – see Appendix 3 for further details.)

WHAT TO CHARGE

You need to find out what other therapists charge in your area – and not just for Reiki, but for other therapies like reflexology and massage – because this will give you an idea about what price you can ask. Your charges will also depend upon whether you are paying for the hire of a room, or whether you are treating people in your own home or in their homes: in the latter case, remember that whatever amount you charge should also cover your transport costs. But don't fall into the trap of thinking that if you undercut all the other local therapists, you'll start to attract their clients. Firstly that is unfair (and will probably make you unpopular in a community that might otherwise be a good support for you), and secondly it indicates that you don't value Reiki – or yourself – enough to charge a sensible price. Moreover, people may assume that as you charge less, you might not be as good as the others!

Some people find charging for Reiki a bit uncomfortable, but money is simply a convenient form of exchange. Sometimes when healing is given freely people will take advantage of the practitioner, calling on their services constantly and expecting to be treated at almost any time, regardless of any other commitments the healer may have. This is one of the reasons why paying money for a treatment, even if it's only a small amount, actually gets the client involved in the process and builds a sense of commitment to taking part in their own healing.

Healing intrinsically *is* freely given. Reiki energy flows regardless of any financial reward. But you deserve to be paid for your time – you would be in any other job – and to be recompensed adequately for the time, effort and money you have put into training and practising and setting up your equipment and premises. The principle is really that we should value ourselves – and value the wonderful energy that is Reiki – and learning to accept money in exchange for Reiki treatments is a part of that valuing. If you still feel a bit awkward about this, then by all means devote some of your time for 'free' treatments, perhaps helping out in a hospice or a nursing home for the elderly. But to be professional about your business you must set proper charges and stick to them.

What you charge for Reiki treatments should be made clear in any leaflets you have, and should be discussed with clients when they make an appointment, including whether you need to be paid in cash, or whether you are prepared to accept cheques, or even, if you are working within a complementary health clinic or spa, if the client can pay with their debit or credit card. This avoids any surprise or embarrassment when the client comes for their treatment and realises they don't have sufficient money on them to pay you!

MARKETING AND PUBLICITY

To get your business off to a good start – and to keep it going – you will need to do at least a small amount of marketing, to make sure that people know where you are and what you do. There are lots of ways to bring your services to the attention of other people, but do be aware that there are also laws relating to advertising and promotional materials – see Chapter 21 for details.

Advertising

Advertising in local newspapers or other publications is rather expensive and is rarely worthwhile, unless it is a specialist publication designed to publicise green issues and alternative health. Entries in directories like Yellow Pages also cost a lot, and you often have to wait at least a year before the new issue comes out – and people rarely consult such directories when looking for a Reiki practitioner. There are a growing number of opportunities to advertise in directories on the internet, and since more and more people are using the internet this may be a better idea; it is usually quite inexpensive and sometimes is free. It is also possible to advertise on your own website. This isn't either as difficult or as expensive to set up as you might imagine, as most website providers offer packages that include software that is as easy to use as most word-processing packages. There are some contact details for website providers in the Resources section.

Publicity Materials

Most small businesses need some form of publicity materials, the most popular being leaflets, posters and flyers. It is certainly worth producing a good, professional leaflet – an A4 piece of paper, folded into thirds, is the most popular size. This should tell people about Reiki, about you and your background and qualifications, how long treatments last, how much you charge, and your contact details and the location(s) of your practice. This can be produced at home if you have a computer and a good printer, especially if you have a desk-top publishing package, although do try to make it look as professional as possible. Also, get someone else to proofread it, as it can be difficult to spot your own mistakes; poor spelling and grammar can put people off, because they make you look at the very least careless, and at worst unprofessional. However, if you don't have much experience at producing such materials yourself, you could get something designed by a local printing firm. Leaflets and flyers could be left at libraries, health food shops, holistic therapy centres, and so on. Do remember to put a poster in your local newsagent's window, as this can be very effective.

Gift vouchers can sometimes be a good idea, so that people can buy a treatment as a present for someone else. It is also sensible to have a few letterheads (they are easy to produce on a computer) so you can send out occasional promotional letters – but do be aware of data protection legislation which gives people the right to request that you do not send them promotional literature (see Chapter 21). Business cards can be useful, too, because you can hand them out to groups if you give a talk, or write the next appointment time on the back before people leave.

Other Ways to Publicise Your Practice

There are other ways to publicise your business, such as taking a stand at holistic health fairs, or giving short talks to groups like the Women's Institute, the National Women's Register, Townswomen's Guild, Lions Clubs, Probus Clubs. Your local gym, holistic health centre or health food shop may host 'taster' days or evenings that you could take part in, although you need plenty of confidence for these. However, the best publicity is *always* 'word of mouth' – building up a good reputation so that your clients come back for more, and recommend you to other people. Remember that Reiki is not about competition – you need to trust in your potential for success, knowing that you will attract the right clients for you. The energy you put out will draw to you those people for whom you are the right person to help them, so even if there is another Reiki practitioner nearby, she or he will attract whoever is right for her or him, too. Just send Reiki to the situation, and visualise nice, friendly people coming to you, and that's what you will get!

COMBINING REIKI WITH OTHER THERAPIES

Reiki works well with virtually all complementary therapies, but particularly with any 'hands-on' therapy such as aromatherapy, reflexology, shiatsu, metamorphic technique, acupressure, cranio-sacral therapy, chiropractic, osteopathy and any other therapy where massage or manipulation are involved. If the therapist is attuned to Reiki, then the energy will automatically flow from the therapist's hands during the complementary therapy session if the client needs it. For therapies which entail taking some form of preparation internally, such as homoeopathy, Bach flower remedies or herbal medicine, the bottle or container can be held in the hands to allow Reiki to flow into the medication.

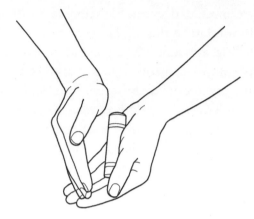

If Reiki is the only therapy you practise, you might consider continuing your personal development by training in one or two others, to extend the service you can offer to your clients. It is important to remember that although Reiki is wonderful, it isn't the *only* thing that can help people, and sometimes an experience of a different therapy can give someone the 'kick-start' they need to continue with their healing. It is essential to realise that all these complementary therapies have particular benefits, and to recognise and respect the contribution of other therapists, whether allopathic or complementary. You should investigate where other therapists are located in your area so that you can recommend them to your clients if necessary.

RECORD KEEPING

You should keep records of every client you treat, for every visit. These records should be

- Straightforward

- Free from any personal views or judgements

- Stored in accordance with the current laws on data protection (see Chapter 21)

Reiki is a healing practice and practitioners should not attempt to diagnose or offer a specific outcome or cure (both of which are illegal unless you are medically qualified), so the information required before a Reiki treatment is simple, and may differ from other complementary treatments. While some practitioners may feel they need more detail, the basic information required was covered in Chapter 18, legal restrictions are covered in Chapter 21, and there is a sample Client Treatment Record sheet in Appendix 6.

You also need to ensure that you comply with the current Data Protection Act and any other current relevant legislation with regard to the storage of data (see Chapter 21), and must keep all your client records under lock and key. You should even make arrangements in your will for what should happen to those records if you die – yes, really! If you are practising outside the UK, please check what regulations apply in your country. (There is more about the ethics involved in record keeping in Chapter 20.)

Insurance, Accounts and Tax

You will also need to be adequately insured to practise, so you must have *public liability insurance, public indemnity insurance* and, if you employ anyone else, *employers' liability insurance* as well – details of what these insurances cover are in Chapter 21. It is good practice to have your insurance certificates available for clients to see, or even discreetly displayed somewhere in your therapy room. Insurance can usually be obtained at a reasonable cost through an umbrella organisation such as the UK Reiki Federation.

It is also vital to keep accounts, although these do not need to be complicated. A simple two-column system will suffice, as shown below, providing that you keep all your receipts and other paperwork relating to your business, such as bank statements, cheque stubs, credit and debit card slips and statements, invoices, gift vouchers and so on. Good record keeping pays dividends, because you will have to calculate how much tax you must pay, and if you haven't recorded all your necessary expenditure you will end up paying too much!

INCOME			EXPENDITURE		
Date	Description	Amount	Date	Description	Amount

Even if you decide to use an accountant to prepare your accounts and tax returns, you will still need all of the above, so it is best to get into good habits straight away. There are lots of books available that show you how to do simple book-keeping; there is online advice on tax issues for small businesses at www.hmrc.gov.uk, and business courses are often offered at local colleges or through your local Business Link (www.businesslink.gov.uk), which will also offer general business support, information and advice, so do an internet search or refer to the Resources section. If you are practising in other countries, please check what tax regulations you will have to comply with there.

LOOKING AFTER YOURSELF

Remember the old adage 'healer, heal thyself'! Running a successful Reiki practice can be hard work, so you really need to look after yourself first ... and always. You won't be much help to other people if you let yourself get run-down or become ill, so it is vital to set in motion those things that can help you to remain healthy, whole and energetic. That means boosting your physical well-being with good nutrition and sensible exercise, but also concentrating on your mental, emotional and spiritual well-being. You work with a wonderful holistic healing energy, so please don't neglect yourself. A daily self-treatment of a minimum of thirty to forty minutes is important – and preferably an hour, when you can – and having a regular Reiki treatment from another practitioner is also excellent. Monthly would be fine, but if you are going through a particularly busy or stressful time, try to make it once a week. If you know other Reiki people in your area, perhaps you could arrange a free 'swap'.

Whether you are just starting out or have been running a busy practice for some time, one of your priorities should be to manage your time effectively to prevent burn-out. If you always find you are rushing around 'chasing your tail', then you need to take stock of your life, and see how you can reorganise things to make your life easier. Many of us tend to take on too much, so we run ourselves ragged, or begin to let other people down, so the first thing to do is to start being assertive, and say 'No' to everything you don't really *want* to do (and probably to some of the things you would like to do, but simply don't have the time for). You will also need to build up your strength and stamina, as standing up doing treatments can be quite tiring otherwise. Taking up yoga, Tai Chi, Qi Gong or a martial art is a good way of strengthening yourself, and getting your energies flowing well.

Your Personal Support System

When you spend a lot of time helping others, it is vital to have your own personal support system – people you can turn to for advice and assistance if you have problems, or need encouragement. Your support group should include your Reiki Master, and perhaps other practitioners, or the members of a Reiki sharing group and the other students you met when you did your Reiki training, as well as family and friends. Something which would undoubtedly help is if you could encourage some family members or friends to train in Reiki, as then you can swap treatments regularly, which would benefit all of you.

Chapter Twenty

PROFESSIONAL STANDARDS, ETHICS AND CODES OF PRACTICE

If you go to a therapist of any kind, what sort of experience do you hope you will have, and how do you want to be treated? Whatever your answer is, that is what it takes to be a good practitioner! Unfortunately, a proficient practitioner needs to be all things to all people, which is a pretty tall order. It means you need to be a good listener, have an understanding and caring nature, be empathetic and sympathetic with people and treat them with respect, and also be knowledgeable, confident and firm enough to command their respect. And, of course, you also need to be thoroughly experienced and good at what you do!

In this chapter we look at professional standards, ethics and codes of practice which are suitable for any practitioner working anywhere in the world, because clients deserve the highest standards when receiving Reiki, wherever they are located. If you are a member of any professional organisation in any country, such as the UK Reiki Federation in Britain, you will find that they have published codes of practice and ethical principles which you will be expected to abide by as long as you are a member, so you should make sure that you know what these are. Most organisations publish their codes of practice on their websites and it would be sensible to print a copy for your own use, and keep it where you can easily refer to it – it is your responsibility to ensure that you abide by it.

The purpose of a Code of Professional Conduct and Practice is twofold:

1. To outline the high standard of professional conduct and practice which practitioners are required to comply with.

2. To inform the public, other professions and employers of the standard of professional conduct and practice they can expect of a registered practitioner.

Whilst there may be slight differences in the approach of each individual professional organisation, the majority will have very similar suggestions for good practice, which will be in line with local and national health regulatory bodies, so this chapter outlines the most common features. However, the Reiki Principles should certainly help to inform your practice!

Just for today, do not anger,
do not worry,
be grateful,
devote yourself to your work,
and be compassionate to yourself and others.

DEALING WITH CLIENTS

As a Reiki practitioner the most important ethical considerations are integrity, respect and confidentiality. The 'status' of being a therapist puts you in a privileged position of trust when you are treating members of the public, because you will be regarded by many as a health professional – which you are not, unless you are medically trained – so whatever you say will be regarded as 'the truth', which is a considerable responsibility. Needless to say, a practitioner must never give the impression that they have medical qualifications if they don't.

To act with integrity, you should make clear to your client what is involved in a Reiki treatment, how long it will last and how much it costs before starting a treatment, and explain what type of client records you keep. It may not be possible initially to estimate how many treatments will be needed, but it is the client's choice whether to take your advice to have further treatments, or not.

The welfare of the client is of paramount importance, and they should always be treated with respect and consideration, and they are entitled to receive safe, competent care in accordance with UK law or the laws in whichever country you practice. (The legal requirements you'll have to meet in the UK are set out in Chapter 21.)

Treatment of Minors

Consultation, assessment and treatment should only be carried out with the full consent of the patient, or the relevant parent or legal guardian in the case of minors – failure to obtain informed consent may lead to criminal or civil proceedings. A person is normally described as a minor if they are under the age of sixteen, but in some countries those under eighteen are considered minors, so this is something you should check. You may also feel it would be advisable to have a parent or guardian present whilst you carry out the treatment. Because Reiki treatments usually involve touch, albeit on a clothed body, having a parent or guardian present as a witness to what you do when treating a child will hopefully avoid any potential misunderstandings or false allegations of impropriety.

Advising a Client

Any advice or treatment should be honestly presented, and in a way which fully respects the client's rights, beliefs and privacy, so that the client is fully informed about what to expect; the practitioner must not attempt to influence a client to do anything against their will, or for the financial or other benefit of the practitioner. Also, a practitioner must never diagnose (unless he or she is also medically qualified), must not countermand any instructions or prescriptions given by a doctor, and must not make any claims of a 'cure'. If at any time you feel that a client should consult a doctor, you can suggest this, but please do so in as calm and tactful a manner as possible. It is not illegal for someone to refuse to consult a conventional medical practitioner, but you must write in the client's notes that you have advised them to do so.

In terms of using Reiki with someone receiving conventional medical treatment, you should *never* advise anyone to stop taking any medicines, or reduce their medication, or to stop seeing their doctor or other health professional. However, if your client is on medication to restore balance in the body, for conditions such as diabetes or high blood pressure, you should advise them to keep a close eye on their results if they self-monitor them, and to check regularly with their doctor in case they need their medication dosage changed. This is because Reiki can often help the body to reach a more appropriate balance, so it can (although it does not always) result in some positive changes.

Another thing to remember is that clients may be nervous when coming for a treatment, so it is important to treat them with gentleness and respect, and to invite them to ask any questions or discuss anything about the treatment which may be worrying them. You will then be able to reassure them so that they can relax and enjoy the treatment.

KEEPING RECORDS

Records should be legible, attributable and kept together with any clinical correspondence relevant to your client. You must keep all information (medical details and appointment records) relating to each client entirely confidential, even from members of their own family, unless you have the client's consent to disclose it or unless you are legally obliged to do so by a court of law. A possible exception to this is if you believe that the client's safety is endangered, or the client has threatened suicide, which you are legally bound to report to an appropriate health professional such as a doctor or psychiatrist. (If you are practising outside the UK, please check what regulations apply in your country.) However, in these cases you are required to inform the client that you have discussed their case with someone else, and must make a note of this on his or her records.

Client records should therefore be kept where other people do not have access to them, and legally you are required to keep such records safely for six years from the time of the last consultation (some insurance companies require you to keep such records for nine years). If you cease to practise, then you must either return the records to the client, if this is practicable, or dispose of them securely after six years either by incineration or shredding. This also means that you should make some provision in your will for the proper disposal of your client records after your death. Your client records – and any lists you keep of the names, addresses and telephone numbers of people who have made enquiries about treatments – are also subject to the Data Protection Act in the UK (please check the position if you practise in other countries), and even if you don't keep these lists on a computer, you may still be required to register with the Data Protection Agency – for further information see Chapter 21.

Your initial client records should include their name, address, telephone number, and a brief case history including any medical problems they have had in the past (and present), any surgical procedures they have undergone, any medication they are taking now (and any previous medication which might be important). You should also include any alternative remedies they are taking, and other complementary therapies they have been, or are currently, receiving. You will also need the name, address and telephone number of their doctor (for emergency use only) – see the Sample Treatment Record in Appendix 6.

Each time a client attends an appointment you should make a note of the date, time, a brief outline of the treatment and any particular results and/or experiences, any advice given, and a record of consent where appropriate. Your records should be clear and comprehensive, but purely factual – there should be no comments or opinions which, even if made in a jocular way, could be misinterpreted. Remember your client has a right to see these records, if he or she requests this, and their accuracy is important because they are admissible as evidence in a court of law: they could be required as part of your defence in the unfortunate (although hopefully unlikely) event of any legal action being taken against you for negligence or injury.

THE THERAPIST–CLIENT RELATIONSHIP

Naturally it is important to be professional at all times, and that includes having set boundaries. For example, it would be unacceptable to exploit your clients either financially or emotionally by insisting on regular appointments, or by making them feel dependent upon you. It is also absolutely unacceptable to interfere with or exploit a client in a sexual manner, and you should never ask a client to remove any clothing other than their coat and shoes.

Because many different types of people may come to you for treatment, it is very important that you are non-judgemental, and do not show any preferences or prejudices, regardless of a person's race, colour, creed, gender or sexual orientation. Your non-judgementalism should also extend to accepting your clients' rights to make their own choices in respect of their health and lifestyles. Whatever opinions you might have on subjects such as smoking, heavy drinking or eating unhealthily, your clients have the right to live their lives in their own way, without being made to feel uncomfortable because of their habits.

Dealing with Unacceptable Behaviour

You do, however, have the right to ask that people do not smoke or drink alcohol on your premises, and to suggest that they should be sober when coming for a treatment. (Smoking is banned in public places in the UK, and even if you are using your own home for treatments, this would then be classed as a business premises, and therefore as a public space.) Of course you also have the right to refuse to treat someone if their behaviour is unacceptable, for example if you suspect they have been taking drugs, or they are drunk, abusive, intimidating, or if they make you feel physically or sexually unsafe. (In the UK a female practitioner does have the right to only treat female patients/clients under the Sex Discrimination Act 1975, Section 35 subsection 2, which gives exception to circumstances where physical contact is involved.) However, it is important that you should deal with such a situation sensitively and in an uncritical way, perhaps by suggesting that the client returns at some future time, or that another therapy or therapist might be better for the person for the time being.

Personal Relationships with Clients

Something else to be aware of is that if you find that during your professional practice, you are becoming involved in a more personal (romantic/sexual) relationship with a client, you should end the professional relationship and arrange alternative care for the client. Where it appears that a client seems to be becoming more closely involved with the practitioner, the practitioner should take care not to encourage the client, and may well be advised to arrange alternative care.

COMPLAINTS OR CLAIMS BY CLIENTS

You should deal promptly and fairly with any complaint or claim made against you by a client. If the situation cannot be resolved easily between you, you should then make it known to your client that your professional association, such as the UK Reiki Federation, or the General Regulatory Council for Complementary Therapies (GRCCT), has a formal complaints procedure. In such cases, you should contact your professional association and also give your client the contact details so that they can fulfil their right to refer the complaint (see Chapter 14).

THE PERSONAL CONDUCT OF PRACTITIONERS

As a Reiki practitioner you must obviously adhere to professional standards relating to your own conduct, not only to ensure that your clients receive the best possible treatment, but also so that you do not undermine public confidence in Reiki. This means you must have high standards of personal hygiene, and must not put your clients at risk by treating them when you are ill, or under the influence of alcohol or drugs. This could potentially result in a charge of unacceptable professional conduct, which may or may not result in criminal proceedings – see Chapters 14 and 21. You must also take care not to mislead clients by using any title or qualification which could be misunderstood to confer medical knowledge, unless of course you are medically qualified.

PUBLICITY AND PROMOTION OF YOUR PRACTICE

As outlined in Chapter 19, in order to run a successful Reiki practice you will need to publicise it, but you must always abide by any rules or regulations in force in the country in which you are operating. This means that any leaflets, flyers, posters or advertisements you produce must comply with the law, must not contain anything which could be construed as indecent or offensive, must not guarantee successful treatment or claim to cure any condition or illness, must be honest and truthful, and should not mislead the public into believing that you have qualifications or experience which you do not, or that your services, skills or personal qualities are superior to other similar therapists. The material should, however, contain your contact details, but you should take care that any business name you use for your practice should not be too similar to that of other practitioners or health professionals, which may cause confusion.

PRACTICE ARRANGEMENTS AND CONTINUING PROFESSIONAL DEVELOPMENT

You are responsible for registering with an appropriate professional association such as the GRCCT, the General Regulatory Council for Complementary Therapies, before beginning to practise, and to renew your registration annually. You should ensure that your premises are well maintained, hygienic, suitably lit, heated and ventilated, and comply with all relevant legislation relating to health and safety. You must also have professional indemnity and public liability insurance, and, if appropriate, employers' liability insurance.

To practise competently, a practitioner must possess the knowledge, skills and abilities required for lawful, safe and effective practice without direct supervision. They must acknowledge the limits of their professional competence and only undertake treatments and accept responsibilities for those activities in which they are fully trained and competent. This also means that they must keep their knowledge and skills up to date throughout their careers in a variety of ways, including by taking part regularly in learning activities that develop their competence and performance. For further information about this, please refer to Chapter 22 on Continuing Professional Development.

If any aspect of practice is beyond a practitioner's level of competence or outside their area of knowledge, they must refer the client to an appropriate practitioner of either complementary or conventional medicine. If in any doubt, the client must be told to consult his or her doctor.

Chapter Twenty-one

LEGAL REQUIREMENTS

The practice of any form of complementary or alternative medicine is governed by a range of legal requirements, mostly for the protection of clients, but also for the protection of practitioners. In this chapter the basic requirements are summarised, but it is your responsibility to make sure that you comply with the law at all times, so it is necessary to regularly check what the up-to-date laws and other relevant regulations are, as these can change. Some helpful websites are given under each section, but don't assume that these are the only sources of information because, again, sometimes changes occur! Also, the details below refer to the legal position in the UK, so if you have a Reiki practice in any other country, please check the relevant laws where you are. As an example, it is illegal in some states in the USA to practise Reiki unless you are a doctor or a minister of religion.

DISCRIMINATION LAWS

If you intend to abide by the ethical principles of integrity, respect and trust outlined in Chapter 20, then obviously it would be wrong to discriminate against any clients on the grounds of age, religious beliefs, disability, gender, race or sexual orientation, and all of these factors are covered by both European and UK equalities legislation – please investigate the legal position on discrimination in any other country you work in so that you can stay within the law.

Discrimination occurs when you are treated less favourably than another person in a similar situation and this treatment cannot be objectively and reasonably justified. The European Convention on Human Rights reflects the core idea that all of us, no matter who we are, enjoy the same human rights and should have equal access to them. In line with this core idea, the Human Rights Act (1998) prohibits discrimination on a wide range of grounds including 'sex, race, colour, language, religion, political or other opinion, national or social origin, association with a national minority, property, birth or other status'. The case law relating to this has shown that the term 'other status' includes, among other things; sexual orientation, illegitimacy, marital status, trade union membership, trans-sexualism and imprisonment. It can also be used to challenge discrimination on the basis of age or disability.

Restrictions

Not all differential treatment is discriminatory. Discrimination occurs when differential treatment cannot be objectively and reasonably justified. Moreover, positive discrimination occurs when a disadvantaged group is treated more favourably in order to overcome an existing situation of inequality. Where it can be objectively and reasonably justified, more favourable treatment in relation to the enjoyment of human rights is permissible under the Human Rights Act.

A milestone along the road to a fairer, more equal Britain, the new Equality and Human Rights Commission, opened on 1 October 2007. This commission is working to eliminate discrimination, reduce inequality, protect human rights and build good relations, ensuring that everyone has a fair chance to participate in society.

Discrimination legislation in the UK covers the following:

- **Age** – It is unlawful for a person's age to be the cause of less favourable treatment in the workplace or in vocational training.

- **Religion and Beliefs** – A person's religion or beliefs, or those of somebody else, should not interfere with their right to be treated fairly at work, at school, in shops or while accessing public services such as healthcare and housing.

- **Disability** – If someone has a physical or mental impairment, they have specific rights that protect them against discrimination (see the next section). Employers and service providers are obliged to make adjustments for them.

- **Gender** – Women, men and transgender people should not be treated unfairly because of their gender, because they are married or because they are raising a family.

- **Race** – Wherever a person was born, wherever their parents came from, whatever the colour of their skin, they have a right to be treated fairly.

- **Sexual Orientation** – Whether a person is gay, lesbian, bisexual or straight should not put them at a disadvantage.

So what are the implications of this type of legislation on a Reiki practitioner? Basically, businesses and organisations, when providing services to people, cannot discriminate unlawfully on the grounds of their disability, race, gender, religion or beliefs or sexual orientation. This applies whether services are provided face to face, by telephone or online, and whether the services must be paid for or are provided free of charge. This means it is unlawful for businesses or organisations, or anyone working for them, to refuse to provide someone with a service, to provide a lower standard of service or to offer a service on different terms than they would to other people. Generally, the law covers services provided by individuals and organisations to the public or any section of the public. In most cases, however, equality legislation does not apply to private members' clubs, and there is currently no legislation outlawing discrimination on the grounds of age in the area of goods and services.

> **Useful Websites**
>
> www.equalities.gov.uk/
>
> http://equalityhumanrights.com

THE DISABILITY DISCRIMINATION ACTS (DDA)

The Disability Discrimination Acts (1995 and 2005) are pieces of legislation that promote civil rights for disabled people and protect disabled people from discrimination. Under the DDA, it is against the law for service providers to treat disabled people less favourably than other people for a reason related to their disability. Service providers have to make 'reasonable adjustments' to the way they deliver their services so that disabled people can use them. Examples of reasonable adjustments include:

- Installing an induction loop (a cable around a listening area linked to an amplifier) for people who are hearing impaired.

- Providing disability awareness training for staff who have contact with the public (training providers can be found on the internet).

- Providing larger, well-defined signage for people with impaired vision (a signage guide is available from RNIB – www.rnib.org.uk).

- Putting in a ramp at the entrance to a building as well as steps.

What is considered a 'reasonable adjustment' for a large organisation like a bank may be different from a reasonable adjustment for a small local shop, or, indeed, a therapy room. It is about what is practical in the service provider's individual situation and what resources the business may have. They will not be required to make changes which are impractical or beyond their means. However, failure or refusal to provide to a disabled person a service that is offered to other people is discrimination, unless it can be justified.

> **Useful Websites**
>
> www.equalityhumanrights.com
>
> www.direct.gov.uk

WORKING WITH MINORS OR VULNERABLE ADULTS

If, as a Reiki practitioner, you get children or vulnerable adults coming to you for treatment, you must ensure that you gain either their consent, if they are competent to give it, or that of a parent, guardian or carer.

Children under the age of sixteen are not automatically presumed to be legally competent to make decisions about their healthcare. However, the courts have stated that those under sixteen will be competent to give valid consent to a particular intervention if they have sufficient understanding and intelligence to enable them to understand fully what is proposed. In other words, there is no specific age when a child becomes competent to consent to treatment; it depends both on the child and on the seriousness and complexity of the treatment being proposed. With all competent children you must respect their request to keep their treatment confidential, unless you can justify disclosure on the grounds that you have reasonable cause to suspect that the child is suffering, or is likely to suffer, significant harm.

If a child is not competent to give consent for themselves, you should seek consent from a person with parental responsibility. Legally you only need consent from one person with parental responsibility, although clearly it is good practice to involve all those close to the child in the decision-making process. The Children's Act 1989 sets out all of the definitions of 'parental responsibility'. Even where children are not able to give valid consent for themselves, it is very important to involve them as much as possible in decisions about their own health, using methods appropriate to their age and understanding to seek their opinion. Where a child has a disability you should take particular care to ensure that the information is provided in a suitable form for them to understand, e.g. using interpreters for those hard of hearing.

Once children reach the age of sixteen they are presumed in law to be competent to give consent for themselves for their own surgical, medical or dental treatment, and any associated procedures. They are deemed competent if:

- They can comprehend and retain information material to the decision, especially as to the consequences of having or not having the treatment in question.

- They can use and consider this information in the decision-making process.

For any other person's consent to be valid, the person must be:

- Capable of taking that particular decision (competent)

- Acting voluntarily (not under pressure or duress), and

- Provided with enough information to enable them to make the decision

It is essential that the information available for people with learning disabilities is appropriate and accessible. It should never be assumed that people are not capable of making decisions just because they have been unable to take a particular decision in the past.

To make decisions about healthcare, children and their parents, or any vulnerable adults and their carers, may need to know the following:

- The benefits and the risks of the proposed treatment

- What the treatment will involve

- What the implications of not having the treatment are

- What alternatives may be available

- What the practical effects on their lives of having, or not having, the treatment will be

You should make sure they have enough time and support to make their decision, and bear in mind that they can withdraw their consent at any time, and if safe to do so, treatment must be stopped. Legally it makes no difference if consent is given in writing, orally, or non-verbally (e.g. by holding out an arm for treatment), but you should record the method of consent in your treatment notes.

Useful Websites

www.dh.gov.uk/en/index.htm

DIAGNOSING ILLNESS AND OFFERING MEDICAL ADVICE

It has been mentioned in other chapters that it is illegal for anyone in the UK who is not medically qualified to diagnose illness or prescribe medication. As this is probably the case in many other countries, if you practise Reiki outside the UK please check on the legal position where you are working. However, there are some other restrictions in the UK which you should note:

- It is illegal to practise dentistry if you are unqualified to do so.

- Under the Venereal Diseases Act 1917 it is illegal to treat for reward, whether direct or indirect (e.g. for a 'contribution'), syphilis, gonorrhoea or soft chancre. It is therefore not advisable to give Reiki knowingly to people suffering from these conditions unless the service is entirely free.

- Except in cases of urgency or sudden necessity, it is illegal for anyone other than a certified midwife to attend a woman in childbirth without medical supervision, or for anyone other than a registered nurse to attend for reward as a nurse on a woman in childbirth or during a period of ten days thereafter (see the box on this in Chapter 16).

- Practitioners should not prescribe or sell remedies, herbs, supplements, oils, etc., unless they have undergone appropriate training and have qualifications which entitle them to do so.

- The Cancer Act 1939 prohibits any advertisement containing an offer to treat any person for cancer, or to prescribe any remedy for cancer, or to give any advice in connection with the treatment of cancer, or to imply that such treatment might result in a cure.

Useful Websites

www.opsi.gov.uk

TREATMENT OF ANIMALS

If you decide to work professionally with animals, you must be aware of and abide by any laws relating to their treatment. In the UK the Veterinary Surgeons Act of 1966 states that anyone treating animals must be a qualified veterinary surgeon, and that no one other than a qualified vet can diagnose problems, carry out tests for diagnostic purposes, advise or carry out medical or surgical treatment or prescribe medication. Indeed, Section 19 of the act makes it an offence for anyone other than a veterinary surgeon to practise veterinary surgery.

However, there are some exceptions to this:

- Practise by veterinary students.

- Medical treatment or minor surgery (not involving entry into a body cavity) given by veterinary nurses under veterinary direction.

- Minor medical treatment given by owners to their own animals of any kind, medical treatment or minor surgery (not involving entry into a body cavity) given to farm animals by their owners or by farm workers, and first aid in an emergency.

- Specified minor surgical operations which may be carried out by any adult, and in some cases by animal husbandry students under supervision.

- Specified invasive operations which can only be carried out by competent people, namely blood sampling of farm animals and badgers, sampling for residues and epidural anaesthesia.

- Physiotherapy, and other manipulative therapy such as osteopathy and chiropractic, provided that the animal has first been seen by a veterinary surgeon who has diagnosed the condition and decided that it should be treated by physiotherapy under his or her direction.

All other forms of complementary therapy in the treatment of animals, including homoeopathy, must be administered by veterinary surgeons. It is illegal in terms of the Veterinary Surgeons Act 1966 for lay practitioners, however qualified in the human field, to treat animals. Moreover, faith healers (a term that would probably include Reiki) are required in the terms of the Code of Practice of the Confederation of Healing Organisations to ensure that animals have been seen by a veterinary surgeon who is content for healing to be given by the laying on of hands.

So basically the Veterinary Surgery Act of 1966 prohibits anyone other than a qualified veterinary surgeon from treating animals, including diagnosis of ailments and giving of advice on such diagnosis. However, the healing of animals by contact healing, by the laying on of hands or distant healing is legal, and to give emergency first aid to animals for the purpose of saving life or relieving pain is permissible under Schedule 3 of the 1966 Act.

The Protection of Animals Act 1911 requires that if an animal clearly needs treatment from a veterinary surgeon the owner must obtain this, so before treating animals you must seek assurance from the owner that the animal has been taken to a vet for examination, diagnosis and treatment, and that the vet is content for Reiki healing to be given. Regulations in other countries may be different, but I would advise you to find out what they are before carrying out any work with animals so that you can stay within the law.

Useful Websites

www.rcvs.org.uk

www.reikifed.co.uk

www.confederation-of-healing-organisations.org

HEALTH, SAFETY AND SECURITY

You are responsible for the health and safety of, and have a duty of care for, everyone affected by your business and its activities. This includes:

• Employees working at your premises, from home, or at another site.

• Visitors to your premises such as clients, their relatives and carers.

• People at other premises where you're working, such as a holistic health centre.

• Members of the public, even if they're outside your premises.

• Anyone affected by products and services you produce or supply.

You should conduct a thorough assessment of the risks your business faces.

• Risk is the chance, high or low, that someone or something could be harmed by a hazard

• Hazard means anything that can cause harm, e.g. chemicals, electricity, a slippery floor, etc.

Wherever you practice, even if it is in your own home, you must have a policy for how you look after health and safety. If you employ five or more people, this policy must be in writing. You also need to comply with certain specific legal requirements, including:

• Recording and reporting accidents.

• Consulting employees or their safety representatives on health and safety matters.

• Ensuring your employees understand and carry out their responsibilities for health and safety, such as following the safety rules you have set up.

Other specific requirements can include registering your business, and taking out employers' liability insurance.

Here are some of the key steps you need to take to meet your legal obligations to protect employee and client health and safety. Make sure you:

1. Check whether you are required to register for health and safety with your local authority or the Health and Safety Executive (HSE). Most businesses are now exempt from this requirement but those using dangerous or

explosive chemicals or operating in high-risk industries may still be required to register or need a licence.

2. Conduct a risk assessment.

3. Consider how your business and its activities affect employee health and safety as part of this assessment.

4. Assess your business's use of hazardous substances and how you can minimise risks.

5. Get the right insurance.

6. Provide the right information to employees and visitors, for example through training, operating procedures and signage.

7. Put in place equipment and procedures to minimise the dangers of fire.

8. Put in place adequate first aid facilities and appropriate accident and incident procedures.

9. Prepare a health and safety policy including key information and procedures. If you have five or more employees, this must be in writing.

Useful Websites

www.businesslink.gov.uk/

www.hse.gov.uk

DATA PROTECTION

The Data Protection Act 1998 gives individuals the right to know what information is held about them, and it provides a framework to ensure that personal information is handled properly. The Act works in two ways. First, it states that anyone who processes personal information must comply with eight principles, which make sure that personal information is:

• Fairly and lawfully processed

• Processed for limited purposes

• Adequate, relevant and not excessive

- Accurate and up to date

- Not kept for longer than is necessary

- Processed in line with your rights

- Secure

- Not transferred to other countries without adequate protection

The second area covered by the act provides individuals with important rights, including the right to find out what personal information is held on computer and most paper records. If an individual or organisation feels they're being denied access to personal information they're entitled to, or feel their information has not been handled according to the eight principles, they can contact the Information Commissioner's Office for help (www.ico.gov.uk). Complaints are usually dealt with informally, but if this doesn't resolve the issue, enforcement action can be taken.

You may need to register as a data controller with the Information Commissioner's Office, although if none of your records are held on computer you do not need to register. The act provides an exemption from notification for some organisations. These are:

- Organisations that process personal data only for:
  a. staff administration (including payroll);
  b. advertising, marketing and public relations (in connection with their own business activity); and
  c. accounts and records

- Some not-for-profit organisations

- Organisations that process personal data only for maintaining a public register

- Organisations that do not process personal information on computer

- Individuals who process personal data only for domestic purposes

The main purpose of the public register is transparency and openness. It is a basic principle of data protection that the public should know (or be able to find out) who is processing personal data about them, plus other details about the processing (such as why it is being carried out). At the time of going to press, if you only hold records of your clients for your own business requirements, such as keeping accurate financial accounts, or for individual mail shots, you are exempt from having to register, but it is worth visiting the self-assessment webpage to determine whether this is the case for you as an individual practitioner. Go to www.ico.gov.uk and look for 'Notification Exemptions: A Self-assessment Guide'.

In addition, the Freedom of Information Act came into force at the beginning of 2005 (although it is retrospective and covers all information, not just that which has been collected since 2005). It provides individuals and organisations with the right to request information held by a public authority. It is therefore unlikely to affect you in your role as a Reiki practitioner, although under the Data Protection Act individuals can request information.

Thanks to the Data Protection Act your clients have the legal right to contact you and request in writing a copy of all of the information you hold on them. They can then request that you change your data so that it is up to date, or more accurately reflects their information. They can also object to the way that you handle the information. You would need to reply within twenty-one days detailing the actions you are going to carry out. In addition, clients can ask that you stop sending them marketing material, e.g. mailshots. In extreme cases they can go to court to claim compensation if the Data Protection Act has not been adhered to.

Useful Websites

www.ico.gov.uk/

www.ico.gov.uk/notify/self/question1.html

THE KEEPING OF FINANCIAL AND OTHER RECORDS

By law, you must keep business records for at least five years and ten months after the end of the tax year the records relate to, and you can be fined for failure to maintain or retain the records you need to make a tax return. You'll need to keep your business records and personal records separate: most businesses find that it helps to have a separate business bank account.

Basic Records

The basic records you must keep will normally include:

- A record of all your sales (and fees received from clients), with copies of any invoices you've issued.

- A record of all your business purchases and expenses.

- Invoices for all your business purchases and expenses, unless they're for very small amounts.

- Details of any amounts you personally pay into or take from the business.

- Copies of business bank statements.

You or your accountant must use these records to create a profit and loss account, which shows the sales income you have received and the expenses you've paid, and what profit or loss you've actually made.

Capital Allowances

It's helpful to keep a separate record of purchases and sales of assets that you use in the business, such as equipment. These need to be treated differently on your tax return. You can claim capital allowances for assets, which means that rather than claiming the whole cost at the time you buy, you reclaim the cost over time – see www.hmrc.gov.uk or www.which.co.uk for further advice.

Other Records You Must Keep

All businesses are different and there are many specific types of detailed records that may need to be kept. Some examples of records you should keep include:

- Cash book

- Petty cash book

- Order notes and invoices

- Copy sales invoices

- Details of any other business income received

- Details of any private money brought into the business

- Till rolls or other form of electronic record of sales

- Details of any other income

- Any cash taken out of the till to pay small business expenses

- Bills and invoices for purchases and expenses

- A record of stock on hand at the end of the year

- All bank and building society statements, credit card statements, pass books, cheque stubs and paying-in slips which include details of business transactions

All this information will be useful in completing your self-assessment tax return. You'll need to keep certain records and hold on to them for several years so that you can back up the information you put on your return.

Records Related to Business and Personal Use

It's important that you keep your business and personal records separate. For assets that you use for both business and personal purposes – for example your therapy rooms if they also include an apartment where you live – you must keep enough records so that you can work out what expenditure relates to business use and what is private. For example, with sales you must keep a record of:

- any stock you take for personal and family consumption

- goods or services you supply to someone else in exchange for goods or services, i.e. barter transactions

Even if you don't record these through a till, you'll need to make a record at the time the transaction takes place of the goods taken or supplied and their retail price.

If you use the same vehicle for both business and private purposes, again you should keep enough details to help you split the total amount you spend between your business and private use. Usually it will be enough to keep a record of business and private mileage and to split the vehicle running costs in the same proportions.

Useful Websites

www.hmrc.gov.uk/index.htm

www.which.co.uk

INSURANCE

All Reiki practitioners must be adequately insured to practise. The insurance policy must state provision for public liability and employers' liability (if personnel are employed) and professional indemnity, as well as provision for professional treatments. Insurance can be provided for Reiki only, or can include other therapies, and can cover most risks associated with working privately, or running a practice. These might include working at premises other than your home or clinic, or the equipment you use in giving treatments. It's important to make sure that you read any policy documents carefully to ensure that you are getting the insurance cover you need.

Public Liability Insurance

Public liability insurance covers your legal liability to pay damages to members of the public for death, bodily injury or damage to their property which occurs as a result of your business activities. It also covers legal fees, costs and expenses such as representation at any coroner's inquest, fatal accident inquiry or other court hearing because of an accident.

Professional Indemnity Insurance

This protects professional businesses against their legal liability towards third parties for injury, loss or damage, arising from their professional negligence or that of their employees. Certain professions must have professional indemnity insurance as a regulatory requirement or as a result of their professional authorisation, including architects, accountants, solicitors, surveyors, insurance brokers, financial advisers – and therapists treating clients!

Employers' Liability Insurance

If you employ anyone, you are responsible for their health and safety whilst they are at work, so employers' liability insurance is compulsory. This will enable you to cover the cost of compensation for your employees' injuries or illness whether they are caused on or off site.

Working from Home

Most household insurance policies can be extended to cover working from home, but you must discuss this with your insurance provider. Household insurance does not normally cover any loss of office equipment, nor will it provide public liability cover. In some cases working from home may even invalidate your household insurance, so you are strongly advised to check with your household insurance provider.

There are some other insurances you might consider, depending on a variety of factors including the location of your practice:

- Loss of cash insurance – provides cover to an agreed limit for the loss of money, whether in transit or from business premises.

- Travel insurance – this is essential if you or your employees travel abroad. Ensure that you are covered for working abroad as well as travelling, if necessary.

- Goods in transit insurance – covers goods against damage whilst being moved.

- A fidelity guarantee – insures against any loss of money or stock as a result of staff dishonesty, such as theft.

- Credit insurance – insures you against debtors who are unable to pay you as a result of bankruptcy.

- Commercial legal insurance – covers legal expenses that may arise out of a change in legislation or penalties resulting from non-compliance.

Useful Websites

www.reikifed.co.uk

www.reikiassociation.org.uk

www.businesslink.gov.uk

LEGAL ASPECTS OF ADVERTISING, MARKETING, AND DISCLAIMERS

Any advertising should comply with the British Code of Advertising Practice and meet the requirements of the Advertising Standards Authority. The main principles of the advertising standards codes are that advertisements should not mislead, cause harm, or offend, and all marketing communications should be legal, decent, honest and truthful. Advertising of Reiki must be discreet and dignified in tone; it should not contain testimonials or claim a cure or mention any disease. It should be confined to drawing attention to the therapy available, the qualifications of the Reiki practitioner and offering general information regarding the treatment process.

The Advertising Standards Authority (ASA) is the independent body set up by the advertising industry to police the rules laid down in the Advertising Code. The ASA regulates the content of advertisements, sales promotions and direct marketing in the UK. They make sure standards are kept high by applying the advertising standards codes, and they can stop misleading, harmful or offensive advertising and can ensure sales promotions are run fairly. They can also help to reduce unwanted commercial mail, either sent through the post, by email or by text message, and they can resolve problems with mail order purchases. There are specific rules for certain products and marketing techniques. These include rules for advertising alcoholic drinks, health and beauty products, adverts aimed at children, motoring adverts, environmental claims, gambling, direct marketing and prize promotions.

The types of advertising and marketing the ASA deals with include:

- Magazine and newspaper advertisements

- Radio and TV commercials (but not programmes or programme sponsorship)

- Television shopping channels

- Posters on legitimate poster sites (but not fly-posters)

- Leaflets and brochures

- Cinema commercials

- Direct mail (advertising sent by post and addressed to you personally)

- Door drops and circulars (advertising posted through the letter box without your name on)

- Advertisements on the internet, include banner ads and pop-up ads (but not claims on companies' own websites)

- Commercial email and SMS text message ads

- Advertisements on CD ROMs, DVD and video, and faxes

What the ASA don't deal with are claims on websites; TV and radio programme sponsorship; shop window displays; in-store advertising; and political advertising.

Probably the most relevant aspects to Reiki practitioners of the Advertising Code are the following:

- All marketing communications should be prepared with a sense of responsibility to consumers and to society.

- Marketers have primary responsibility for ensuring that their marketing communications are legal. Marketing communications should comply with the law and should not incite anyone to break it.

- Marketing communications should contain nothing that is likely to cause serious or widespread offence. Particular care should be taken to avoid causing offence on the grounds of race, religion, sex, sexual orientation or disability. Compliance with the Code will be judged on the context, medium, audience, product and prevailing standards of decency.

- Marketers should not exploit the credulity, lack of knowledge or inexperience of consumers.

- No marketing communication should mislead, or be likely to mislead, by inaccuracy, ambiguity, exaggeration, omission or otherwise.

- Marketing communications must not omit, hide or provide in an unclear, unintelligible, ambiguous or untimely manner, material information if that omission or presentation is likely to affect consumers' decisions about whether and how to buy the advertised product or service, unless the information is obvious from the context.

Useful Websites

www.asa.org.uk/asa/

www.reikiassociation.org.uk

www.reikifed.co.uk

COMPLAINTS PROCEDURES

Hopefully you will never receive any complaints from clients, but if you do, you need to realise that there are legal issues to comply with, in addition to any disciplinary proceedings which may be instigated by or through your professional association.

When someone buys goods or services from a trader, they are making a legally binding contract, and the law they can look to for protection is the Supply of Goods and Services Act 1982. People are advised to first speak to the trader (therapist) about the problem as soon as possible, although letters of complaint can also be effective. The person who is complaining must state what they want you to do, such as give them another treatment, a refund, or compensation, and by when this action should take place – which must be a reasonable time period.

Disputes and/or Disciplinary Proceedings

Your professional association or regulatory body, such as the UK Reiki Federation or the GRCCT (General Regulatory Council for Complementary Therapies), will have specific procedures to resolve any complaint from a client about one of their members, so you should check what these procedures are. Usually they will require a copy of the complaint in writing, and the professional association or regulatory body will then conduct a full investigation into the complaint. This may result in the permanent or temporary exclusion from the association of that member if such action is appropriate. However, the member will be able to appeal against this decision, and in the event of serious misconduct and permanent exclusion the ex-member may be able to apply for their exclusion to be reviewed after a predetermined period of time.

Useful Websites

www.tradingstandards.gov.uk/

www.uklegislation.hmso.gov.uk/

www.grcct.org.uk

www.reikifed.co.uk

www.reikiassociation.org.uk

You need to remember that it is entirely your responsibility to ensure that you comply with any and all laws relating to your practise of Reiki in whichever country you work, and to make sure that you keep up to date by regularly checking for any new or revised information. The websites given above will certainly help with this in the UK, but you may need to look at other sources as well.

Chapter Twenty-two

CONTINUING PROFESSIONAL DEVELOPMENT (CPD)

If you are working as a registered Reiki practitioner in the UK you will need to demonstrate that you are keeping up with changes and developments both in your field of practice and the law, and that you are continuing to develop professionally, and this is what CPD – Continuing Professional Development – is all about. However, making sure you continue to develop professionally shouldn't be confined only to Reiki practitioners in the UK! In order to give clients the best possible experience of Reiki it is important for any therapist to keep up to date with developments in their field of expertise, wherever they work, and this chapter will give you some ideas of the type of CPD which might be beneficial to you.

WHAT IS CPD?

CPD is a career-long process where trained and qualified people in many different professions undertake a range of learning activities through which they can continue to increase and enhance their skills and abilities, and ensure that they maintain their capacity to practise safely, effectively and legally within the scope of their profession. All professional and/or registered Reiki practitioners must commit to undertake CPD as a condition to continuing their membership of their professional association or regulating body, and provide evidence that they are doing so.

CPD FOR PROFESSIONAL/REGISTERED REIKI PRACTITIONERS

Members of the public who go for treatments will expect that professional/registered Reiki practitioners have a high standard of relevant professional knowledge, skills and competence. In order to satisfy these expectations, the Reiki practitioner will need to update their knowledge and understanding by undertaking CPD throughout their working life so that they can continue to practise safely. It is important to review their knowledge and experience so that they can adapt to factors that could affect their practice which they may not previously have come across.

Who Benefits?

The benefits of CPD extend to:

- **The Public** – who are reassured that the person treating them is maintaining and developing their knowledge and skills on an ongoing basis.

- **The Reiki Practitioner** – who gains confidence and satisfaction from their additional knowledge, experience and understanding, knowing that they will be able to offer their clients the best possible care. In addition, taking part in CPD shows their commitment to their chosen profession.

- **The Employer** – because it ensures that the Reiki practitioners who work within their organisation are capable, competent and well trained.

- **The Profession** – because increasingly professional bodies are being required to demonstrate that their members are undertaking CPD in order to maintain best practice, to reassure the public and give them confidence in the service.

PLANNING YOUR CPD

In order to decide what CPD would be appropriate for you, you need to reflect on and assess your own learning needs and interests. You may find it helpful to discuss this with friends and colleagues. You need to think about how you can build effectively on your strengths, and limit any factors that might be inhibiting your effectiveness, including factors affecting your own health such as workload and stress levels. In addition, you might also build on ideas for improvement identified through appraisals, if you work for an employer, and identify any available training courses pertinent to your needs. You will also need to consider advances in knowledge and practice in relation to technology, legislation and your own discipline, as well as your own preferred learning style. For instance, do you like attending courses, working through distance-learning materials, shadowing someone else working in your area of expertise, researching from books or journals, watching DVDs, or any other method of learning?

Whatever form of CPD you choose, it won't be sufficient to just attend a course, or read a book or an article. To make the CPD effective you need to set yourself learning objectives – what you hope to gain from it – and then reflect on what you have learned afterwards, assessing how it has contributed to your self-development. CPD isn't just about the number of hours you do, but also about the quality of the activities you undertake. Both your learning objectives and reflections should be written down in a file or notebook, because you need to have documentary evidence of having undertaken some CPD – it may be required periodically by your professional association or regulatory body to support your continuing membership. Afterwards, of course, you should use your experiences to either reinforce your current practice or to introduce changes which will enhance your practice in some way.

In most cases, your professional association will require a minimum number of hours of CPD. In the case of Reiki the recommendations are that you should undertake twelve hours of CPD each year, a minimum of six hours of which should be directly Reiki related, and a maximum of six hours could be other related topics which will enhance your knowledge, experience and professionalism. This could include such things as studying for qualifications in another therapy, learning meditation techniques, or research into a specific health topic that interests you, for example.

EXAMPLES OF CPD ACTIVITIES

There are many different activities which could be classed as CPD. However, core training, which in the case of Reiki means Reiki 1 or Reiki 2 courses, does not count as CPD. Here are some ideas of what would be regarded as CPD activities:

- **Work-based Learning** – Shadowing another practitioner; case studies; discussions/meetings with colleagues; secondments; project work; involvement in committees; coaching from colleagues.

- **Professional Activity** – Mentoring; tutoring, teaching or lecturing; taking part in Reiki sharing groups; being an examiner or assessor; giving presentations at conferences.

- **Formal/Educational** – Attending courses, workshops or retreats; undertaking research; attending conferences or seminars; distance learning; further training in Reiki techniques or other relevant subjects such as anatomy and physiology, first aid, communication skills, marketing, etc.

- **Self-directed Learning** – Reading books, journals or articles; reviewing books or articles; updating your knowledge via the internet, TV, or DVDs or through voluntary work.

PROVIDING EVIDENCE OF CPD

Writing down your learning objectives and reflections on your CPD activity has already been mentioned, but there are also other ways of providing additional evidence of any CPD you have undertaken.

- **Material Acquired from Others** – Course certificates, letters from clients, carers, students or colleagues; testimonials.

- **Material Demonstrating Reflection and Evaluation** – Personal development plans; evaluation of courses/conferences/seminars attended; documentation from appraisals, clinical supervision or job evaluation.

- **Material You Have Produced** – Critical literature reviews; project reports; course assignments; notes from your presentations; articles written for publication; research papers; clinical guidelines; information leaflets.

Whatever evidence you provide, it should be dated, and kept safely, as it may have to be produced (or copies of it sent) to your professional association or regulatory body when renewing your membership.

One point to consider is that if you wish to be on the National Register of Reiki Practitioners, CPD is an excellent way to increase your skills and knowledge and thereby ensure that you are practising in accordance with the National Occupational Standards (NOS) for Reiki. It is likely to be a requirement of any regulatory body – and is already a requirement of the GRCCT – that registrants guarantee that within three years of being registered they will have completed sufficient additional training to comply with all of the NOS. (If you are not sure whether your existing qualification or award is sufficient, please contact either your professional association, or the GRCCT administration department.)

It is possible that the requirements for CPD may change from time to time, so please ensure that you check at least annually with your professional association or the GRCCT to make sure you comply with current requirements. Useful website sources of information include those of the Reiki Council (www.reikicouncil.org.uk), GRCCT (www.grcct.org.uk), and the UK Reiki Federation (www.reikifed.co.uk).

Part Five

BECOMING A
REIKI MASTER (LEVEL 3)

The Different Types of Master Training –
Master Practitioner and Master Teacher

•

The Master Symbol

•

Attunements

•

Teaching Reiki Level 1 Courses

•

Teaching Reiki Level 2 Courses

•

Teaching Reiki Master Level

Chapter Twenty-three

REIKI 3 TRAINING (MASTER PRACTITIONER/ MASTER TEACHER)

Becoming a Reiki Master can be a truly wonderful and life-enhancing experience, but it certainly isn't just about gaining an extra qualification. It can be immensely rewarding, incredibly satisfying and often filled with delight, but the process of becoming a Reiki Master can potentially be physically, mentally, emotionally and spiritually demanding, so the decision to train as a Reiki Master should not be taken lightly, or without adequate thought and preparation. Moreover, one important thing to remember is that receiving a Master attunement does not make you a Reiki Master! It is just the beginning of a long journey *towards* the mastery of Reiki. But you can do your best to live up to it, to 'walk your talk', to gradually 'become' Reiki, so that it forms a vital and inexorable part of your life.

At Master level, personal and spiritual development are no longer optional: they are essential. Reiki will lead you towards a more spiritual way of being, through experiences that will give you a greater level of wisdom and understanding about yourself, and about other people. To become a Reiki Master is to become the *embodiment* of Reiki – the embodiment of love, light, healing, harmony and balance. That might perhaps seem a bit daunting, especially at first, but taking on the role of Reiki Master means being someone who lives with Reiki as an essential part of their daily lives, as well as someone who has plenty of knowledge and experience of using Reiki in different ways. However, please realise that no Reiki Master knows *everything* about Reiki! Reiki is itself a teacher, so the longer a Master uses and teaches Reiki, the further along the path *towards* mastery they go, and for each

Master, that is a very personal journey, because each Master has a different starting point.

Each of us has a unique set of life experiences, and it is inevitable that these will influence how, when and why we came to Reiki. And of course being a Master isn't just about knowing how to attune someone, or how to carry out a Reiki class. It's also about knowing how to lead someone towards their own personal and spiritual fulfilment – without judgement or censure, but with love and compassion. That is passing on the essence of Reiki, and that's what you get better at as the years go by!

WHAT DO YOU NEED TO KNOW?

Obviously to take Reiki 3 training you need first to have taken Reiki 1 and Reiki 2, and preferably to have practised self-treatments and treatments on other people for a while, because if you do plan to teach others, you will need a fairly broad experience from which to impart your knowledge. It is an advantage to have a basic understanding of energy theory, including the human energy field – auras, chakras and meridians (see Appendix 2) – as well as a thorough knowledge and understanding of Reiki theory and practice:

- What Reiki is, its origins and history (Chapter 4)

- The Reiki Principles (Chapter 5)

- The three Reiki 2 and one Master level Usui Reiki symbols and their mantras and how to use them, and possibly other symbols, depending upon the system of Reiki you use (Chapters 11, 12 and 13)

- How to carry out a self-treatment (Chapters 7 and 12)

- How to carry out treatments on other people in a chair and on a therapy couch, including the appropriate hand positions (Chapters 6, 8 and 12)

- How to carry out distant treatments (Chapter 13)

- How Reiki can be used as emergency treatment (Chapters 7, 8 and 12)

- How Reiki can be used on animals, plants and inanimate objects (Chapters 9 and 12)

- How Reiki can be used to heal emotional, psychological and spiritual problems and other situations (Chapters 10 and 12)

- How to carry out attunements at each level (not described in this manual)

- How to advise your students if they wish to practise professionally (all chapters in Part Four).

You also need to know how to run a small business, including the relevant UK and European legislation (or the legislation in any other country you work in), ethics and codes of practice, how to communicate effectively and appropriately to create professional relationships, the importance of confidentiality, how to reflect on your practice and identify development needs, and how to look after your own physical, mental, emotional and spiritual health and well-being to support yourself and your work. You will find some relevant information on these topics in Part Four, because whether you're running a professional Reiki practice, or running a business teaching Reiki, you'll need similar skills.

Some Reiki Masters have a thorough knowledge of other complementary therapies, some have been meditating and pursuing a spiritual path for many years, some have a psychic background, whilst for others their Reiki 1 course was their first major step along their spiritual path. Reiki Masters come from all walks of life, including commerce and industry, the legal professions and the armed forces, the caring professions and agriculture, and from all age groups – from their twenties to their eighties and over. This diversity means that there is bound to be a Reiki Master somewhere whose approach will appeal to you, and who will therefore be just the right person to guide you through your personal Reiki path. Eventually, if you decide to become a Reiki Master, you will be the right person to guide others on their Reiki journeys!

CHOOSING YOUR TYPE OF TRAINING AND INITIATING MASTER

Reiki Master training in the West can be minimal and take a very short time, or it can be very comprehensive and take a long time – or anywhere in between those two points. For example, some Masters insist that you should have at least three years' experience of Reiki, preferably working at least some of that time as a professional practitioner, before they will accept you for Master training; others have no minimum time requirements, and some even actively encourage every Reiki 2 student to become a Reiki Master as soon as possible.

The system for Master training that was most prevalent until the mid-1990s was that of Reiki Alliance Masters (see Chapter 4), who usually train by the apprenticeship system where a student Master works alongside a fully trained and experienced Master for at least a year. They gradually learn how to organise and teach classes for Reiki 1 and 2 by observing, and then take over certain parts of the class as they gain knowledge and confidence. When their initiating Master considers them ready, they are taught the Master symbol, and receive the Master attunement, and are taught (and practise at Reiki classes alongside their initiating Master) the attunement processes for the first two levels. Often the Master attunement process is not taught until several years later, when the newly qualified Master has acquired plenty of experience.

However, it is much more usual nowadays to learn how to be a Reiki Master in the same way as you learn the skills required for the Reiki 1 and Reiki 2 levels – by attending a short course. Obviously what can be taught will be limited by the amount of time the course takes, and since this varies between one day and one week (sometimes longer), with most probably taking an average of three days, there is considerable variation in content, style and quality of training, as well as in cost. There are as many variations in Reiki Masters as there are in any other profession. There are some excellent Reiki teachers who charge moderate prices, whereas there are others who have little experience and offer inadequate information and poor support, yet who charge high prices. It is your responsibility to find the Master who is right for you, so do contact a few before you decide, and perhaps retake either a Reiki 1 or a Reiki 2 course with them, or at least have a Reiki treatment from them, so that you can get to know them a bit first.

WHAT CAN BE INCLUDED IN REIKI MASTER TRAINING?

Quite often Reiki Master training is divided into several parts:

Master Practitioner or Reiki 3A

The prerequisite for this level of training is to have taken a Reiki 2 course. The Master Practitioner course is usually taken over one or two days, and students are taught the Usui Master symbol and receive instruction in some advanced Reiki techniques which use the Master symbol, to enhance their practise of Reiki. This level is sometimes called Advanced Reiki Training, or ART, especially in the Usui/Tibetan system of Reiki, developed by the American Reiki Master William Lee Rand.

Master Teacher or Reiki 3B or Reiki 4

Depending upon the length and content of this course, the prerequisite for this training might still be Reiki 2, or it might require a student to have already taken Reiki 3A above, which would then be followed by a further Reiki Master Teacher two-day training course, where students are taught and given some time to practise the attunement processes for all three Reiki levels. This final stage might also include some additional symbols – for example, in the Usui/Tibetan system there are a further two symbols that are not a part of traditional Usui Reiki.

Other Masters offer longer Master Teacher courses of anything from three days up to a week or more, and which sometimes also include a period of apprenticeship, either using preparatory distance-learning materials or 'shadowing' a qualified Reiki Master during some Reiki 1 or Reiki 2 courses, so that the student has the opportunity to review and increase their knowledge of the whole Usui Reiki system. These courses will normally cover the traditional Usui Reiki from the Western (Takata) lineage, but may also include techniques and attunement methods from traditional Japanese (Doi) lineage Reiki, or the Usui/Tibetan system (Rand lineage). Some Reiki Masters offer very intensive and energetically challenging Reiki Master courses that not only include Usui and Usui/Tibetan symbols and attunement methods, but also extend the students' knowledge to other types of Reiki (at Master level) in addition, such as Tera Mai®, Sekhem, Karuna Reiki™ and Jin Kei Do, including any extra symbols and different attunement processes those systems use. (See Appendix 1 for brief descriptions of these different Reiki systems.)

There are obviously some basics which *must* be included in Reiki Master training, and other aspects which would be advantageous but which are not essential. Here is a checklist that you might find useful when making your decision on where to go for training.

The Essentials

1. The Usui Reiki Master symbol:
   - How to draw the symbol
   - The mantra for the symbol
   - Attunement to the symbol
   - Ways of using the symbol, including advanced Master Practitioner techniques for treatments

2. The personal and environmental preparations needed before carrying out attunements

3. Usui Reiki 1:
   - Learning and practising the four attunement method (or single attunement for Usui/Tibetan Reiki Level 1 – see below)
   - What to include in teaching Reiki 1 (for individuals and groups)

4. Usui Reiki 2:
   - Learning and practising the single attunement method
   - What to include in teaching Reiki 2 (for individuals and groups)

5. Usui Reiki 3 (Master):
   - Learning and practising the single attunement method (does not have to be learned at same time as Reiki 1 and 2 attunement methods)
   - What to include in teaching Reiki 3 (Master) level (for individuals and groups)

6. Developing the Master–student relationship

7. The business responsibilities of being a Reiki Master

8. The ongoing responsibility for personal and spiritual development

Possible Additions to the Training

Other opportunities might also be offered to you as part of your development, such as observing and co-teaching of Reiki 1 and Reiki 2 courses after training with your initiating Master, and some courses will include special meditations and advanced Reiki techniques, but this will largely depend upon the knowledge and experience your initiating Master has. Those who have been Masters and practitioners for many years, and who perhaps have trained in various Reiki systems including the traditions from Japan, will obviously be able to offer students more than a recently trained Master. However, if you feel drawn to a particular Master, perhaps because of their personality or other factors, then that is likely to be the best person for you, regardless of how much experience they have. (You can, of course, add to your own knowledge by reading books about Reiki, such as *The Basics of Reiki, Reiki for Life* and *Living the Reiki Way* by Penelope Quest.)

There are a number of Masters who include some traditional Japanese techniques in their Reiki Master training, such as methods of meditation and energy cleansing, plus a form of blessing or spiritual empowerment called Reiju, which Reiki students in Japan would receive on a regular basis to enhance their flow of Reiki and to aid their spiritual development. In the West the method of performing Reiju isn't known by many Masters, but when it is, it tends to be used during Reiki sharing groups or other gatherings of Reiki students or Masters, on either a regular or occasional basis.

The Usui/Tibetan Reiki System

If you are learning the Usui/Tibetan Reiki system, then you will also need to know how to draw the Tibetan Master symbol (which is not the same as the Usui Master symbol) and the Fire Serpent symbol, and will need to be attuned to those symbols. In addition, this system uses four versions of the Antahkarana symbol (an ancient healing and meditation symbol that has been used in Tibet and China for thousands of years) but no attunement to this symbol is required. There are also some techniques which use the additional Usui/Tibetan symbols, notably for balancing and clearing chakras, or for a healing attunement.

Moreover, the Usui/Tibetan system has different attunement methods to the traditional Usui Reiki, including a technique called the Violet Breath. Instead of four attunements for Reiki 1, the Usui/Tibetan system has a single, integrated attunement, although sometimes this is repeated four times, to emulate the traditional Usui Reiki system. (It should be noted that many modern Reiki Masters don't actually realise that they are not teaching the traditional Usui Reiki, as the Usui/Tibetan system has become so widely practised.)

There should be ongoing support for each student from the Master who trained them, especially for the first few years as they establish their own teaching practice. It would be an advantage to have some qualifications or experience in teaching or training, acquired before or after your Reiki Master course, because this will give you more confidence. However, some students initially take Master training for their own spiritual development, deciding not to teach, at least for a few years. It's a good idea anyway to take the pressure off yourself, and not to decide straight away when you're going to begin attuning other people. Take some time to get used to the higher vibrations, the greater flow of energy. Begin using the Master symbol, familiarising yourself with its power. Meditate on it. Practise attunements over a pillow or a teddy bear, until you feel confident that you can remember all the steps of the process. There's no hurry. You're going to be a Reiki Master for the rest of your life!

THE MASTER SYMBOL

The Master symbol comes from the Japanese kanji, and is the fourth in the Usui system of Reiki. There are two very similar versions in common use today, one of which consists of twenty-two strokes while the other has seventeen. It is described as 'a Zen expression for one's own true nature or Buddha-nature', of which one becomes aware during the experience of enlightenment or 'satori' and one translation of its four-syllable mantra is 'treasure house of the great beaming light'. These definitions indicate how profound this symbol is, as its use gives us direct and immediate connection to the Light, the Source, the Master within – the essence of 'enlightenment'. In fact, it represents that part of the self which is already completely enlightened, so when we use the Master symbol, we are actually connecting in a profound way with our Higher Self – that enlightened part of our being which has total wisdom and understanding. The Master symbol brings in even higher and purer dimensions of light and healing – Reiki – to assist with self-awareness, personal growth, spiritual development, intuition and a deep understanding of 'being'. It is not appropriate to print the Usui Master symbol or its mantra in this manual as it should only be revealed to and used by trained Reiki Masters.

The Master symbol can be used to bring Light into any situation; it is an essential part of each Master's development to use this symbol to surround themselves with higher and finer energy vibrations as often as possible, to help with self-cleansing and self-purification (on spiritual levels) to help to create a more harmonious and balanced life. Meditating on this symbol can bring enormous benefits, as it directly enters the consciousness to allow Light to enter even the darkest and most deeply buried blockages, whether those blockages are on a physical, mental, emotional or spiritual plane. It can also sometimes be used in combination with the other Reiki symbols, when it will increase their effectiveness and allow them to act from only the very purest and highest motivations.

There are various ways of using the Master symbol, and it can be drawn in the same way as the other symbols – with the whole hand, or fingers, or eyes, or visualised. It is multi-dimensional energy, having height, width and depth, but also operating in time, space and light. It can appear to be any colour but the most usual are white, gold, purple, violet, turquoise, pink or rainbow-coloured. You can draw it in the air and then 'step into it'; you can visualise it filling your whole being; you can imagine breathing it in with each breath; and you can draw the symbol and chant its mantra (when you're alone!) to purify and fill your body and the space where you are with light, love and peace, before and after any activity. It also plays a part in the attunement process for all levels of Reiki, as well as helping the Reiki Master to create a unique sanctified space in which to carry out the sacred ceremony of initiation.

THE ATTUNEMENTS

As mentioned earlier, if you take a course to qualify as a Reiki Master Practitioner, you would not at that stage learn how to carry out attunements. Those are only taught when you train to be a Reiki Master Teacher. As that training should be in person with a qualified Reiki Master, it is not appropriate to describe any of the attunement processes in this manual, whether for the traditional Usui Reiki, the Usui/Tibetan Reiki system, or the Reiju empowerments from the Japanese traditions.

HOW TO PREPARE FOR MASTER TRAINING

Some Reiki Masters ask that you carry out some preparation before taking Master training, others don't feel that is important, but here are some ideas which you can follow if you feel drawn to them.

It can be an advantage to raise the vibrations of your energy bodies – physical, mental, emotional and spiritual – so that you will be better prepared for the power of the Master energy coming through you. Your preparations could include daily meditation (which might include meditating on each of the Reiki 2 symbols, or on the five Reiki Principles), plus self-treatments with Reiki, and practice of Hatsurei-ho (see Appendix 3), plus weekly Reiki treatment 'swaps' whenever possible, either with another practitioner, or with the Master who will be training you. This will enable you to get to know each other more, and if they have trained in the Japanese traditional techniques this would also give you the chance to receive regular Reiju attunements to increase the flow of Reiki.

You might also look at other possibilities for self-improvement and growth, perhaps by reading spiritually inspired books (there are suggestions in the Resources section at the back of this manual), or by attending personal growth groups or workshops – plus, of course, thinking about the ethics, responsibilities and commitment of being a Reiki Master. It would also be useful to look at what experience you already have, and to thoroughly practise all the techniques detailed in this manual! If you have practised Reiki professionally for several years this would obviously be of greater benefit to your future students than if you had done only an occasional Reiki treatment on family or friends, because you would then have a wealth of experience to share with them. Equally, if you confidently and regularly use the Reiki symbols, this will enable you to teach them more effectively.

AFTER REIKI MASTER TRAINING

Like the other Reiki courses, after being attuned as a Reiki Master you will go through another twenty-one-day clearing cycle, although this one does tend to be a bit deeper in its effects, as one might expect, since the Master energy has a very high vibration. With this in mind, it is probably better not to attune anyone else for at the very least a month, and preferably six months or longer after you've completed your Master training. Of course you might not choose to attune anyone for many years, preferring to use the higher energies and the Master symbol for your own personal and spiritual development, and in your Reiki treatments on yourself and others, and that's fine. You are still working with the energy. So let yourself go at a pace that suits you, and don't feel pressurised by family or friends, who might be looking forward to you attuning them. Only do it when you feel it is right, and trust your inner instincts, your intuition, to let you know when that is.

As already mentioned, one of the imperatives when you become a Reiki Master is to work with Reiki on your personal and spiritual development, allowing it to teach you who you really are. This divinely directed energy has the power to transform you and change your life, increasing your self-awareness, your intuition, and bringing a greater happiness and contentment. It is therefore necessary to prioritise Reiki; you should give it time in your life, and use tools such as meditating on the Reiki Principles, and the four Reiki symbols and their mantras (and particularly the Master symbol).

Because the Master symbol works at very high and fine vibrational frequencies, it can connect you in a deep way with aspects of your Higher Self/Higher Consciousness, and this can result in a very profound personal connection to the Source (God), leading to intense and wonderful experiences of enlightenment. You might like to try an alternative meditation technique, which is to 'walk' the symbol. Imagine the Master symbol drawn on the ground, and walk the shape of each stroke, chanting the sacred mantra as you go. This can be done inside but seems to be even more powerful if done outside, perhaps in a private area of a garden, or in a clearing in a wood.

Other aspects of Reiki as a spiritual discipline are daily self-treatment (preferably for at least an hour), thinking about and putting into practice the Reiki Principles on a daily basis, performing at least one Hatsurei-ho each day, plus self-cleansing with Reiki (see Appendix 3) and using Reiki as a normal part of your everyday life so that it becomes your automatic response to anything and everything. You can start and end each day by first placing your hands in the Gassho (prayer) position for a few moments, and then drawing (or visualising) the Master symbol and chanting its mantra, with the intention that Reiki should fill your being and your day (or night). This is a really powerful way of enhancing your spiritual growth, especially if you combine it with some suitable affirmation(s) for your personal and spiritual healing, guidance and well-being.

The more you use Reiki, the more your energy channels will be cleared, opened and expanded so that you can receive increasing amounts of energy. Eventually you integrate Reiki into the many layers and energy fields that make up your whole self, both energetic and physical, and when that happens, your total being becomes Reiki, so that everything and everyone within your expanded energy field will be touched by the vibration of Reiki. You will be spreading healing, harmony and balance wherever you go.

Chapter Twenty-four

TEACHING REIKI
LEVEL 1/FIRST DEGREE

TEACHING AS A REIKI MASTER

Teaching a course for the first time can be very daunting. Not only do you have your course content to remember, but you have to deliver the information in an easily understandable way – and you have people to deal with too! With that in mind it's easy to forget that your students may find the idea of learning a new skill as daunting a proposition as well, so try to remember that it's also part of your role to put the students at ease as soon as they arrive.

The Master relationship that you have with your students, and the way in which your students view you, will have a considerable impact on how they react to and understand Reiki. If you come across as being much cleverer or more spiritually advanced than your students, you may make them feel in some way inferior, which will make it more difficult for them to ask you questions; they will feel they have to look up to you, putting you on a pedestal, rather than simply treating you as a teacher with knowledge which they don't yet have. However, if you become too 'chummy', 'all mates together', you may find it harder to gain their respect or trust – or even to get their attention to tell them something when they are busy chatting!

It's important to remember that everyone is a unique individual with something to contribute to a Reiki class – and that you will learn from your students as well as them learning from you. You have some specific knowledge and experience which they are keen for you to share with them, but you will find that each one of them, at some time during the course, will say or do something which contributes to your learning, too, and it's crucial to value and acknowledge this with gratitude. That in no way belittles your credibility. Instead it will actually add to your standing within the group, because your students will then see that you have the strength and confidence to accept other people's ideas as an on-going part of your personal and spiritual development.

Remember too, that teaching is often the best way to learn, so sometimes it pays to focus on what you, yourself, are saying in a class. Often as you describe examples or ideas, you will have sudden insights about how they relate to something which is going on in your life at that time. True learning about Reiki begins not when you have received the Master attunement, but after you start teaching others!

It is an important part of your role as a Reiki Master to allow students to contact you after a class has finished, so that they can ask questions if they need to. This might be unusual in courses for other therapies, but Reiki isn't just another therapy – it's a healing system and a way of life. The connection your students have with you is different from that students have with other teachers, because you are linked through Reiki, so there needs to be a greater level of after-care. Of course you can set limits; you don't want phone calls early in the morning or late at night. But you need to be there for them – although you're unlikely to find it such a big deal, because generally only a few students will call upon your help, and often that's just for reassurance.

It can be really nice to develop friendships with your students, and holding regular 'Reiki sharing' afternoons or evenings can be a good way of doing this. There is a word of caution here, however. Occasionally a student can become too 'needy' and overly identified with you, phoning you too often and being a bit 'clingy'. You will need to tackle this situation calmly but firmly, politely pointing out that it is inappropriate for them to keep contacting you so regularly, and steering them towards helpful books, or even a counsellor if you feel that would assist in that particular situation.

Another obvious point is that you must always follow the highest ethical and professional standards in your dealings with any students. It is unacceptable to exploit your students financially, emotionally, or sexually. If an attraction develops between you and a student, it needs to be treated in a very sensitive and professional manner, and it might be best to seek the advice of your professional association or an independent third party.

As an additional note: if someone is drunk, abusive, intimidating, or if they make you feel physically or sexually unsafe, either in a Reiki class, or at a later time, then of course you must take steps to ensure your own safety, in as sensitive a way as possible.

PREPARING FOR TEACHING

At some point in your past you will have seen and experienced different teaching/lecturing/training styles, whether at school, college, within the workplace, at a night class that you've taken, or during the Reiki courses that you attended before becoming a Reiki Master. All of these experiences will stand you in good stead when developing your own style as a Reiki Master Teacher, as you'll no doubt remember the good techniques that helped you retain information, and a few of the bad techniques that you noticed along the way that you will want to avoid! A good style to aim for is one that involves the students as much as possible, i.e. make it an interactive course for them, rather than one where they just sit and listen to you. This is generally the best way for people to learn, as when they 'do' something they are more likely to remember it. Have a look at some suggested activities mentioned below (page 257) for ideas on how you can keep your students motivated and involved in the course.

One of the best pieces of advice about teaching is that preparation is *everything*. When you've been a student in the past and you've attended a course where it all went smoothly, you might not have realised it, but there would undoubtedly have been a huge amount of preparation involved beforehand, which would have given the impression that running the course was extremely easy. That's the ultimate aim for every teacher, but the preparation does take time, so you'll need to plan for that.

Let's take a look at what needs preparing before running a Reiki 1 course:

- Administration, e.g. sending out leaflets and booking forms, confirming bookings and keeping a list of students due to attend

- Course joining instructions (including course timings and directions to the venue) being sent to students

- Your subject knowledge (if there are any gaps!)

- Finding and getting to know your venue (this could be your front room)

- Students' course documentation (this will hopefully be *The Reiki Manual* that you're reading now!) or notebook

- Any additional course handouts or paperwork (such as teaching notes, activities, etc.)

- Course equipment (such as therapy couches, pillows, blankets)

When you send your joining instructions to your prospective students, it may be helpful to mention useful items for them to bring, e.g. a notebook, pen, lunch (if not provided), and advice on wearing comfortable layers of clothing, etc.

If you have spent time preparing all of the above your course should go smoothly, giving you a much more pleasant experience of teaching for the first time. It is a good idea to prepare a list of everything you'll need on a course, for example, candles, incense, CD player and CDs, blankets, etc., to make sure you don't forget anything. Keep a copy of the list to make sure you've got it for next time, and keep adding to it if you find you've forgotten something. There's a suggested list included in Appendix 7.

If you're not already used to teaching groups of people you might choose to teach just one person at a time, although it is certainly easier to teach at least two people simultaneously, so they can practise on each other. If you enjoy working with groups, it is best to start with perhaps four or six people, but it may be better to avoid teaching more than ten at a time, for energetic and practical reasons. It is possible that students in very large groups might at some time in the future be excluded from registering as professional practitioners in the UK due to the National Occupational Standards (see Chapter 14), as it might be viewed that they wouldn't have received sufficient individual attention and tuition. It can also be jolly hard work teaching large groups, especially when it comes to the time and energy it takes to do the attunements!

There are plenty of books that offer further tips on how to teach, some of which are listed in the Resources section.

HOW TO TEACH REIKI 1

The Reiki 1 course is ideal for people who just wish to use Reiki on themselves, their friends and family, as well as being the essential foundation for those who want to go on to become professional Reiki practitioners.

The course should be about covering the basics, so the order of the subjects that you teach needs to be logical. It's easy to forget what it was like to not know anything about Reiki and 'blind' your students with lots of detail and information that they won't be able to process without a good introduction, so a useful subject to start with would be 'What is Reiki?' Keep the explanation to layman's terms initially, even if you have a deeper understanding of energy, metaphysical illness and/or life messages and soul purposes, and then build on this explanation throughout the course. This could be the first exposure to Reiki that some students have had, so their initial impression of Reiki is all down to you!

The Reiki 1 course is traditionally held over two days – roughly sixteen hours of contact time – although some Masters also like to hold an introductory evening beforehand, to allow people to learn something about Reiki and to experience it for themselves. This wouldn't necessarily be confined only to those people who had booked on to the course, so it might encourage more bookings for your next course. When planning the rest of the course, take a look at the sample timetable on page 256 for some ideas about the order of the course content.

At this level it is important that students learn what Reiki is, its history and development, its effects, when and how it can be used, the difference between 'healing' and 'curing' and how to give themselves a self-treatment, as well as how to treat other people, animals and plants. There should be a brief explanation of what an attunement is, and the twenty-one-day clearing process, so that students are prepared for what they might experience – but, of course, don't give away any sacred information.

If you are teaching traditional Usui Reiki there should be four separate attunements, which should be at least three hours apart (and preferably four), to allow the energy to settle. (Usually two are performed on day one and two on day two.) You could also space the attunements out over more days, e.g. one a day for four consecutive days, or even one a day over a period of weeks, e.g. four Saturdays, provided each attunement is properly sealed. (You should have been taught how to do this, but if you're not sure please contact your Reiki Master for further instructions.)

There should also be time for questions and for students to practise treatments on themselves and on their fellow students. You will need to demonstrate each type of treatment first, and then supervise their practice. A self-treatment, allowing the students two to three minutes for each hand position, will take about thirty minutes; a treatment of a person seated in a chair will also take about thirty minutes if you allow about three minutes in each hand position; and a full treatment of someone lying on a therapy couch will take between forty-five minutes and an hour, depending on how much time you have available – five minutes in each hand position is ideal, and that will take sixty minutes. It's very important to give people time to practise treatments. Firstly, it gives them confidence that they can really do this (!), because they get feedback from other students; and secondly it helps to 'fix' the hand positions in their minds. Moreover, any active participation is always beneficial to the learning process.

Reiki 1 Theory – Chapters to Refer To

When you decide on the exact subject content to cover on your course, the following chapters of this manual may be helpful in gathering together all of the theory that you need, and of course you can refer to them in class if each of your students has a copy.

Subject	Chapter
What is Reiki?	3
History and origins of Reiki	4
Reiki training structure	2
Attunements	3
The Reiki Principles	5
Hand positions	6
Self-cleansing	Appendix 3
Self-healing	7
Treating others with Reiki	8
Using Reiki creatively	9 and 10

SAMPLE COURSE TIMETABLE

As you may know, different Reiki Masters offer both residential and/or non-residential Reiki 1 courses, often over a weekend, so an example of a typical two-day course programme is given below. The exact timings will depend upon how much content and how many activities you want to include, but you would probably start each day at about 9.00 a.m. and end at about 6.00 p.m. As a general rule you should schedule in a mid-morning and mid-afternoon break, as well as about an hour for lunch. This helps the brain recover between sessions!

DAY ONE

Morning
- Agenda for the day
- Introduction to what Reiki is, how it works, and its holistic effects
- History and origins of Reiki
- Reiki training structure (why Reiki is so quick to learn and so easy to use)
- What is healing?
- What are attunements?
- The twenty-one-day clearing process
- First attunement to the Reiki healing energy

Afternoon
- The Reiki Principles and precepts
- Importance of self-cleansing (discussion)
- Second attunement
- Importance of self-healing (discussion)
- Demonstration and practise of self-treatment with Reiki (including hand positions)
- Ways of using Reiki creatively, including with animals and plants, food and drink, inanimate objects, etc., using Reiki on situations, and how Reiki can become a tool to change your life
- Session summary

DAY TWO

Morning
- Agenda for the day
- Third attunement
- Treating other people with Reiki (discussion); including what can be treated, how often, preparation and equipment required, discussion of contraindications or cautions, etc.
- Demonstration and practise of treatment with a seated person (including hand positions)

- Demonstration of a full Reiki treatment with a person lying on a therapy couch (including hand positions)

Afternoon
- Fourth attunement

- Practical session where each student both gives and receives a full Reiki treatment

- Question and answer session

- Certification

- Session summary

SUGGESTED ACTIVITIES

Rather than just 'talking at' your students, getting them to participate in an activity helps them to learn, keeps them focused, and should also keep them enthusiastic about the course content as they will be enjoying themselves! Activities can be as simple as asking open questions (who, what, where, which, why, when, how) for them to discuss in small groups, or asking the group as a whole to work together to send Reiki to a situation.

Depending on what you decide to cover in your course, some of the following activities may be useful for you to include.

Icebreaker

1. After introducing yourself and running through the course agenda, ask each student to tell the rest of the group:

- Their name

- Where they've travelled from for the course

- Why they've decided to do the Reiki 1 course

- (Optional) An interesting fact about themselves, which can be as silly or as serious as they want!

This will help the group to bond as there's bound to be common ground between them, and if you choose to include the interesting fact, there's generally one funny one, and one very interesting one, both of which could lead to further bonding chats during coffee breaks.

General Reiki

2. In groups of two to four people, distribute photos of Mikao Usui, Chujiro Hayashi and Hawayo Takata, with their names written/printed on separate pieces of paper, and ask the students to match the photos and the names.

3. Get each student to create a diagram or plot their Reiki Master lineage, so they can see how they're connected to the founder of Reiki – Mikao Usui.

4. Get each student to send Reiki to a situation of their choice, for at least five minutes, so that they've had experience of doing so. You can provide post-it notes for them to write the situation down on, and then get them to hold the note between their hands whilst they send Reiki to the situation.

5. After a practical session get each student to write in their course documentation or notebook: 'Giving/Receiving Reiki I felt… [they write what they experienced].'

6. In groups of two to four people, ask the students to list or demonstrate to each other the sequence of self-treatment hand positions.

Attunement

7. Following each attunement, give the students time to think about the experience, and then get them each to write in their course documentation or notebook: 'During my attunement I experienced… [they write what they experienced].'

Reiki Principles

8. In groups of two to four people, ask the students to think of examples of how they are going to adopt each of the Reiki Principles into their life, e.g., 'I will no longer get angry when I'm stuck in traffic.'

Course Summary

9. To make it a fun (but educational!) end to the course, you can divide the group into two teams and run a Reiki quiz. This could be in any format that you're able to produce, e.g. a standard 'pub quiz' format, or *Mastermind* type of questioning, or a *Blockbusters* type of game, etc. Use a format that you feel happy to present, but also one that feels like it is still honouring the Reiki subject.

OPTIONAL EXTRAS

As a Reiki Master, you will want to run your course your own way, so you may feel like including some extra sessions. For example, once you've explained what Reiki is, you may find it useful to introduce people to energy, and in particular to how students can detect and sense the aura and chakras (see Appendix 2). This can be really helpful because your students will begin to understand what Reiki is – a spiritual energy – even before you start talking about it in any detail. It's also a fun thing to do, and it helps to further the bonding in the group. You may also want to include details of any Japanese techniques that you have learned, such as the practice of the Japanese Reiki Shower technique, and Hatsurei-ho, a Japanese meditation and energy cleansing technique (see Appendix 3).

The important thing is that, by the end of your course, you need to feel satisfied that you have provided the best Reiki 1 course that you could have done, so tailor the course content as you see fit.

Optional Extras – Activities

10. When talking about energy and how it affects us all, get the group to try and sense their own and each other's auras by using dowsing rods, pendulums or their hands. Some people may also be able to see them.

11. Get each student to practise giving themselves a Reiki Shower (see Appendix 3), so that they'll have experience of an energy cleansing and protection technique.

Chapter Twenty-five

TEACHING REIKI
LEVEL 2/SECOND DEGREE

HOW TO PREPARE FOR TEACHING

Preparation is key to teaching a successful course, as we saw in the previous chapter, but experience is also valuable. It would be well worth teaching a few Reiki 1 courses before you attempt to run a Reiki 2 course, as it will give you a good grounding in the type of questions you'll be asked, and any practical issues you may encounter. Just to reiterate the advice from the previous chapter – you may like to start with teaching one or two people, then groups of four to six and gradually work your way up to about ten people once you've had more experience of dealing with groups (although you should note what was said in the previous chapter about National Occupational Standards and large groups).

Again, it's useful to have a list of everything that you need for your Reiki 2 course as it can be overwhelming trying to remember everything. The checklist provided in Appendix 7 should be useful. As mentioned in the last chapter, when you send your joining instructions to your prospective students, it may be helpful to mention useful items for them to bring, and advice on wearing comfortable layers of clothing.

What you would need to do to prepare for teaching a Reiki 2 course is identical to that for a Reiki 1 course, so please see the beginning of Chapter 24 to help with that. However, the subject knowledge that you may need to revise will be slightly different.

HOW TO TEACH REIKI 2

Reiki 2 is about students taking their skills further, learning the three Usui symbols and their mantras, and what they can do. It is the second stage in their commitment to Reiki, and is therefore more taxing spiritually, emotionally and psychologically. The Reiki 2 attunement expands the students' flow of Reiki, both for themselves and their development as healers, and for those they treat, and of course the ability to send distant treatments is a phenomenal benefit!

You will need to make sure that they know the symbols well enough to use them. You could teach them this by getting the students to do a self-treatment on Day One of the course, using the Power symbol (because that's the easiest to remember), and setting a test on the morning of Day Two to make sure they know all three symbols. This is important for you, to check their progress and put right any potential problems, and for them, because they gain confidence in their own ability so that they are better able to spend the rest of the day using the symbols on the other students for hands-on and distant treatments.

To practise the distant treatments, you may like to have half of the students lie on therapy couches in one room, and then take the other half into another room and talk them through a distant treatment, using a correspondence (such as a teddy bear or a pillow). This 'proves' to them that distant treatments work, as the students are always excited and amazed by what they experience!

However, a two-day course, even with practical sessions, isn't really enough to make the theory and symbols 'stick', so before you issue them with their Reiki 2 certificate, you may want to ask them to complete a practice journal of simple case studies, such as:

- At least six full hands-on treatments using the Reiki symbols (treating a minimum of three different people).

- At least six full distant treatments on people (treating six different people – some of these could be 'swaps' with other students from their course, to acquire some good quality feedback).

- Using the Reiki symbols on at least three personal and three global situations.

You could give them blank treatment diary sheets (there's a sample in Appendix 5) to record their case studies in and ask them to send them back to you. After you have read and approved the sheets you could return them to the students with their certificates. It can be helpful if you clarify the timescale that these actions should be completed within – three to six months is usually enough time for the students to complete the tasks on their own, whilst ensuring the course content is still fresh in their minds.

It would be useful to review the hand positions when demonstrating the hands-on treatment, because these are the same as those taught for Reiki 1.

Reiki 2 Theory – Chapters to Refer To

When you decide on the exact subject content to cover on your course, the following chapters may be helpful in gathering together all of the theory that you need. And your students can refer to them too, if they each have a copy of this manual.

Subject	Chapter
Hand positions	6
Reiki symbols	11 and Appendix 4
Attunements	3
Creative uses of the Reiki symbols	12
Space clearing/cleansing	12
Energy cleansing techniques	Appendix 3
Self-treatments	7 and 12
Treatments on others	8 and 12
Distant healing	11 and 13
Twenty-one-day clearing process	2
Western vs. Japanese training	2
Professional practice	14 to 22

SAMPLE COURSE TIMETABLE

As with Reiki 1, timings will depend upon how many activities you plan to include, and you will need to schedule in a mid-morning and mid-afternoon break, as well as an hour for lunch. As previously mentioned, this helps the brain recover between sessions.

DAY ONE

Morning
- Agenda for the day
- Brief review of Reiki 1 theory and hand positions
- The three Reiki 2 symbols (Power/Focus, Mental & Emotional/Harmony, and Distant/Connection) and their mantras (theory and practice)
- Reiki 2 Attunement
- Personal time following attunement to allow for private meditation, learning the Reiki symbols or just having some 'personal space'

Afternoon
- Creative uses of Reiki symbols and mantras
- Using Reiki symbols for space clearing and creating sacred space
- Using Reiki symbols during hands-on treatments
- Self-treatment – demonstration and practise, using the Power symbol and its mantra
- Reiki 2 techniques to treat others (discussion)
- Session summary

Evening
- Students should be encouraged to spend time learning the symbols and mantras so that they can use them confidently in Day Two's practical hands-on and distant healing sessions.

DAY TWO

Morning
- Agenda for the day
- Reiki symbols test

- Using Reiki symbols for chakra clearing and balancing (see Appendices 2 and 3)

- Demonstration and practise of a hands-on treatment using the Reiki symbols

Afternoon
- Distant healing – the ethics and practice, on individuals or multiple people at the same time

- Using a 'correspondence' for distant healing

- Programming distant treatments for a future/past time

- Demonstration and practise of how to perform a standard distant treatment

- Question and answer session

- Twenty-one-day clearing process and Reiki case study journals

- Certification requirements

- Course summary

You may want to inform students before a course that practice time is available on the course, but that it is *essential* to put aside time over the following few months to practise both hands-on and distant treatments and to complete a case studies journal before a Reiki 2 certificate can be awarded.

(**Note:** currently, each Reiki Master creates and issues his or her own certificates.)

SUGGESTED ACTIVITIES

As mentioned in the previous chapter, getting students to participate in the course as much as possible will help keep them motivated, and will aid the learning process. It may be useful to have a few 'revision' activities (that cover Reiki 1 subjects) at the beginning of your Reiki 2 course. This will help you to see if there are any gaps in the students' knowledge, and it will act as a good refresher for them all. (Refer to the previous chapter for some ideas for useful Reiki 1 revision activities.)

Some of the following activities may be useful to you on a Reiki 2 course:

Icebreaker

1. See the icebreaker activity in the previous chapter.

Revision of Reiki 1

2. Have a large outline of a human body laid out on a therapy couch, and a set of photocopies of left and right hands. Ask the group to work together to agree on which hand positions go where, and in which order they should be carried out.

General Reiki

3. Get each student to write down their own phonetic way of saying the Reiki symbol mantras.

4. Get the group as a whole to cleanse the room energetically with the Power symbol.

5. Get each student to send Reiki to a personal or global situation of their choice using the appropriate Reiki 2 symbols, for at least five minutes, so that they've had experience of doing so. You can provide Post-it notes for them to write the situation down on, and then get them to use this whilst they send Reiki to it. If there is any global situation that is prevalent at the time of your course you may want to specify which situation they are to send Reiki to, for example a recent earthquake or an ongoing war.

6. After a self-healing session, get each student to write in their course documentation or notebook: 'During self-healing I felt... [they write what they experienced].'

7. After a practical session, get each student to write in their course documentation or notebook: 'Giving/receiving Reiki using my Reiki 2 knowledge was the same as/different to Reiki 1 because... [they write what they experienced].'

8. In groups of two to four people, ask the students to discuss the ethics of distant healing/treatments in the following situations:

- A baby in a neo-natal unit
- An elderly relative in hospital
- An unconscious friend in hospital
- A friend in a damaging/unhappy relationship
- A friend of a friend who's ill
- A relative going on active service, for example, in the Middle East

Attunement

9. Following their attunements, give the students time to think about the experience and get them to write in their course documentation or notebook, 'During my attunement I experienced… [they write down what they experienced].'

Course Summary

10. Refer to the previous chapter for ideas for a course summary activity.

OPTIONAL EXTRAS

Again, there may be additional content that you wish to include in your course. Some Reiki Masters include how to do a Mental and Emotional Treatment, which uses the Reiki symbols, during their Reiki 2 course (*Reiki for Life* by Penelope Quest has details of this technique). Other items you may like to include are:

- Hatsurei-ho and the Reiki Shower technique (see Appendix 3)

- Psychic protection together with energy cleansing, as being vital for energy workers (refer to Appendix 3)

- Using the Power symbol for cleansing and protecting spaces

You may also want to incorporate a 'pre-course' evening session, if you feel there is the need to devote more time to subjects than a two-day course would usually allow.

Optional Extras – Activity

11. Find a large picture of the human body or draw an outline of a body on a flip chart. Then make up two sets of cards – one set made up of one card per chakra colour, whilst the other set of cards will have the names of the chakras printed/written on them, one name per card. Get the group to work together to pin/stick the correct chakra colour and name to the appropriate part of the human body picture (see Appendix 2 for information about chakras).

Chapter Twenty-six

TEACHING REIKI LEVEL 3/REIKI MASTER

PREPARING TO TEACH MASTER-LEVEL REIKI

To teach at this level, experience is vital. It would be worth you teaching multiple Reiki 1 and 2 courses, probably over a number of years, before you attempt to teach a Reiki Master course.

In order to teach Reiki Masters, you obviously need a thorough understanding of Reiki theory and practice:

- What Reiki is

- The three Reiki 2 symbols and the one Usui Reiki Master symbol, their mantras and how to use them

- How to carry out treatments in a chair and on a therapy couch

- How Reiki can be used as emergency treatment

- How Reiki can be used on animals, plants and inanimate objects

- How to carry out attunements at each level

- How to advise students if they wish to practise professionally

It would be useful if you were familiar with other relevant topics too, such as energy theory, including the human energy field; methods for energy cleansing and psychic protection; the healing process and the mind/body connection with health and illness; and meditation and visualisation techniques.

You will also need to know how to run a small business, including all the relevant UK and European legislation, ethics and codes of practice; how to communicate effectively and appropriately to create professional relationships; the importance of confidentiality; how to reflect on your practice and identify development needs; and how to look after your own physical, mental, emotional and spiritual health and well-being to support yourself and your work. These are all skills you will need to pass on to your students.

It is even more important during a Reiki Master course that you lead by example, as you are literally being seen as the 'Master' expert by your students. If you have any friends or family members who are trained teachers, speak to them for guidance about how to deliver the course, including how to 'train the trainer', i.e. how to coach other people in teaching. Find out what has been their most valuable lesson throughout their teaching career. Listen to their tips about what works, and take their advice about what it's best to avoid!

If teaching is a skill that is new to you, refer to the Resources section at the back of the book, as in this chapter there is only room for very general advice about the actual mechanics of teaching.

From a course resource point of view, the list of what you would need to prepare is identical to that mentioned in previous chapters. However, the subject knowledge that you may need to revise will be more advanced.

HOW TO TEACH A REIKI MASTER COURSE

The teaching standards when delivering Reiki courses should be as high as for other subjects, so it's important to ensure that any potential Reiki Masters you may be training are not only serious about and committed to Reiki, but are also fully prepared for their role as teachers of this amazing energy healing and spiritual development system. However, although one of the major focuses of the Reiki Master training is to prepare people to teach Reiki, it's important to remember that some potential students wish to take this training for their own personal and spiritual development, and don't, initially, wish to teach. That's perfectly acceptable – although it is likely, at some time in the future, that they might change their mind and start teaching, even if it is only a few people!

Reiki Master Theory – Chapters to Refer To

When you decide on the exact subject content to cover on your course, the following chapters may be helpful in gathering together all of the theory that you need, and it would certainly be beneficial if all of your Master students had their own copy of this *Reiki Manual* for use during their training and afterwards.

Subject	Chapter
Reiki theory for Reiki 1 and Reiki 2	3 to 13
Practitioner training and National Occupational Standards (NOS)	14 to 22
Running a business	19
Legal responsibilities	21
Human energy system	Appendix 2
Cleansing techniques and psychic protection	Appendix 3

MASTER PRACTITIONER OR MASTER TEACHER?

The first thing you have to decide is whether you are going to teach Reiki Master as a single level, referred to as Reiki Master Teacher, or whether you want to split it into two parts. When this happens the first part is called Reiki Master Practitioner (or, alternatively, Reiki 3A or Advanced Reiki Training), and the second part Reiki Master Teacher.

Whichever way you decide to teach Reiki Master, this level is about the students' commitment to Reiki as a way of life, and as the teacher of this level your dedication also needs to be apparent. The students will be looking to you to be a good example of 'living what you love' and 'walking your talk'!

It is important to keep the course as practical as possible, i.e. you should include the students by making them 'do' the course through activities and practice sessions. This chapter contains lots of ideas for how to do that. However, it is more difficult with this level to provide sample timetables, because the ways in which Masters choose to teach can differ greatly, especially in the amount of time taken. Instead there are lists of essential and optional topics to be covered, and suggestions on how to put a course together.

REIKI MASTER PRACTITIONER

There isn't really a lot of theory to teach at Master Practitioner level, and because of this you might choose to include some of the 'optional extras' referred to later, so this course could probably be fairly easily fitted into one or two days. However, you might consider suggesting a minimum time lapse, and possibly a minimum level of experience of carrying out treatments, between taking a Reiki 2 course and a Reiki Master Practitioner course.

Sample Core Course Content

- Introductions, and course agenda

- The Usui Master symbol and its mantra (plus time to learn and practise these)

- Attunement to the Usui Master symbol

- Symbol test (possibly also including the three Reiki 2 symbols)

- Ways of using the Usui Master symbol – in meditation, for self-treatments and treatments on others, for working on problems and situations

- Demonstration and practise using the Usui Master symbol in treatments

- Course summary and presentation of certificates

Optional Extras

Some of these are always included in Advanced Reiki Training (ART), which comes from the William Rand lineage, so if this is your lineage you will have been taught these on your own Usui/Tibetan Reiki Master course – they are marked with an asterisk. Other subjects will depend on the extent of your knowledge and experience outside traditional Reiki, so only include them if you feel comfortable and confident about using and teaching them.

- Revision of Reiki 1 and Reiki 2 theory, especially the hand positions for treatments, and the Reiki 2 symbols and their uses

- Understanding energy, and the body's energy system – the aura, chakras and meridians

- Understanding the mind/body connection and its relationship to health and illness

- Understanding the body's healing processes and how Reiki can help

- Energy cleansing techniques such as the Hatsurei-ho and Reiki Shower (see Appendix 3)

- Scanning techniques to detect imbalances in a client's energy field *

- Using Reiki with crystals, and creating a crystal grid *

- Aura cleansing with Reiki (also called Reiki Psychic Surgery) *

- Moving meditation *

REIKI MASTER TEACHER

If you are teaching this as one complete course (rather than as two separate levels), you need to include all of the essential topics shown in the Reiki Master Practitioner section above. Of course you might choose to also include some of the optional extras, so you will need to allow one or two days of training to cover this. However, as this level is specifically to prepare people to teach Reiki, you might consider getting your students to prepare themselves for the course by revising all the Reiki 1 and 2 theory (and Reiki Master Practitioner, if they have done that), perhaps by giving them a copy of this manual, and by encouraging them to read other relevant books, such as *Living the Reiki Way* and *Self-Healing with Reiki* by Penelope Quest, or others recommended in the Resources section at the back of this manual.

You might also, as with Master Practitioner training, suggest a minimum time lapse between the students taking their Reiki 2 course and taking the Reiki Master Teacher course, to allow them to gain adequate experience. One, two or three years are the most usual minimums, although some Masters don't specify a particular time lapse. In addition, you might encourage your students to gain some experience or qualifications in teaching or training, not necessarily as a prerequisite for the course, but perhaps before they actually start to teach.

Structuring Your Course

Course agendas for Reiki Master Teacher can vary enormously between Reiki Masters, usually depending upon how they themselves were trained. As mentioned above, sometimes the course is split into Master Practitioner, followed by Master Teacher, but if you choose to teach both together there are still a number of ways to do this.

1. As an apprenticeship of at least a year, with a student shadowing you on the courses you teach, together with some one-to-one time on the specific Master-level theory and practice

2. Part apprenticeship, part course, where the students are required to work through some preparatory distance-learning materials based on the theory and practice of Reiki 1 and 2. This means they would complete a variety of tasks and activities and answer questions which would be submitted to you for assessment in advance of the course-based part of the training. It's important for a Reiki Master to provide regular email and/or telephone support to students during this distance part of the training. The second part would be a course (residential or non-residential) over a minimum of three, and up to seven, ten or even fourteen days (although it could be split between multiple weekends), where the Master-level theory and practice is covered and where the Master attunement is given. It would only be on successful completion of both of these parts that the students could be considered to have 'passed', and become Reiki Masters.

3. As a stand-alone course lasting anywhere between three and fourteen days (depending upon how much content you want to put in it), which could be residential or non-residential.

It should be noted that a short course, such as that in 3 above, even with practical sessions, isn't really enough time to cover all of the information students need to become Reiki Masters. So before students attend your Reiki Master course you could ask them to fulfil some basic requirements, such as:

- Potential students must have a minimum of two years' experience of using Reiki at Reiki level 2, including experience as a professional practitioner (because even a short time working as a practitioner will add depth and understanding to their work as a Reiki Master)

- Having some qualifications or experience in teaching or training is also highly recommended, although perhaps not essential, as some students initially take this course for their own spiritual development, deciding not to teach for a few years

Sample Core Course Content

Whichever method of training you choose, you will need to cover some essential topics. (It may also include some optional topics or activities.)

- Introductions, and course agenda

- A review of the whole Usui Shiki Ryoho system (from Mrs Takata's lineage), including symbols, treatment methods, hand positions and training

- Understanding the development of Reiki in the West and in Japan

- All of the theory and practice outlined above under 'Reiki Master Practitioner'

- Understanding the attunement process, and the essential personal and environmental preparations needed

- Demonstration and practice of the four-attunement method for traditional Usui Reiki 1, or single-attunement method for Usui/Tibetan Reiki 1 (on a correspondence, e.g. a teddy bear, and on fellow students)

- What to include and how to teach Reiki at level 1 (for individuals and groups)

- Demonstration and practice of the single-attunement method for Reiki 2 (on a correspondence, and on fellow students)

- What to include and how to teach Reiki at level 2 (for individuals and groups)

- Demonstration and discussion (or practice) of Master attunement methods and training

- Understanding and working with the Reiki Principles in today's world, and your commitment to self-healing and Reiki as a way of life

- How to establish and run a successful Reiki teaching business, including legal responsibilities, keeping records, marketing, etc.

- Time for questions

- Course summary and presentation of certificates

You might decide to delay the presentation of a Master Teacher certificate until the student has completed some additional tasks after the course, such as an attunement under observation by you.

Optional Extras

Some of these, marked with an asterisk, are always a part of the Usui/Tibetan Reiki Master course, so you will have been taught those when you trained as a Reiki Master Teacher in that lineage, whereas others will depend upon the breadth of your own knowledge and experience outside traditional Reiki theory.

- Reiki and the human energy system (possibly including dowsing with rods and pendulums), and the links with health and well-being

- The necessity of, and methods for, energy protection and cleansing for yourself and your environment

- Developing your intuitive skills for healing work and personal awareness (including scanning with hands and/or pendulums)

- Several special meditations and some time for reflection

- Discussion of the changes in training which may be necessary in the future for potential UK registration of Reiki practitioners (please check the regulations in your own country if you teach outside the UK)

- A Reiki Master's need for a 'support system' and ongoing need for self-awareness, personal growth and spiritual development

- The two- and three-attunement methods for Reiki 2

- An opportunity to take part in one or more 'Reiki shares'

- An opportunity for the students to have some observed teaching practice

- What is included in Japanese Reiki training for the three levels – Shoden, Okuden and Shinpiden

- How to work with the Reiki Principles as a daily spiritual practice – and learning them in Japanese

- Demonstration and practice of the Reiju blessing/spiritual empowerments from the Japanese lineage

- Demonstration and practice of other techniques from the Japanese lineage

- Demonstration and practice of the Usui/Tibetan additional symbols and mantras – the Tibetan Master symbol and the Fire Serpent symbol *

- Additional Master attunement to the Tibetan Master symbol and the Fire Serpent symbol *

- How to use the ancient Anthakarana symbols to assist with healing *

- The Violet Breath *

- A Healing Attunement *

- Demonstration and practice of the Usui/Tibetan attunement for Advanced Reiki Training (ART) *

- Demonstration and practice of the Usui/Tibetan attunement for Reiki Master (i.e. including the additional symbols) *

- The Microcosmic Orbit Meditation *

- Energy cleansing using the Native American herb mix 'smudge' *

Following any of the course structures mentioned above, you may want to award your students with their certificate at the end of the formal course. Alternatively, you could choose to issue them after an interval of between three and twelve months, to allow time for your students to practise and gain experience.

SUGGESTED ACTIVITIES

As mentioned in previous chapters, getting students to participate in the course as much as possible will help keep them motivated, and will aid the learning process. Indeed, when teaching Reiki Masters to teach others it's even more important that they have experience of 'doing' the activities that they in turn may get their students to undertake. It may be useful to have a few 'revision' activities that cover both Reiki 1 and Reiki 2 subjects during the Reiki Master course. This will help you to see if there are any gaps in the students' knowledge, and it will act as a good refresher for them all. Refer to Chapters 24 and 25 for additional revision activities for these levels.

Some of the following core activities may be useful to you on a Reiki Master course:

Icebreaker

1. Refer to Chapter 24 for a good 'icebreaker' activity to introduce students to each other.

Revision of Reiki 1 and 2 Knowledge

2. Any of the activities given for Reiki 1 or Reiki 2 mentioned in the previous two chapters can be used as revision.

General Reiki

3. If possible, schedule in some Reiki 'share' sessions during the Reiki Master course, which will remind the students what it's like to be a Reiki client, and it will also relax them during what can be an intensive course.

4. Get each student to write and lead a short meditation with the group.

5. Ensure each student has sufficient practice of carrying out attunements at all levels of Reiki.

Teaching Practice

6. It is advisable that your students have experience of 'teaching' by the end of the course, as they may be passing on this knowledge to others when they eventually teach their own Reiki courses. If time allows, try and schedule in two sessions where each student teaches the group:

   - **Session One:** Ask each student to choose any subject covered in Reiki 1 or Reiki 2 courses, and prepare a fifteen-minute session where they will teach this subject to the rest of the group, followed by a five-minute question and answer session.

     After the session, ask the student how they felt their session went, and what they would keep the same and what they would change about the next time they taught that subject.

     Ask the group to give positive/constructive feedback on the student's delivery of the session.

   - **Session Two:** Allocate a subject (of your choice, not theirs!) to each student and ask them to prepare another fifteen-minute teaching session, this time incorporating any suggestions that were made during the previous feedback session.

     Following the session ask the student how they felt this session went compared to their previous one, and what they felt they did well.

     Ask the group to give positive/constructive feedback on this session compared to the student's first one.

Attunement

7. Following the Master attunement(s), give the students time to think about the experience; get them to write in their course documentation or notebook: 'During my attunement I experienced… [they write what they experienced].'

Course Summary

8. At the end of the course ask the students to share with the rest of the group what they will remember most about the course, and one action point that they will take away from it.

At this level it is perhaps even more important that your Reiki Master students know that they can have post-course support from you, because it can feel quite daunting to realise the responsibility they have taken on – potentially to lead others on their Reiki journeys. You could provide them with a contact list of their fellow students (if permission has been given), so that they can keep in touch, and you might also arrange a follow-up get-together of the students on the course, perhaps three or six months later, for some additional training, or just to socialise and swap experiences. In addition, it is good to keep in regular touch with them yourself by email and/or telephone – not too often, but perhaps every couple of months, just to check how they're getting on, and to invite them to ask about anything they're not sure of. And, of course, let them know that they can contact you with any queries whenever they need to. If you've spent quite a few days with your students you will, hopefully, have got to know them pretty well, and often your Reiki Master students become your friends, which can be really nice!

Part Six

APPENDICES

APPENDIX 1

STYLES OF REIKI

There are many different styles and systems of Reiki practised today around the world. There are Reiki systems that come directly from Japan (generally referred to as Eastern Reiki or Japanese Reiki), Reiki systems that come from Japan via (mainly) the USA (generally called Western Reiki), as well as Reiki systems that combine Eastern and Western Reiki, such as Gendai Reiki. There are also Reiki systems that have evolved from Western Reiki, such as Karuna Reiki® and Tera-Mai™.

Each person practising Reiki should be able to trace his or her lineage of teachers back to Dr Usui. In the West this lineage usually runs through Mrs Takata and one or more of the twenty-two Reiki Masters she taught, but it can sometimes be through other students of Dr Hayashi. In the Eastern system the lineage can be through other students taught by Dr Usui, or through the Usui Reiki Ryoho Gakkai – the organisation set up to preserve Dr Usui's teachings.

The following is an alphabetical list of the main Reiki styles that can be found today, with some brief details about each. It is designed for information purposes only and is not intended to be a list of recommended styles. People practising Reiki styles or systems with the same name may actually teach very different things, so it is up to you to research and decide which might be right for you – and new Reiki styles do crop up from time to time! Where possible, websites have been included, but an internet search will usually provide more information, as well as details of individual teachers of each system.

ANGELIC REIKI

A modern style of Reiki, combining the Usui and Shamballa lineages with what is described as an angelic vibration through Archangel Metatron. (Shamballa Reiki is supposed to originate from the ancient land of Atlantis.) **Websites:** www.angelicreikimagic.com and www.angelicreiki.info.

BUDDHO ENERSENSE©

This system claims to be derived from Buddhist Lamas in Nepal, Tibet and Northern India, and was inaugurated by the Venerable Seiji Takamori, a Buddhist monk. It is a system of spiritual discipline related to healing, involving meditation practice and empowerments, using ancient symbols, mantras, yantras and other aspects of Buddhist teachings and philosophy. (See also Reiki Jin Kei Do.)
Website: www.healing-touch.co.uk

EASTERN REIKI

A modern term, indicating any Reiki lineages that do not include Chujiro Hayashi. There is no generic website.

GENDAI REIKI-HO

A system founded in Japan by Hiroshi Doi who trained with Mieko Mitsui, Kimiko Koyama, Hiroshi Ohta and Chiyoko Yamaguchi.

Gendai Reiki-ho techniques are based on both traditional Japanese Reiki Ryoho and Western-style Reiki techniques. Its goal is to achieve a state of great spiritual peace.
Website: www.gendaireiki.net

HAYASHI REIKI KENKYUKAI

Hayashi Reiki Kenkyukai means the 'Hayashi Reiki Research Society', and is a term used by Chujiro Hayashi for what he taught. There is no current website.

JAPANESE REIKI

A modern term, usually indicating that the practitioner or Master is practising or teaching Western Reiki with the addition of specific techniques from

Japan that were brought into the West in the late 1990s, mostly by the author Frank Arjava Petter and the Japanese Reiki Master Hiroshi Doi.
Website: www.reikidharma.com

JIKIDEN REIKI

A style of Reiki whose title means 'directly taught Reiki', with the lineage coming through Chujiro Hayashi, Wasaburo Sugano, Chiyoko Yamaguchi and Tadao Yamaguchi. It concentrates on treatment, but does also encourage the broadening of spiritual awareness.
Website: www.jikidenreiki.co.uk

KARUNA REIKI®

Karuna means 'compassion', and this healing system was developed by William Lee Rand. It is based on two levels and nine new symbols in addition to one Usui symbol and two Tibetan symbols, and the attunement system is different to that of Usui Reiki. It is normally only available to people already qualified as Reiki Masters, and it seems to activate a different type of healing energy to that brought in by Usui Reiki. It has an interesting spiritual dimension.
Website: www.reiki.org

KOMYO REIKI

In Japan, the word Komyo means 'enlightenment', so the name Komyo Reiki can be translated as 'Enlightenment Reiki'. Its lineage comes through Chujiro Hayashi, Wasaburo Sugano, Chiyoko Yamaguchi and Hyakuten Inamoto, so it has a very similar origin to Jikiden Reiki, but is closer in content to some other Western/Japanese-style Reiki lineages.
Website: www.komyoreiki.com

RAKU KEI REIKI

Raku Kei Reiki has been called 'The Way of the Fire Dragon', and encompasses the energies of the Fire Dragon. This style of Reiki was developed by Iris Ishikuro, Mrs Takata's sister, and Arthur Robertson, and it is supposed to be an advanced Reiki originating in Tibet. Aspects of it are also included in Usui/Tibetan Reiki developed by William Lee Rand. It is normally only taught to qualified Reiki Masters from other lineages. There is no direct website, but an internet search will reveal individual teachers.

REIDO REIKI

A blend of traditional Japanese Reiki and Western Reiki which emphasises meditation and 'living a Reiki way of life'. It was developed by Fuminori Aoiki, whose lineage is Chujiro Hayashi, Hawayo Takata, Barbara Weber-Ray, and it consists of seven levels.

Website: more information can be found on www.aetw.org

REIKI JIN KEI DO

Reiki Jin Kei Do is a spiritual lineage and system of Reiki that emphasises the development of compassion and wisdom within one's own life. Its lineage is Chujiro Hayashi, Venerable Takeuchi, Seiji Takamori, Ranga Premaratna. (See also Buddho Enersense.) Jin is the Japanese word for 'compassion' and represents the Buddhist concept of universal compassion for all beings. Kei is the Japanese for 'wisdom' and represents the Buddhist understanding of universal wisdom, which is the product of deep spiritual practice. Do is the Japanese for 'way' or 'path'.

Website: www.omahhum.org; www.healing-touch.co.uk

REIKI PLUS®

The Reiki Plus® system, developed by David Jarrell, is said to embody the philosophy of 'Freedom through Responsibility', the key teaching of Saint Germain, described as the Ascended Master, World Server and Master of the Seventh Ray. The lineage is through Chujiro Hayashi, Hawayo Takata and Virginia Samdahl/Barbara McCullough/Phyllis Lei Furumoto, and it is based on Western Reiki with additional metaphysical elements.

Website: www.reikiplus.com

SEICHEM

See Tera Mai® Seichem

SEKHEM

Pronounced 'say kem', and also known by the initials SKHM, and similar to Seichem, this is apparently an ancient Egyptian system of healing wisdom. The current system was founded by Patrick Ziegler based on his experiences in the Egyptian Great Pyramid. Sekhem is an Egyptian word meaning 'power' or 'might', and is the Egyptian equivalent of 'ki'. There is no generic website, but an internet search will reveal individual teachers.

TERA-MAI™ REIKI/TERA MAI® SEICHEM

Founded by Kathleen Milner, whose lineage comes through Patrick Ziegler, Tom Seaman and Phoenix Summerfield, Tera-Mai Reiki is also sometimes called Tera Mai Seichem. It includes attunements to earth, air, water and fire energies, and has up to thirty-one symbols.
Website: www.kathleenmilner.com

TIBETAN REIKI

A generic term that covers lineages through Hawayo Takata, Iris Ishikuru and Arthur Robertson, so it includes elements from Raku Kei Reiki and Usui/Tibetan Reiki. There are a number of additional levels as well as a number of different symbols, one of which is said to ignite the Kundalini energy. There is no generic website.

TRADITIONAL JAPANESE REIKI

A school of Reiki developed by Dave King in Canada, incorporating information from the Hayashi line in Japan that does not include the Takata lineage.
Websites: more information can be found on www.aetw.org and www.usui-do.org

TRADITIONAL REIKI

Traditional Reiki generally refers to the practices of the Reiki Alliance and those Masters who follow closely the Hawayo Takata/Phyllis Lei Furumoto lineage.
Websites: www.reikialliance.com and www.reikialliance.org.uk

THE RADIANCE TECHNIQUE® (TRT®)

A style of Reiki also referred to as Authentic Reiki® or Real Reiki®. It has seven levels apparently passed on by Mrs Takata to its founder, Barbara Weber-Ray, who claims to be Mrs Takata's successor.
Website: www.trtia.org

USUI-DO (TRADITIONAL JAPANESE REIKI)

This system is from the Japanese lineage through Chujiro Hayashi (but not through Hawayo Takata) and was developed by Dave King and Melissa Riggall. It is very different from other Reiki styles, as it has no Masters, and the attunements are regarded simply as ceremonies. The whole system is driven solely by the intent of the practitioner who has at his or her disposal a number of 'tools' that affect the way the energy is directed. There are seven levels in a similar ranking system to that used in Japanese martial arts. **Website:** www.usui-do.org

USUI REIKI RYOHO

The 'Usui Spiritual Energy Healing Method'. It is the term used by people with lineages running through the Usui Reiki Ryoho Gakkai organisation in Japan, through the lineage of Kan'ichi Taketomi and Kimiko Koyama, as well as through Hiroshi Doi's Gendai Reiki organisation (see Gendai Reiki). There is no website currently available.

USUI REIKI RYOHO GAKKAI

This is a closed society in Japan that was set up to continue the teachings of Mikao Usui. Lineages come through the past (and present) presidents of that society, Juzaburo Ushida, Kan'ichi Taketomi, Yoshiharu Watanabe, Hoichi Wanami, Kimiko Koyama, Masayoshi Kondo, and their students. There is no website currently available.

USUI REIKI/TRADITIONAL USUI REIKI

A term used by many Reiki Masters to indicate that they teach Reiki, but they may not confine themselves to any one system, so they may teach elements from a number of different Reiki styles. There is no generic website.

USUI SHIKI RYOHO

What is usually referred to as traditional Reiki in the West, with the lineage from Mikao Usui, Chujiro Hayashi and Hawayo Takata to Phyllis Lei Furumoto, Mrs Takata's granddaughter. Furumoto and another of Takata's Masters, Paul Mitchell, set up 'The Office of Grand Master' – a term meaning the recognised lineage bearer, which her followers use to describe Phyllis

Furumoto – which has outlined what they call the four aspects (healing practice, personal growth, spiritual discipline, mystic order) and nine elements (oral tradition, spiritual lineage, history, principles, form of classes, money, initiation, symbols, treatment) of the Usui Reiki system, all of which they believe should be incorporated into Reiki training and practice. Masters who belong to the Reiki Alliance generally follow this system of teaching in three levels with four symbols. Some independent Reiki Masters also use this system with some minor adaptations.
Website: www.usuishikiryohoreiki.com

USUI/TIBETAN REIKI

A style founded by William Lee Rand incorporating elements from Raku Kei Reiki, Usui Shiki Ryoho and, since the early 2000s, Japanese techniques. Lineages come from Chujiro Hayashi, Hawayo Takata, Iris Ishikuro, Arthur Robertson, Diane McCumber/Marlene Shilke; Phyllis Lei Furumoto, Carrel-Ann Farmer, Leah Smith; and more recently, Hiroshi Doi. The system is based on four levels – Reiki 1, 2, Advanced Reiki Training (ART), Reiki Master – incorporating the four traditional Usui Reiki symbols, and two additional symbols said to be from Tibet.
Website: www.reiki.org

APPENDIX 2

THE SCIENCE OF ENERGY AND ITS RELATIONSHIP TO REIKI

The science of energy isn't strictly a part of Reiki theory. However, an understanding of it can inform your practice and potentially help your students, and your clients and recipients too.

ENERGY THEORY

Scientists have confirmed that everything in the universe is made up of energy, vibrating and oscillating at different rates. One theory is that all energy exists on a continuum from the most dense and least conscious, or what we call physical matter, to the least dense and most conscious, which we call spiritual.

Low Vibrations   High Vibrations

Dense Energy ←——————————————————→ **Spiritual Energy**

(Matter)   (Consciousness)

Why is this of any interest to people learning or using Reiki? Because Reiki is a spiritual energy that vibrates at a very high rate, and it works at an energetic level with both the physical matter of the body and the electromagnetic energy of the energy field which surrounds and interpenetrates the physical body. Understanding this will help you to understand why Reiki can help your healing on many different levels, from the physical to the mental, emotional and spiritual aspects of each individual.

HUMAN ENERGIES

The physical body seems solid, yet every cell within it is actually energy or light, vibrating at a slow enough frequency to make it into visible physical matter. The human body, and the energy field which surrounds it, is made up of electromagnetic energy, and every person has a unique vibrational energy signature, or frequency, in the same way as we all have unique finger-prints or DNA. Drawing more energy of a higher vibration into yourself – like the high spiritual energy we call Reiki – raises the energetic vibrations of your whole body to a higher level, and as the higher the frequency, the less dense and therefore more conscious the energy is, this process also raises your consciousness, enabling you to become more spiritually aware – a process of 'enlightenment'.

THE HUMAN ENERGY FIELD

The human energy field comprises both the physical body and an energy body surrounding and within it, which is made up of much finer, lighter and higher vibrations. This energy body is made up of three parts:

1. Outside your physical body is a field of energy called **the aura**, or auric field

2. Internally you have a host of energy channels flowing through your body called **meridians**

3. Connecting the internal and external energy fields is the third part, a series of active energy centres known as **chakras**

Perhaps the easiest way to understand this is to think of the parts of the energy body in similar terms to parts of your physical body. The aura could be described as the energy equivalent of your whole physical body; the chakras could correspond to your brain, heart and other major organs; and the merid-ians are similar to your veins and arteries, but instead of blood, they carry energy – the life-force we call Ki.

The energy that comprises the human energy field has various names, depending upon the culture or spiritual tradition – **Ki** (Japanese), **Qi** or **Chi** (Chinese), **Prana** (Indian), **Light** or **Holy Ghost** (Christian) – or it may simply be called **life-force**. This life-force flows within the physical body through the energy centres called chakras and the energy pathways called meridians, as well as flowing around the body in the aura. When your Ki, or life-force, is high and flowing freely, you feel healthy, strong, confident, full of energy, ready to enjoy life and take on its challenges, and you are much less likely to become ill. If your Ki is low, or there is a restriction or blockage in its flow, you feel weak, tired and lethargic, and are much more vulnerable to illness or 'dis-ease'.

The Aura

The aura is a field of energy or light which completely surrounds the physical body above, below and on all sides. It is as much a part of you as your physical body, but the higher frequencies of the energies that make up the aura mean it is harder to see with the naked eye, although it can be detected by some scientific equipment, and a representation of the aura can also be photographed using a special Kirlian camera (named after two Russian researchers; this uses a process that records on photographic film the field radiation of electricity emitted by an object to which an electric charge has been applied).

The aura is made up of seven layers, with the inner layers closest to the physical body comprised of the densest energy, and each succeeding layer being of finer and higher vibrations. Most people have an oval (elliptical) aura, which is slightly larger at the back than at the front, and fairly narrow at the sides, which also stretches above the head and below the feet. See illustration opposite.

People's auras vary in size, but the outer edge of the aura can be anywhere from 1 to 2 metres (3 to 6 feet) from the physical body, to 20 metres (66 feet) or more in front and behind the body. Your aura is not always the same size, however, as it can expand or contract depending upon a variety of factors such as how healthy you are, how you are feeling emotionally or psychologically at any given moment, or how comfortable you feel with the people in your immediate surroundings.

The aura is spiritual energy (or life-force, or Ki), which is present around each of us from birth (and before birth, as the foetus develops) until around the time of our death. Usually just before death only a narrow band of spiritual energy remains, down what is referred to as the 'hara line', linking all the chakras in the centre of the body; after physical death, no aura can be detected, because the life-force no longer exists. However, in a living person the outer edges and the individual layers of the aura can be detected using dowsing rods or a pendulum, and they can also be sensed with the hands. The densest layers, nearest the body, can also be seen with the naked eye by

most people with a little practice, and some very psychic people can see the whole energy body quite clearly.

The Chakras

Chakra is a Sanskrit word meaning 'wheel', 'disc' or 'vortex', and very intuitive people describe the chakras as funnel-shaped energy points, similar in shape to a tornado or whirlpool, with the narrowest point near the body, and the widest visible point between 30 and 60 cm (12 to 24 inches) away from the body. See illustration overleaf.

The chakras are energy centres located at various points around the energy body where the spiritual energy of your aura, the Ki or life-force, circulates actively. There are seven major chakras in the human body, at:

1. The perineum, near the base of the spine

2. Near the navel

3. At the solar plexus

4. In the middle of the chest

5. In the throat

6. The centre of the brow

7. The crown of the head

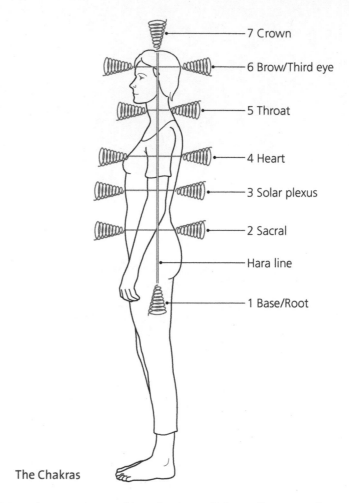

7 Crown

6 Brow/Third eye

5 Throat

4 Heart

3 Solar plexus

2 Sacral

Hara line

1 Base/Root

The Chakras

In addition there are a number of minor chakras, for example in the palms of the hands, on the knees and on the soles of the feet. A healthy chakra vibrates evenly in a circular motion, either clockwise or anti-clockwise, and this can be detected by using a pendulum held over the chakra point. Sometimes people can actually feel the energy moving with their hands. The outer edge of the chakra can be only a few inches from the body or several feet away, depending upon that person's physical, mental and emotional state. Most people have alternating clockwise and anti-clockwise chakras, but some have a few consecutive clockwise chakras, then a few anti-clockwise ones, and other people have all their chakras circulating in the same direction.

Chakras are intimately connected with our physical health, as each is linked with specific parts of the body, and to systems within the body. When a particular chakra is healthy, balanced and open, so are its connected body parts, but if a chakra is blocked, damaged or too closed, then the health of the connected body parts and systems will begin to reflect this. Our energy field, including the chakras, is affected by everything which happens to us, good and bad. (For more information please refer to either *The Basics of Reiki*, or *Reiki for Life*, both by Penelope Quest.)

When we are attuned to Reiki, it flows through our energy system, flowing in through our crown chakra at the top of the head, and down the hara line to the heart chakra, and from there along the meridians to the minor chakras in the palms of each hand (as illustrated in Chapter 3). When we use Reiki for self-healing, it will flow around the whole of our physical body and aura, helping to break through energy blockages and remove negative energy.

DETECTING THE AURA

Sensing the Aura with Your Hands

Something you might like to try is sensing your own aura between the palms of your hands. Hold your hands out in front of you with the palms facing each other, about 60 cm (2 feet) apart, and *intend* to detect your auric energy – it is your intention which switches on this ability, just as it is your intention that switches on the flow of Reiki.

Now close your eyes, so that you have fewer distractions and can concentrate on any sensations in your hands and fingers, and then slowly bring your hands closer together. You may find that your palms get warm, or your fingers begin to tingle, and as your hands get quite close together you may feel a resistance between them, almost as though you have a balloon between your hands. That's your auric energy!

Seeing Auras

To see your own aura it is easiest to look at either (or both) of your hands. Hold your hand out at arm's length away from you, with the fingers spread wide apart, preferably with a plain background behind. Some people find it easiest with a light background, whilst others prefer something dark, so just experiment. What you are looking for is a faint outline close to and surrounding the fingers, which usually appears as lighter than your finger colour although sometimes it is more like a slightly darker smudgy line.

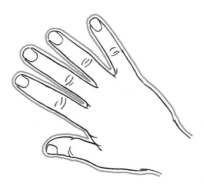

It's important to be relaxed about this – a soft gaze is more likely to achieve results than a fiercely concentrated stare. If at first you don't succeed, try a different kind of background or better lighting; daylight is better than artificial light, and fluorescent lighting can make it particularly difficult. Please don't expect to see masses of brightly coloured light. The auric field is usually softly coloured, but it is very subtle and is often 'sensed' rather than seen, so don't be disheartened if you can't see anything clearly!

When you've successfully seen the aura around your own fingers, you might like to look for other people's auric fields. It is unusual to see auras all the time. Most people 'switch on' this ability by actively looking, so you're unlikely to notice them whilst wheeling your trolley around the supermarket! It is easiest to see when a person is involved in something important to them, such as giving an impassioned speech, because the aura seems to intensify at such times. It can be seen as a soft white or golden glow, and is most easily seen around their head and shoulders, like the 'halo' seen in old paintings of spiritual people. Again, it will probably be best if they have a plain background behind them, but the more practice you have the easier it gets, and eventually you will probably begin to see (or sense) shades of other colours, too.

ENERGY PROTECTION AND CLEANSING TECHNIQUES

Whatever level of Reiki you have – 1, 2 or 3 – it is useful to include regular energy protection and cleansing into your daily self-healing routine, whether you intend using Reiki on other people or not. Being attuned to Reiki raises your body's energy vibrations, and as the energetic oscillations become faster, this makes your whole energy field lighter and less dense as you gradually become more and more 'enlightened'. This not only increases your spiritual awareness, but also means that your whole energy field can become more permeable, and therefore potentially more vulnerable to denser, negative energies.

The negative energies that can impact on your energy field can be either internal or external:

- **Internal** – Anything you think, feel, say or do which is negative, e.g. vengeful thoughts, feelings such as sadness or bitterness, constant complaining.

- **External** – Anything you hear, see or experience negatively from other people (e.g. sad or distressed people) or in negative places (e.g. hospitals, or at funerals), as well as negative news, ideas or images from newspapers, TV, radio and films.

ENERGETIC PROTECTION

Protecting yourself energetically doesn't have to be complicated. You can use your thought energy (which is very powerful) to visualise protective barriers around you, and of course you can use Reiki, with or without the symbols. Here are a few ideas you can use every morning, especially before leaving home, although you can also use them at any time you feel particularly threatened, such as when going into some stressful situation or if you have to deal with very negative people in a work or social situation.

- Imagine yourself in a bubble of white or golden light which is above, below and on all sides of you, and is filled with Reiki; the edges of the bubble are permeable only by love, light, Reiki and positive energies.

- Imagine yourself inside a bubble of light filled with Reiki, and imagine that the bubble is closely surrounded by a fine mesh made of gold, which is only permeable by love, light, Reiki and positive energies.

- If you ever feel really threatened, do all of the above, and then outside your bubble of light filled with Reiki and covered with gold mesh imagine a ring of fire, and outside that imagine a shiny eggshell made of mirror glass or shiny silver, with the mirrored side facing outwards. This effectively forms an energetic boundary around you, so that any negative thoughts sent your way will only rebound back to the sender, because they are reflected by the mirrored surface.

- If you have level 2 Reiki, you can draw a large Power symbol in front of you and step into it, saying its mantra three times. Imagine being wrapped inside the Power symbol so that it is in front, behind, above, below and on each side of you, and intend that the Reiki protects you from any negativity or harm.

Each of the above methods is useful in different situations, so use your intuition to decide which is the most appropriate at any particular time.

ENERGY CLEANSING

As well as protecting yourself from negative energies, it is also necessary to cleanse your whole energy body (as well as your physical body) every day, and often several times a day, depending upon what you are doing. One of the main aspects missing in the Reiki traditions in the West has been self-cleansing; what was usually taught was that 'Reiki is its own protection'. Essentially this is true, because Reiki will fill the energy field of both the practitioner and recipient, but this does not totally cleanse each person's energy field, nor does it prevent negative energies from one aura being transferred to another, although no negative energy travels through the Reiki channel – Reiki is always a pure, wise, loving and compassionate energy.

It is interesting that the 'new' techniques that have come from Japan since the late 1990s include a number of cleansing methods which would be used by Japanese Reiki students on a daily basis. Dr Usui would have been well aware of the need for energetic cleansing because of his knowledge of martial arts and other energy practices, so it is probably not surprising that he included a number of techniques which are similar to some from the Qi Gong (Ki-ko) traditions. Below are the two main cleansing techniques from the Japanese Reiki traditions: the Reiki Shower floods your energy field with Reiki to cleanse and revitalise it, and the Hatsurei-ho combines cleansing with meditation and healing.

The Reiki Shower Technique

You can use this technique almost anywhere for cleansing yourself. It also helps to centre yourself, raising your consciousness and bringing you into a pleasantly meditative state.

1. Make yourself comfortable, either sitting or standing. Place your hands in Gassho (prayer position) and centre yourself, slowing down and deepening your breathing, and then *intend* to use Reiki to cleanse and activate your whole energy field.

2. Separate your hands and lift them above your head, as high as possible, keeping them 30–40 cm (12–15 inches) apart, palms facing each other.

3. Wait for a few moments until you begin to feel the Reiki building up between your hands, and then turn your palms downwards so that they are facing the top of your head. Visualise Reiki flowing out of your hands, and intend that you are receiving a shower of Reiki energy that flows over and through your whole physical and energetic body, cleansing you and removing any negative energy.

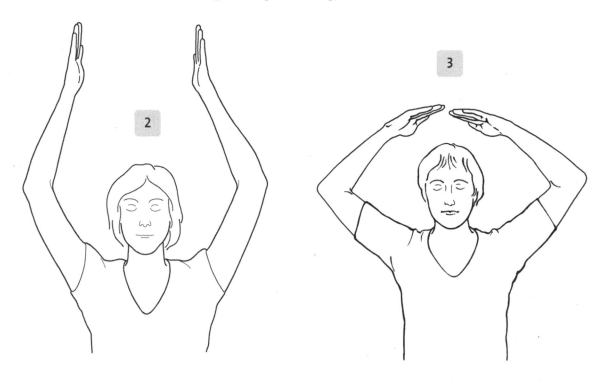

4. When you sense the Reiki energy flowing over and through you, move your hands, palms still facing towards you, and begin to draw them slowly down in front of your face and body, keeping your hands 30–40 cm (12–15 inches) away from your body. Intend that Reiki is flowing from your hands, and continuing to cleanse and revitalise you as you draw your hands all the way down your body, and then down your legs to your feet, eventually turning your palms to face the floor and either touching the floor to ground the energy, or gently throwing the energy off your hands so that any negative energy flows out and into the earth below, for transformation. See illustration on opposite page.

5. Repeat this exercise a few times – three is usually enough – and then clap your hands a few times to disperse any residual energy. Finally place your hands together again in the Gassho position, and spend a few moments experiencing gratitude for the Reiki.

Hatsurei-ho

Hatsurei-ho, pronounced 'hat soo ray hoh', is a very valuable cleansing technique, and although the length of the description may make it look a bit complicated, actually it's fairly simple. It can take as little as ten minutes, or you can spend longer if you wish.

   The technique is split into three parts, and its basic functions are:

• to cleanse the outer part of your energy body (the aura) with dry bathing or brushing (Kenyoku-ho),

• to cleanse the inner part of your energy body with the cleansing breath (Joshin Kokyu Ho), and

• to allow you to bring more Reiki into yourself for your own personal healing (on all levels – physical, emotional, psychological and spiritual), and to send Reiki out for global healing (Seishin Toitsu).

It isn't essential to learn the Japanese names for the different parts of Hatsurei-ho, but you can do so if you wish.

1. Kihon Shisei ('key hon she say') – Standard Posture
Sit down and make yourself comfortable, allow yourself to relax and close your eyes. Focus your attention on your Tan-dien point, which is 3–5 cm (1–2 inches) below your navel, and with your hands on your lap, palms facing downwards, spend a few moments bringing your breathing into a slow, steady rhythm as you centre yourself and intend to begin the Hatsurei-ho.

2. Kenyoku-ho ('ken yo koo ho') – Dry Bathing or Brushing Off
   a. First place the fingers of your right hand near the top of your left shoulder, with the palm of your hand facing the floor, fingers and thumb close together, and draw your hand diagonally down quickly and positively across your chest down to your right hip. At the same time, expel your breath rapidly, making a loud sound throughout the movement, e.g. 'Haaah'. See illustrations overleaf.

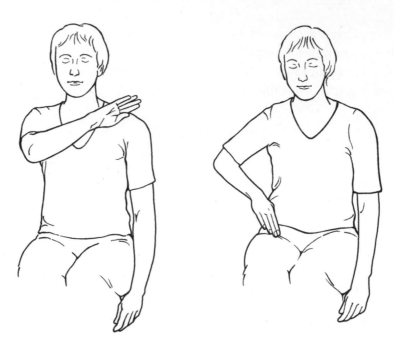

b. Now do the same thing on the other side, placing your left hand on your right shoulder, and quickly brush down diagonally from the right shoulder to the left hip, again exhaling noisily.

c. Repeat the action, with your right hand on your left shoulder, brushing diagonally from your left shoulder to your right hip and exhaling loudly.

d. Next place your right hand on your left shoulder again, but this time draw your right hand quickly and positively down the outside of your left arm, all the way to the fingertips of your left hand, whilst expelling your breath noisily, as before.

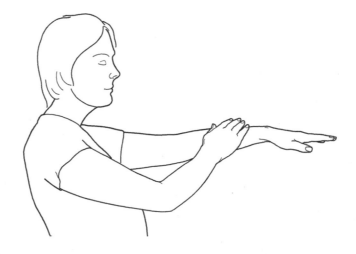

e. Repeat this process on the other side, with your left hand on your right shoulder, brushing down quickly and positively to the fingertips of your right hand, expelling your breath loudly as before.

f. Complete this process by once more sweeping your right hand down your left arm from shoulder to fingertips, again exhaling loudly.

(It may seem strange that each action is done three times, rather than an even four, but the reason is that in Japan there is superstition about doing things four times, as the word for the number four is the same as the word for death!)

3. Connect to Reiki
Now raise both your hands high up in the air above your head, with your palms facing each other, 30–40 cm (12–15 inches) apart, and visualise and feel the light and vibration of Reiki flowing into and between your hands, running through your whole body.

4. Joshin Kokyu Ho ('joe shin koh kyoo ho') – The Cleansing Breath
Lower your arms and put your hands on your lap, this time with your palms facing upwards, and let yourself breathe naturally and steadily through your nose. Then say to yourself:

I now breathe in Reiki for my cleansing, so that as the Reiki flows around my body and aura, it breaks through any blockages and picks up any negativity, so that as I breathe out, the Reiki takes the blockages and negativity away, to beyond my aura where they can be safely healed and transformed.

As you breathe in, visualise Reiki as white light pouring into you through your nostrils and through your crown chakra, filling your head, neck, shoulders, arms and hands with Reiki, and then flowing down your back, chest, waist, hips, abdomen and down into each leg, all the way down to the tips of your toes. Then imagine the Reiki spreading out, expanding to fill the whole of your aura, and intend that as the Reiki flows through the whole of your physical body and energy field, it is cleansing you.

Continue this process for two or three minutes, or up to twenty minutes or more if you wish, breathing in Reiki to cleanse you, and breathing out Reiki so that it takes away any negativity. Finally, when you feel ready, take a really deep breath and blow out the rest of the negativity, and then move on to the next section.

5. **Gassho ('gah show') – Prayer Posture**
Put your hands together with the palms and fingers flat against each other, in the Gassho prayer position, and hold them in front of the centre of your chest, at about the level of your heart chakra (see page 297).

6. **Seishin Toitsu ('say shin toy itsoo') – Concentration or Meditation**
Then say to yourself:

Now I breathe in Reiki for my own healing – healing on all levels, physical, emotional, psychological and spiritual, wherever I need Reiki at this time – and as I breathe out I can share the wonderful gift of Reiki, allowing it to flow in all directions to heal the planet, the people, the animals, birds, fish and other creatures, the trees, crops and other plants, and anything else that needs Reiki at this time.

Keeping your hands in the Gassho position, take your focus away from breathing through your nose, and imagine that you are breathing through your hands, and as you breathe in, visualise the light of Reiki flowing in through your hands directly into your heart chakra. Imagine it filling your heart chakra and then sense it flowing into your hara line, the energy line that connects all the chakras from the base up to the crown; visualise it flowing up and down your hara line, so that your hara line is filled with light, and see or sense the Reiki spreading out to fill the whole of your physical body and your aura with its healing, balancing and harmonising energy.

Then imagine that as you breathe out, Reiki can flow beyond your aura in all directions, to heal anything on this beautiful planet Earth that needs Reiki at this time.

Continue this process for two or three minutes, or up to twenty minutes or more if you wish, and let your mind settle into a peaceful, meditative state.

7. Gokai Sansho ('goh keye san shoh')

In the traditional way, Japanese Reiki students would at this point say the Reiki Principles aloud three times, as instructed by Dr Usui – obviously in Japanese. This is an important part of your spiritual practice, so you may feel you would like to do this in Japanese (see the phonetic pronunciation in Chapter 5) or in English – whichever English version of the Principles you prefer.

8. Mokunen ('moh koo nen')

Place your hands back onto your lap with the palms facing downwards, and intend that the Hatsurei-ho is now complete. When you feel ready, open your eyes and rub or gently clap your hands together a few times to bring you back to a greater state of physical awareness.

You are now ready to get on with your day. However, to continue your spiritual practice this is an ideal time to carry out a self-treatment, placing your hands in each position on your head and body for between three and five minutes in each position, or longer if you prefer, depending on how much time you have available.

APPENDIX 4

THE REIKI LEVEL 2 SYMBOLS

SYMBOL NUMBER 1 – THE POWER/FOCUS SYMBOL

Mantra: Cho Ku Rei (Pronounced 'Choh Koo Ray')

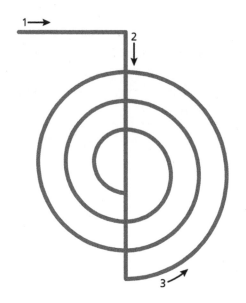

SYMBOL NUMBER 2 –
THE MENTAL AND EMOTIONAL/HARMONY SYMBOL

Mantra: Sei He Ki (Pronounced 'Say Heh Kee')

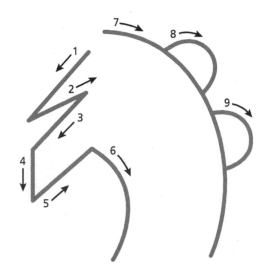

SYMBOL NUMBER 3 –
THE DISTANCE/CONNECTION SYMBOL

Mantra: Hon Sha Ze Sho Nen
(Pronounced 'Hon Shah Tzay Show Nen')

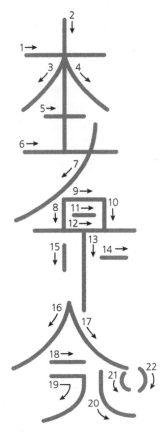

APPENDIX 5

SAMPLE REIKI DIARY/
TREATMENT JOURNAL

One of the features of Reiki 2 is that there is more to 'learn' than at Reiki 1. It is therefore important to put aside time over the following weeks and months to practise using the symbols to reinforce your learning so that you don't forget the symbols or how to use them. Many Reiki Masters ask that you carry out a specific number of full hands-on treatments and distant treatments on people (friends and family) as well as practising using the symbols to help to heal both personal and global situations, before they will issue you with your Reiki 2 certificate. They might also specify the length of time within which you need to complete this practice; three to six months is often recommended.

You may be provided with a Practice Journal to record your experiences and keep track of how many treatments you have done, similar to the sample pages that follow, and these can act as a useful informal 'appointments' list, too. When you have completed the number of case studies required by your Reiki Master (between six and twelve individual hands-on treatments and a similar number of distant treatments, is typical), you would then send your completed Practice Journal to them for assessment and, provided they are satisfied with the record of your work you have submitted, they would usually return your Practice Journal to you, together with your Reiki 2 certificate.

If you have any problems in completing your schedule of treatments, or you are uncertain about any points which you learned during your Reiki 2 course, then, of course, please get in touch with your Reiki Master. Most things can be resolved easily if you just talk them over.

REIKI 2 PRACTICE

FULL 'HANDS-ON' TREATMENTS USING SYMBOLS

PRACTICE SESSION 1

Date and Time: Name:

Details of the Experience (For You and the Recipient)

PRACTICE SESSION 2

Date and Time: Name:

Details of the Experience (For You and the Recipient)

REIKI 2 PRACTICE

FULL 'DISTANT' TREATMENTS ON PEOPLE

PRACTICE SESSION 1

Date and Time: Name:

Details of the Experience (For You and Feedback From the Recipient)

PRACTICE SESSION 2

Date and Time: Name:

Details of the Experience (For You and Feedback From the Recipient)

REIKI 2 PRACTICE

USING REIKI SYMBOLS ON PERSONAL/GLOBAL SITUATIONS

PRACTICE SESSION 1

Date and Time: Name:

Details of the Situation and any Experiences and/or Results

PRACTICE SESSION 2

Date and Time: Name:

Details of the Situation and any Experiences and/or Results

SAMPLE TREATMENT
RECORD SHEET

CONFIDENTIAL	
CLIENT NAME:	**DATE:**
CLIENT ADDRESS:	**CONTACT IN EVENT OF EMERGENCY:**
PHONE:　　　　　**D.O.B:**	
EMAIL:	

REASON FOR SEEKING REIKI TREATMENT:

☐ Have you advised the client that whilst they may request help for a particular condition, Reiki may or may not address this problem?

OTHER ALLOPATHIC OR COMPLEMENTARY TREATMENT/MEDICATION BEING USED:

☐ Have you advised the client that it would be good practice to inform their doctor/practitioner that they are receiving Reiki as well?

MEDICAL HISTORY/LIKELY REACTIONS:

OTHER RELEVANT INFORMATION:

SPECIFIC COMFORT NEEDS DURING TREATMENT:

treatment record sheet continues

RECORD OF REIKI TREATMENTS		
Date	Observations during treatment/ advice to client after treatment	Feedback given by client

APPENDIX 7

SAMPLE EQUIPMENT LISTS

PREPARING TO TREAT OTHERS

If you are preparing for a treatment, the list below may help you to gather together all of the equipment that would be useful.

ITEM	TICK IF PACKED/ AVAILABLE
Therapy couch, cover & blanket	
Pillows (2) & pillowcases (2)	
Tea-lights & holders AND/OR Candle & holder	
Matches	
CD player & CDs	
Leaflets/Business cards (if appropriate)	
Treatment Record Sheet (if appropriate)	
Business receipt book (if appropriate)	
Box of tissues	
Clock OR watch	
Bottled water, glasses	

PREPARING TO TEACH A REIKI COURSE

If you are running a Reiki course, use a checklist similar to the one below to ensure you have all the necessary equipment.

COURSE TITLE:	DATE:
ITEM	**TICK IF PACKED/ AVAILABLE**
List of attending students (including their contact details)	
Therapy couches	
Couch covers & blankets	
Pillows & pillowcases (2 of each per couch)	
Tea-lights & holders AND/OR Candles & holders	
Incense, holder & matches	
CD player & CDs	
Handouts, e.g. course agendas, Reiki symbols, activity sheets	
Course manuals, e.g. copies of *The Reiki Manual*	
Case study diaries/treatment journals	
Certificates & pens	
Leaflets/Business cards	
Reiki/Other books	
Photographs of Grand Masters (Usui, Hayashi, Takata)	
Box of tissues	
Post-it notes	
Business receipt book	
Flip chart & pens	
Clock OR watch	
Refreshments, e.g. teas, coffee, milk, sugar, biscuits, bottled water	

APPENDIX 8

REVISION QUESTIONS ANSWERS

CHAPTER 3: WHAT IS REIKI?

Answers

1. 'Spiritual energy' or 'Universal life force energy'

2. The Japanese alphabet/calligraphy

3. Because it affects/works on the whole person – body, mind and spirit

4. Warmth or tingling, seeing beautiful colours, recovering forgotten memories, feeling emotional, feeling the urge to laugh, slight shaking, gurgling stomach, etc.

5. Physical, emotional, mental and spiritual

6. For ever! Once you have been attuned you will always be able to access Reiki

CHAPTER 4: THE ORIGINS AND HISTORY OF REIKI

Answers

1. Japan

2. Dr Mikao Usui

3. The first names given to the three levels of Reiki teaching that we know today – Reiki 1, 2 and Master

4. An organisation of Reiki Masters first formed in 1983

5. Through a series of 'attunements'

CHAPTER 5: THE REIKI PRINCIPLES OR IDEALS

Answers

1. A position with your hands clasped in prayer

2. These may vary, but will be similar to:

   Just for today: do not anger;
   do not worry;
   honour your parents, teachers and elders;
   earn your living honestly;
   and show gratitude to every living thing.

CHAPTER 6:
THE HAND POSITIONS FOR REIKI TREATMENTS

Answers

1. Twelve

2. About five minutes

3. Close to the hand, i.e. not sticking out

4. Move one hand at a time, and move them gently so the recipient is not disturbed

5. *Male*: one hand on each hip bone
   Female: same as above, or in a V shape from the hip bones towards the pubic bone (but not too low down)

6. They would not be able to lie down on their stomach in a conventional way, so the treatment could be given when they were lying on their side, or if they were seated in a chair

CHAPTER 7: USING REIKI FOR SELF-HEALING

Answers

1. It means you are treating yourself as a priority, and it will support all aspects of your physical, emotional, psychological and spiritual self-healing programme

2. The life-force energy which flows within your physical body and surrounds it as your aura

3. *Highest* and *greatest* good

4. No, as Reiki may first work on levels that you may not be aware of, e.g. it may work on emotional issues before tackling a physical problem

5. At any time and anywhere – providing it is appropriate, and not dangerous to do so, e.g. not when driving!

CHAPTER 8:
USING REIKI TO TREAT FAMILY AND FRIENDS

Answers

1. About an hour

2. No. Whatever healing takes place is not under your control

3. Not always (refer to the chapter in full for more information)

4. No, not unless you are medically qualified

5. Under the head, and supporting the knees when recipient is lying on their back, then under the ankles when they are lying on their front

CHAPTER 9:
USING REIKI WITH ANIMALS, PLANTS AND OBJECTS

Answers

1. Usually with a hands-on approach, if safe to do so

2. Usually with hands-on approach, working along one side of the horse first, then the other side

3. By placing your hands either side of the bowl or tank and letting the Reiki flow

4. By distant healing, intending that Reiki flows to an animal for its highest and greatest good, or indirectly by giving Reiki to its food and drink

5. No one other than a qualified vet can diagnose, carry out tests, advise or carry out medical or surgical treatment or prescribe medication. In situations where it's your own animal/pet, or if it's an emergency, it appears to be legal to offer treatment then

6. Give Reiki whilst holding a packet of seeds, or a tray of seedlings, or the pot of a house plant. Alternatively, Reiki the water before watering plants

7. Answers can include: to fix inanimate objects if they're faulty, increase the nourishment of food and drink, and balance the ill effects of additives

CHAPTER 10: USING REIKI TO HEAL PERSONAL AND GLOBAL SITUATIONS

Answers

1. 'I am in a fulfilling, loving relationship' – because it is personal, really positive and fully in the present

2. You can send Reiki to environmental situations; or you can visit a place of power, e.g. a stone circle, and allow Reiki to flow; or you can send Reiki into the earth, i.e. downwards; or hold something in your hands to represent the earth and send Reiki

3. Yes, by holding a piece of paper with the details of the situation on it, and intending Reiki to go to that issue

4. No. Reiki will always work towards the greatest and highest good, but that may be in a way that we wouldn't necessarily choose!

CHAPTER 11: THE REIKI SYMBOLS

Answers

1. One – they will have been taught the other three at Reiki level 2

2. Historically they were not shown to anyone who hadn't undertaken the Reiki 2 or Master course, and they were not recorded anywhere for people to stumble across them. Also, in the Japanese culture the words 'secret' and 'sacred' are interconnected, so it would have been unnatural for them to openly discuss things which were part of a spiritual tradition

3. A word or sound that is repeated to aid concentration in meditation; it can also translate as 'instrument of thought'

4. Distant symbol, Harmony symbol, Power symbol

5. The Focus symbol

6. When doing a standard Reiki treatment, or when carrying out a distant treatment, or when sending Reiki to a situation. It can be used in all Reiki

situations to intensify the Reiki (refer to the chapter in full for more information)

7. For example: to help relationship problems or difficulties; to help with nervousness issues; to help to heal addictions; to improve memory and concentration; to enhance affirmations; to help forgive yourself and others (refer to the chapter in full for more information)

8. The Distant symbol

CHAPTER 12: USING THE REIKI SYMBOLS FOR YOUR-SELF AND OTHERS

Answers

1. Three

2. The Power symbol

3. The Distant symbol

4. Draw a Power symbol in the air in each corner, on each wall, and on the ceiling and floor

CHAPTER 13: DISTANT TREATMENTS AND HEALING WITH REIKI

Answers

1. General distant healing can be given by anyone who has been attuned to Reiki at any level. A distant treatment can only be given by those who have completed Reiki 2, and who therefore are able to use the Reiki symbols

2. *Reiki 1*: by holding a photo of the person, or a piece of paper with their name on it, or visualising them in your hand, and sending Reiki to the photo/paper/vision
   Reiki 2: by the same methods as above, but used in conjunction with the Distant and Power symbols, or by using a 'correspondence' such as a teddy bear

3. Yes!

4. To arrange a suitable time with the recipient when they can be sitting or lying down quietly, and to get some feedback from them afterwards

GLOSSARY

Affirmation A positive statement, usually said aloud, to encourage a positive state of mind.

ART Advanced Reiki Training in the Usui/Tibetan Reiki system (equivalent to Reiki 3, Master Practitioner level).

Attunement Performed by a Reiki Master to a Reiki student, this is the process of passing on the ability to be a channel for Reiki energy.

Aura The energy field surrounding the human body.

Centring yourself The process whereby you prepare yourself to channel Reiki by quietening your mind and steadying your breathing, so that you become calm and relaxed.

Chakra A Sanskrit word meaning 'wheel' or 'vortex' used to describe energy centres in the human energy field. There are seven main chakras in the body, located at the base of the spine, the navel, the solar plexus, the chest, the throat, the brow and at the top of the head.

Channelling The process by which people receive information during a state of meditation or trance.

Chi See Ki.

Chi Kung See Qi Gong.

Connection symbol Also called the Distant symbol; see Symbols.

CPD Continuing Professional Development – the process where you improve your professional knowledge by additional learning or practice, and can provide evidence of your achievements.

Crystals Semi-precious stones such as quartz and amethyst, that can be 'filled' with Reiki so that the energy is released slowly for healing purposes.

DDA Disability Discrimination Act – the legal framework in the UK which businesses have to abide by when treating clients who have a disability.

Distant healing The process of Reiki healing that takes place when the recipient and the Reiki practitioner are in different locations.

Distant symbol Also called the Connection symbol; see Symbols.

Distant treatment A Reiki treatment given when the Reiki practitioner is not present with the recipient, or at a different time to when the Reiki treatment was 'sent'.

Empowerment symbol Also called the Master symbol; see Symbols.

Energy body See Energy field.

Energy cleansing A variety of methods (including Reiki) used to clear negative or disharmonious energy from a person's energy field.

Energy field A field of electromagnetic energy that surrounds and interpenetrates the physical body, often referred to as the energy body, aura, or auric field.

First Degree Reiki See Reiki 1.

Focus symbol Also called the Power symbol; see Symbols.

Fourth Degree Reiki See Reiki 4.

Gassho position Having your hands clasped in prayer.

General Regulatory Council for Complementary Therapies (GRCCT) An independent organisation acting as a regulator for all registered therapists of complementary therapies.

Grand Master The title given by the Reiki Alliance to the person believed to be the 'successor' of Mrs Takata.

Hand positions A sequence of recommended placements for Reiki practitioners' hands when giving a Reiki treatment.

Hands-on treatment A Reiki treatment carried out when a Reiki practitioner is in the room with the recipient, and performs a 'laying on of hands' to give Reiki.

Harmony symbol Also called the Mental and Emotional symbol; see Symbols.

Hatsurei-ho An energy cleansing and meditation technique using Reiki.

Healing crisis The process a body can go through following its first exposure to Reiki, in order to eliminate toxins from the body and achieve optimum health.

Higher Self Another term for the 'Soul' or 'Spirit' of an individual person.

Holistic An approach that looks at the whole person and their lifestyle and beliefs, not just the physical symptom they are exhibiting, in order to eradicate illness and produce well-being.

Ideals See Principles.

Independent Reiki Masters Reiki Masters who are not affiliated to the Reiki Alliance and who teach Reiki in their own way.

Japanese Reiki techniques A range of methods for using Reiki that comes from the Reiki traditions and lineage in Japan.

Kanji The calligraphic representation of the Japanese alphabet.

Ki The energy that permeates all living things; it operates at high vibrations and fast frequencies that make it difficult to see, but it can be detected by various forms of electro-magnetic equipment.

Lineage The line of descent that you can trace from the founder of Reiki, Dr Mikao Usui, through to your Reiki Master and yourself.

Mantras Sacred names of the Reiki symbols; a word or sound that is repeated to aid concentration in meditation.

Master symbol Also called the Empowerment symbol; see Symbols.

Mental and Emotional symbol Also called the Harmony symbol; see Symbols.

Meridians Pathways in the body along which energy (Ki) flows.

National Occupational Standards (NOS) A set of guidelines devised to regulate the practise of Reiki in line with other branches of complementary therapies.

Notifiable disease An infectious or contagious disease which must be reported immediately to a medical practitioner.

Okuden The Japanese name for the level we call Reiki 2.

Power symbol Also called the Focus symbol; see Symbols.

Prana See Ki.

Precepts See Principles.

Principles Principles for living a good life that Dr Usui introduced to his students: 'Today do not be angry, do not worry, be grateful, work hard and be kind to people.'

Qi See Ki.

Qi Gong A Chinese meditative and martial arts technique using a series of slow movements and controlled breathing to encourage the circulation of energy around the body.

Radiance Reiki A Western form of Reiki developed by Dr Barbara Weber-Ray, one of the Masters taught by Mrs Takata.

Red flag symptoms Symptoms that indicate the sufferer requires immediate medical treatment.

Reiji A technique from the Japanese Reiki tradition that encourages the ability to intuitively detect where illness is in the body.

Reiju A form of spiritual empowerment or attunement used in Japan with Reiki students.

Reiki A Japanese word meaning 'Spiritual Energy' or 'Universal Life Force Energy'; also used to describe the system of healing we call Reiki.

Reiki 1 The first course a Reiki student usually attends, where they learn how to practise Reiki on themselves and others, using a set of hand positions, and where they are attuned to receiving Reiki energy.

Reiki 2 The second course a Reiki student usually attends, where they learn how to give Reiki using symbols, and how to send distant Reiki, in addition to receiving further attunements.

Reiki 3 The course that a Reiki 2 student or Reiki practitioner would attend to become a Reiki Master Practitioner (or sometimes a Reiki Master Teacher, see Reiki 4), which would include receiving further symbol(s) and attunement(s).

Reiki 4 Often attended in conjunction with Reiki 3, this is a course that teaches Reiki Master Practitioners to be Reiki Master Teachers, so that they may in time also pass on the teachings.

Reiki Alliance The organisation set up in the West in the 1980s by most of the twenty-two Reiki Masters taught by Mrs Takata.

Reiki Council The lead advisory body for the profession of Reiki in the UK (formerly the Reiki Regulatory Working Group).

Reiki Master The term used to describe someone who has undertaken additional training at Reiki level 3 to become a Reiki Master Practitioner, and/or also Reiki 4 to become a Reiki Master Teacher.

Reiki Master Practitioner A Reiki student or practitioner who has attended a Reiki 3 course (or equivalent).

Reiki Master Teacher A Reiki student or practitioner who has attended a Reiki 3 and Reiki 4 course (or equivalent) and who is qualified to teach Reiki to others.

Reiki practitioner Someone who practises Reiki. They may have attended a Reiki 1 and/or a Reiki 2 course, and they may or may not fulfil all the requirements of the National Occupational Standards.

Reiki Regulatory Working Group (RRWG) See Reiki Council.

Reiki sharing group A gathering of Reiki practitioners who give Reiki to each other, usually on a voluntary basis.

Reiki Shower An energy cleansing technique using Reiki.

Reiki student Someone who is learning Reiki or attending a Reiki course.

Second Degree Reiki See Reiki 2.

Self-treatment Placing your hands in various positions on your body and allowing Reiki to flow into yourself.

Sending Reiki The process of allowing Reiki to flow to someone, either for general healing or for a distant treatment, when not actually with the recipient.

Sensei The Japanese term for 'Respected Teacher', or 'Master'.

Shinpiden The Japanese name for what in the West is called Reiki 3/Reiki Master.

Shoden The Japanese name for what in the West is called Reiki 1.

Spiritual Empowerment See Attunement.

Symbols Sacred shapes which, when drawn, change the way in which Reiki works. There are four symbols in Usui Reiki, three are taught at Reiki 2 (Power, Mental and Emotional, Distant) and one at Reiki Master level (Master).

Tai Chi A Chinese martial art usually practised for health reasons. It consists of slow movements where the mind can be focused solely on the actions of the body, bringing about inner calm.

Teaching notes Self-written documentation to help you deliver a course, usually including the running order of the course, key information to give, and prompts to help you remember facts or actions to perform.

Therapy couch An item of equipment usually provided so the Reiki client can lie down during the treatment.

Third Degree Reiki See Reiki 3.

Twenty-one-day clearing cycle A form of 'energetic spring cleaning' where Reiki helps to cleanse and clear your physical and energy bodies after you have done a Reiki course.

Usui Reiki Ryoho Gakkai An organisation founded in Japan in the 1920s that was dedicated to preserving Dr Usui's original Reiki teachings.

Usui/Tibetan Reiki A style of Reiki founded by the American Reiki Master William Lee Rand.

Visualisation A form of meditation, sometimes called an 'inner journey', where someone imagines or 'visualises' a beautiful landscape, or a sequence of events, that can bring insight and inspiration, and help to calm the mind.

Voluntary Self-Regulation (VSR) Regulation of complementary therapies undertaken voluntarily by practitioners, rather than being imposed by government.

Western Reiki A term used to describe the styles of Reiki that are practised in the West, e.g. Usui Reiki, Usui/Tibetan Reiki.

World Health Organization (WHO) A world-wide organisation that monitors health and illness trends, and advises on global health matters.

RESOURCES

USEFUL ADDRESSES AND WEBSITES

For information about Reiki courses, shamanic retreats and other workshops with Reiki Master Penelope Quest, and for details of all her books:

Websites: www.reiki-quest.co.uk and www.penelopequest.com
Email: info@reiki-quest.co.uk

For details of other Reiki Masters and practitioners, and useful information about Reiki and other forms of healing, you might like to try the following organisations and websites (contact details correct when going to press):

UK Contacts

The UK Reiki Federation
Website: www.reikifed.co.uk
Email: enquiry@reikifed.co.uk

The Reiki Association
Website: www.reikiassociation.org.uk
Email: co-ordinator@reikiassociation.org.uk

The Reiki Council
Website: www.reikicouncil.org.uk
Email: info@reikicouncil.org.uk

The General Regulatory Council for Complementary Therapies (GRCCT)
Website: www.grcct.org
Email: admin@grcct.org

The Reiki Alliance – UK and Ireland
Website: www.reikialliance.org.uk
Email: mail@reikialliance.org.uk

Complementary Therapists Association
Website: www.complementary.assoc.org.uk
Email: info@complementary.assoc.org.uk

Federation of Holistic Therapists (FHT)
Website: www.fht.org.uk
Email: info@fht.org.uk

British Complementary Medicine Association (BCMA)
Website: www.bcma.co.uk
Email: chair@bcma.co.uk

Reiki Healers and Teachers Society (RHATS)
Website: www.reikihealersandteachers.net
Email: info@reikihealersandteachers.net

Institute for Complementary Medicine (ICM)
Website: www.i-c-m.org.uk
Email: info@i-c-m.org.uk

Open Reiki Group
Website: www.connect2reiki.co.uk

Independent Professional Therapists International (IPTI)
Website: www.iptiuk.com

Tera-Mai™ Association
Website: www.maverickbadgemakers.sslpowered.com/**teramai**/
tma-home.php

Royal College of Nursing (RCN) Complementary Therapy Forum
Website: www.rcn.org.uk

National Federation of Spiritual Healers
Website: www.nfsh.org.uk; www.thehealingtrust.org.uk

The Confederation of Healing Organisations
Website: www.confederation-of-healing-organisations.org

USA and Canada Contacts

The Reiki Alliance – Worldwide
Website: www.reikialliance.com
Email: info@reikialliance.com

Usui Shiki Ryoho (The Office of the Grand Master – Phyllis Furumoto and Paul Mitchell)
Website: www.usuireiki-ogm.com

The International Center for Reiki Training (William Lee Rand)
Website: www.reiki.org
Email: center@reiki.org

International Association of Reiki Professionals (IARP)
Website: www.iarp.org
Email: info@iarp.org

Southwestern Usui Reiki Ryoho Association
Website: www.reiho.org
Email: adonea@msn.com

The Radiance Technique International Association Inc. (TRTIA)
Website: www.trtia.org
Email: TRTIA@aol.com

Reiki Outreach International
Website: www.annieo.com/reikioutreach

The Reiki Foundation
Website: www.asunam.com/reiki_foundation.htm
Email: asunam@msn.com

Reiki Center for Healing Arts
Website: www.reikifranbrown.com
Email: revfranb@pacbell.net

Tera-Mai™ Healing Center
Website: www.kathleenmilner.com
Email: kathleenmilner@earthlink.net

Canadian Reiki Association
Website: www.reiki.ca
Email: reiki@reiki.ca

Usui-Do (Traditional Japanese Reiki)
Website: www.usui-do.org
Email: askme@usui-do.org

Worldwide Contacts

Australian Reiki Connection
Website: www.australianreikiconnection.com.au

International House of Reiki (Frans and Bronwen Stiene)
Website: www.reiki.net.au
Email: info@reiki.net.au

Reiki New Zealand Inc.
Website: www.reiki.org.nz
Email: info@reiki.org.nz

Reiki Dharma (Frank Arjava Petter)
Website: www.reikidharma.com
Email: Arjava@ReikiDharma.com
(Available in English, Spanish and German)

The World Health Organization
Website: www.who.int

Other Useful UK Organisations

Advertising Standards Authority: www.asa.org.uk/asa/

British Red Cross (first aid training): www.redcrossfirstaidtraining.co.uk

Business Link: www.businesslink.gov.uk/

Government Equalities Office: www.equalities.gov.uk/
www.equalityhumanrights.com
www.direct.gov.uk

Health Protection Agency: www.hpa.org.uk

Health and Safety Executive: www.hse.gov.uk

HM Revenue & Customs: www.hmrc.gov.uk/index.htm

Information Commissioner's Office (formerly the Data Protection Agency): www.ico.gov.uk/

Office of Public Sector Information: www.opsi.gov.uk www.uk/legislation.hmso.gov.uk/

Office of Qualifications and Examinations Regulation (Ofqual): www.ofqual.gov.uk

St John Ambulance (first aid training): www.sja.org.uk

Skills for Health (UK NOS criteria): www.skillsforhealth.org.uk

The Royal College of Veterinary Surgeons: www.rcvs.org.uk

Trading Standards Institute: www.tradingstandards.gov.uk/

Website Providers: There are many companies providing both website hosting and easy-to-use programs to build your own website, both in the UK and in other countries:

www.oneandone.co.uk

www.fasthosts.co.uk

www.host-review.co.uk

www.webhosting.reviewitonline.net

FURTHER READING

The following books are our recommendations from the many available on each subject. We have placed them under headings to make it easier to find the topics you want to pursue, but many of them cover several categories.

Reiki

Ellis, Richard, *Reiki and The Seven Chakras*, Vermilion, 2002

Hall, Mari, *Reiki for Common Ailments*, Piatkus, 1999

Hall, Mari, *Reiki for the Soul*, Thorsons, 2000

Lubeck, Walter and Petter, Frank Arjava, *Reiki Best Practices*, Lotus Press, 2003

Lubeck, Walter, Petter, Frank Arjava and Rand, William Lee, *The Spirit of Reiki*, Pilgrims Publishing, 2004

Quest, Penelope, *Reiki for Life*, Piatkus, 2002

Quest, Penelope, *The Basics of Reiki*, Piatkus, 2007

Quest, Penelope, *Self-healing with Reiki*, Piatkus, 2009

Quest, Penelope, *Living the Reiki Way*, Piatkus, 2010

Steine, Bronwen and Frans, *The Reiki Sourcebook*, O Books, 2003

Steine, Bronwen and Frans, *The Japanese Art of Reiki*, O Books, 2005

Energy, Auras and Chakras

Brennan, Barbara Ann, *Hands of Light: Guide to Healing Through the Human Energy Field*, Bantam Books Ltd, 1990

Chopra, Deepak, MD, *Quantum Healing*, Bantam Books, 1990

Eden, Donna, *Energy Medicine: Balancing Your Body's Energy for Optimal Health, Joy and Vitality*, Piatkus Books, 2008

Emoto, Masaru, *The Hidden Messages In Water*, Pocket Books, 2005

Feinstein, David, Eden, Donna and Craig, Gary, *The Healing Power of EFT and Energy Psychology*, Piatkus Books, 2006

Hunt, Valerie V., *Infinite Mind – Science of the Human Vibrations of Consciousness*, Malibu Publishing Co, 1996

Kingston, Karen, *Clear Your Clutter with Feng Shui*, Piatkus, 2008

McTaggart, Lynne, *The Field: The Quest for the Secret Force of the Universe*, Element, 2003

Simpson, Liz, *The Book of Chakra Healing*, Gaia Books Ltd, 2005

Webster, Richard, *Dowsing for Beginners*, Llewellyn Publications, 1996

General Healing and Self-help

Angelo, Jack, *Your Healing Power*, Piatkus, 2007

Chopra, Deepak, *Perfect Health*, Bantam Books, 2001

Chopra, Deepak, *Reinventing the Body, Resurrecting the Soul: How to Create a New Self*, Rider, 2010

Edwards, Gill, *Living Magically*, Piatkus, 2006

Edwards, Gill, *Stepping Into the Magic*, Piatkus, 2006

Edwards, Gill, *Life is a Gift*, Piatkus, 2007

Gawain, Shakti, *Living in the Light*, New World Library, 1998

Holden, Robert, *Shift Happens*, Hay House, 2010

Jeffers, Susan, *End the Struggle and Dance with Life*, Hodder Mobius, 2005

Jeffers, Susan, *Feel the Fear and Do It Anyway*, Vermilion, 2007

Scovel-Shinn, Florence, *The Game of Life and How to Play It*, Vermilion, 2005

Anatomy and Physiology

Connor, Jeanine, Morgan, Kathy and Harwood-Pearce, Venetia, *Anatomy and Physiology for Therapists*, Heinemann Educational Publishers, 2006

McGuinness, Helen, *Anatomy and Physiology: Therapy Basics*, Hodder Education, 2006

Waugh, Anne and Grant, Alison, *Ross and Wilson Anatomy and Physiology in Health and Illness*, Churchill Livingstone, 2006

Caring for Your Physical Body

Batmanghelidj, Dr F, *Your Body's Many Cries for Water*, Tagman Press, 2007

Bloom, William, *The Endorphin Effect*, Piatkus, 2001

Holford, Patrick, *The Optimum Nutrition Bible*, Piatkus, 2004

Holford, Patrick, *The 10 Secrets of 100% Healthy People*, Piatkus, 2010

Roizen, Michael F. and Oz, Mehmet C., *You, The Owner's Manual*, Piatkus, 2005

Thomas, Chris and Baker, Diane, *Everything You Always Wanted to Know About Your Body but So Far Nobody's Been Able to Tell You*, Capall Bann Publishing, 1999

Thomas, Chris and Baker, Diane, *The Sequel To Everything*, Capall Bann Publishing, 2001

Metaphysical Causes of Disease

Dethlefsen, Thorwald and Dahlke, Rudiger, MD, *The Healing Power of Illness*, Vega Books, 2004

Hay, Louise L., *Heal Your Body*, Hay House UK, 2004

Hay, Louise L., *You Can Heal Your Life*, Hay House Inc., 2004

Shapiro, Debbie, *The Bodymind Workbook*, Chrysalis Books, 2002

Shapiro, Debbie, *Your Body Speaks Your Mind*, Piatkus, 2007

Shapiro, Debbie, *Healing Mind, Healing Body: Explaining How the Mind and Body Work Together*, Collins and Brown, 2007

Spiritual Development

Hicks, Esther and Jerry, *Ask and It Is Given*, Hay House, 2005

Hicks, Esther and Jerry, *The Amazing Power of Deliberate Intent*, Hay House, 2006

Myss, Dr Caroline, *Anatomy of the Spirit*, Bantam Books, 1997

Roberts, Jane, *The Nature of Personal Reality*, Amber-Allen Publishing, 1994

Roman, Sanaya, *Spiritual Growth*, H J Kramer, 1989

Roman, Sanaya, *Soul Love*, H J Kramer, 1997

Ruiz, Don Miguel, *The Four Agreements*, Amber-Allen Publishing, 1997

Tolle, Eckhart, *The Power of Now: A Guide to Spiritual Enlightenment*, Hodder Mobius, 2001

Tolle, Eckhart, *A New Earth: Awakening to Your Life's Purpose*, Penguin Books, 2006

Walsch, Neale Donald, *Conversations with God – Books 1, 2 and 3*, Hodder & Stoughton, 1996, 1997, 1998

Starting a Business

Lester, David, *Starting Your Own Business*, Crimson Publishing, 2007

Rickman, Cheryl D. and Roddick, Dame Anita, *The Small Business Start-up Workbook*, How To Books Ltd, 2005

Williams, Sara, *The Financial Times Guide to Business Start Up*, Financial Times/Prentice Hall, 2009

Communication

Boyes, Carolyn, *Body Language*, Collins, 2005

Brounstein, Marty, *Communicating Effectively for Dummies*, John Wiley & Sons, 2001

Davis, Martha, Paleg, Kim and Fanning, Patrick, *The Messages Workbook: Powerful Strategies for Effective Communication at Work and Home*, New Harbinger Publications, 2004

Denny, Richard, *Communicate to Win*, Kogan Page, 2006

Fine, Debra, *The Fine Art of Confident Conversation: How to Improve Your Communication Skills and Build Stronger Relationships*, Piatkus Books, 2008

Mahoney, Terry, *Making Your Words Work: Using NLP to Improve Communication, Learning and Behaviour*, Crown House Publishing, 2007

Pease, Allan and Barbara, *The Definitive Book of Body Language*, Orion, 2005

Teaching/Training Techniques

Biech, Elaine, *Training for Dummies*, Wiley Publishing Inc., 2005

Gravells, Ann, *Preparing to Teach in the Lifelong Learning Sector*, Learning Matters Ltd, 2008

Reece, Ian and Walker, Stephen, *Teaching, Training and Learning: A Practical Guide*, Business Education Publishers Ltd, 2007

Sacred Sites and Stone Circles

Burl, A., *A Guide to the Stone Circles of Britain, Ireland and Brittany*, Yale University Press, 2005

Carmichael, David L. et al. (eds.), *Sacred Sites, Sacred Places*, Routledge, 1997

Ordnance Survey, *Ancient Britain (Historical Map)*, Ordnance Survey, 2005

INDEX

Note: Page numbers in **bold** refer to diagrams and photographs.